WARDROBE
CRISIS

WARDROBE CRISIS

HOW WE WENT FROM
SUNDAY BEST TO FAST FASHION

CLARE PRESS

Skyhorse Publishing

Skyhorse Publishing books may be purchased in bulk at special discounts for
sales promotion, corporate gifts, fund-raising, or educational purposes.
Special editions can also be created to specifications. For details, contact the
Special Sales Department, Skyhorse Publishing, 307 West 36th Street,
11th Floor, New York, NY 10018 or info@skyhorsepublishing.com.

Skyhorse® and Skyhorse Publishing® are registered trademarks of Skyhorse
Publishing, Inc.®, a Delaware corporation.

Visit our website at www.skyhorsepublishing.com.

10 9 8 7 6 5 4 3 2

Library of Congress Cataloging-in-Publication Data is available on file.

Cover design by Rain Saukas

Print ISBN: 978-1-5107-2342-9
Ebook ISBN: 978-1-5107-2343-6

Printed in the United States of America

'If you want social justice, be a public servant.
Fashion is ephemeral, dangerous and unfair.'
—*Karl Lagerfeld*

'It's only in the last 150 years we've had the resources to fuel this
consume-discard society. Well, guess what? That party's over.'
—*Yvon Chouinard*

'Who is more demented? The world of the insane
or the world of the insanely fashionable?'
—*Simon Doonan*

Contents

Foreword

by Sarah Wilson

There's a conversation I feel we need to have. The Zeitgeist is so ripe for it. And, yes, we're all having a Wardrobe Crisis.

If I were to kick off such a conversation, I'd probably cut to the chase with this hoary barbecue stopper: Why do we consume? On my blog, where I often write about minimal living and sustainable practices, commenters get positively outraged when I raise the issue. Like I've asked them to stop taking in air.

Many of my friends and peers will cross suburbs to buy the right organic tomato, and will opine righteously about open-cut mining, and yet fail to question their handbag addiction or their excessive shoe collection. The topic makes them uncomfortable. And yet we need to ask ourselves these questions.

Why do we shop the way that we do? What is it doing for us? What's it doing *to* us, to the planet, and to our collective happiness? Why is the amassing of more and more 'stuff' seen as normal? Why is a fashion shopping obsession seen as something fun, perhaps a bit hapless, but definitely status-serving when added to the description in your Instagram bio?

Decluttering has become just another opportunity to buy more stuff – storage boxes and fancy wardrobe solutions and, of course, replacement items when you realise you actually did need that backless, strapless bra contraption you tossed last week. The best antidote to our current Wardrobe Crisis is to be a mindful consumer in the first place.

By now most of us have read the studies that tell us shopping is no surefire route to happiness. Often, quite the opposite. We're also aware of the fact that much of the fashion we consume is getting cheaper and more disposable, and that the global fashion industry is increasingly reliant on unsustainable practices.

And yet this is not an anti-fashion book. Clare lives and breathes fashion, and delivers a persuasive argument for its power as a both a creative force and an agent for change.

For many of us, what we wear is an expression of ourselves. Even I am not entirely immune to the allure of quality, crafted fashion ... and the perfect pair of green shorts. So I guess the next question we need to ask, in the conversation that we need to have, is this: *How should we consume our clothes?*

Mercifully, Clare has stepped up to lead this one, and to stimulate the conversation. Which big issues are key for the fashion industry of the future? What are designers doing to revolutionise it? Which retailers are stepping up? How should we buy our wool, our cotton, our synthetics and our silks? How should it be produced, woven, dyed, printed and sewn? And how can we make greener choices when it comes to what we wear?

I now hand the barbecue-stopping baton over to her ...

Sarah Wilson, January 2016

Introduction

Since when was too much not enough?

This was my canary-in-the-coalmine moment. It was the summer of 2013 and I was dressing for a party. For the life of me I could not find a particular gold lamé blouse with a ruffled collar I'd worn precisely twice before. I wore a different metallic blouse, but I was sad about the ruffles.

The next day I was walking past my local laundry when the owner darted into the street and caught me by the coat tails.

'Get off!' I said. 'This coat is brand new.'

'You left your stuff here before Christmas,' she said. 'You pay.'

Sixty bucks later, I stumbled out carrying what felt like a body bag, complete with cadaver. Through the sweating plastic I spied the ruffled blouse. It was snagged on one elbow.

I had a memory flash of an elderly neighbour darning socks, then couldn't work out if she really had lived next door or if I'd just seen her on the telly. I mean, who darns? I've chucked stuff out on the mere rumour of a hole; bet you have too. And apparently I value my clothes so little I can forget about huge piles of them languishing in the laundromat.

3

I didn't mend the blouse (I stuffed it in a charity bin), but I did mend my ways after that.

Until the next time.

I was about to start a new job, when I had a brainwave. 'Skirts! That's what I need.' More specifically, several new versions of a skirt I already owned, but in different fabrics.

I spent hours combing stores, both online and on the street: Zara, which injects new stock twice weekly; H&M, which had recently taken over the entire 5000-square-metre Melbourne GPO building; Net-A-Porter, which presented me with 291 high-end skirt options, by some of its 1200-plus different brands (although some of these skirts, I have to say, would be more accurately termed belts). I tried Topshop, which – as its creative director Kate Phelan once told me – drops in the region of 7000 new garment styles each year. Finally, I scoured ASOS, which broke down my choices by colour, price (from $11.76!) and style (A-line, mini, midi, maxi, pencil, skater). Nada. Hated them all. Was it really possible I couldn't find a single skirt I liked?

I asked my friend Liane Rossler, who runs sustainable design collective Supercyclers, if she had any tips – and she told me about the rats. Apparently they get more excited about the anticipation of food than they do when it comes to actually eating it. It's science, and stuff.

'The feeling of desire, of anticipation, sometimes that's better than the actual getting,' she said. 'Maybe it's the chase that excites you?'

'I'm not seeking thrills,' I snapped. By this point I was shouting and people were beginning to stare. 'I'm desperately seeking skirts.'

'Doesn't look that way to me,' she said, with a knowing smile.

By the time I'd put my bags down to free a hand to slap her with (there was a fair bit of collateral shopping damage, you see, an unavoidable side effect of the skirt hunt), she'd already started to walk away.

'When you're faced with too much of something, you start to want it less,' she called over her shoulder.

What she didn't say, though fair enough if she had, was: Where'd I think I was going to hang all these new acquisitions? That body bag of dry cleaning turned out to be the nail in my wardrobe's coffin. One night the wardrobe keeled over and carked it. At first I didn't realise its rail had snapped clean because there were so many garments shoved in there, they held themselves up without hangers.

I have a surfeit of clothes. An embarrassment of them. I have, too, my excuses. I never did hold with Quentin Crisp's claim that 'fashion is what you adopt when you don't know who you are'. My clothes do their bit to define me. I worked at *Vogue*, and you can't do that without 'investing' in luxury brands. For a time I also ran my own label, so I made yet more clothes, and collected vintage samples for inspiration. I was so brilliant at that last bit I had to hire two storage units to house them, which I still maintain. And now ignore. I have no idea what's in those boxes and bags. One day, an archaeologist will dig them up and wonder what strange circus troupe wore bloomers with velvet capes.

It is a common affliction, this obsession with getting more clothes. The average woman wears just 40 per cent of those she owns. I have a friend who collects navy and white striped T-shirts.

'But they're all the same,' I told her.

'No, this one has longer sleeves,' she said.

A colleague, who claims she's 'not really into fashion', has seven pairs of jeans. Our parents had the milkman and the newspaper delivery boy – we have the DHL van from Net-A-Porter.

I've just finished reading Elizabeth Cline's insightful book *Overdressed*, about fast fashion in the US, in which she mentions quite casually that American houses built in the last fifteen years now routinely come with walk-in robes the size of second bedrooms. I once had my own wardrobe photographed for a magazine called *Shop Til You Drop*. Heck, I started a blog called 'Wardrobe Spy' with she of the striped shirts. Then one day I literally woke up and thought, 'There are millions living in slums and I have a special drawer just for belts – there's something wrong with this equation.' I still love fashion, it is both my livelihood and an endless source of fascination to me, but when it comes to acquiring as opposed to admiring it, there is such a thing as too much. And too much rarely makes us feel good. You binge; you get a hangover.

According to British journalist Lucy Siegle, author of *To Die For*, 'We have more clothes than at any other time in history, but have become less and less fulfilled and secure in our purchases, precisely because we have become such passive consumers. We watch, we follow, we pick off the rail and – herdlike – we find ourselves at the cash till.'[1]

At the same time, we are becoming less and less connected to the origins of these purchases. How often do we ask the questions: Who made our clothes? Where did they make them, how and from what? How is it possible that we can buy a brand new garment, even one bedazzled by hand with sequins, for less than the cost of a cooked breakfast?

Ninety-two per cent of the clothing sold in Australia is manufactured overseas. Over the past twenty years, our fashion shopping habits have changed beyond recognition. We now shop online, at our desks and on our phones, choosing fashion items from all over the world with nary a thought for where they come from (and how many air-miles they clock up in the process). We are buying more from luxury brands, but much, much more from the lower-priced sector. We buy clothes on a whim, because they are so accessible and seemingly so affordable (though the true cost of a garment is rarely expressed by its retail price – more on that later). Sometimes we buy clothes with the express intention of wearing them just once or twice; we buy clothes to throw away.

Each year Australians send $500 million worth of clothing to the tip. Oxfam says 9,513 garments are thrown into British landfill every five minutes. Americans dump an estimated ten million tonnes every year, some of it brand new with the tags still on. Clothes are increasingly designed with disposability in mind, something that's been dubbed 'the Primark effect' after the Irish discounter that is so polarising in Europe (you either love it for its three-for-a-pound flip-flops, or loathe it for its supply chain issues). As small-scale garment manufacture dwindles in the global north, fast fashion, built on cheap labour in the south, booms.

The 'fast' bit relates to the speed with which the high street market leaders 'translate' trends off the catwalks into garments on the shop floor. High fashion still sticks to the traditional seasonal calendar, showing the Spring collections in September for delivery into stores around March. The carousel spins around again for Autumn, which shows in February, for August deliveries. But in the past decade or so, the Pre-collections, which cover the shoulder seasons (known as Pre-Fall and Resort or Cruise), have grown in both size and prominence. The next wave is 'Pre-pre collections'. Makes you dizzy, doesn't it?

In contrast, fast fashion lead times range from six weeks to a few days. Zara stores receive new styles twice a week. The Korean American owned Forever 21 chain has gained traction since the early 2000s by dropping new styles daily in the US. Even the mid-priced high street stalwart Cue, tiny in comparison to these behemoths and Ethical Clothing Australia accredited, has weekly stock injections.

Too fast?

Around the time Topshop stopped being seen as naff in Britain (approximately 1998), the meaning of the word 'fashion' changed. Forget the elevated world of Parisian designers. Now we accept it to mean simply 'clothes', and bandy it about as a catch-all term for anything with an ad campaign we dress ourselves in, not just the high-end stuff but cheap knock-offs, mid-range high street apparel, gear we wear to play sport and go to the beach in, workwear, childrenswear, accessories, vintage.

Bearing that in mind, the biggest fashion brand in the world is Zara. Its Spanish parent company Inditex produces more than 948 million garments a year. In 2014, it operated 6,683 stores globally, in eighty-eight markets, and had increased its retail footprint by 10 per cent on the previous year. Forbes estimates that Inditex's founder, Amancio Ortega, is personally worth about $68 billion.

H&M is the second biggest player. What began in 1947 with a single womenswear store in the Swedish town of Vasteras is now a global juggernaught operating in more than forty-eight countries. H&M Group's stated goal for 2013 was to grow by 10 to 15 per cent across both sales and number of product lines, opening 325 new stores that year.

To launch into Australia in 2014, they threw a party in their first Melbourne store for the sorts of people who post a lot on Instagram (fashion editors, LA pop band Haim, Miss Universe), flying them in for drinks among the racks of cheap rayon tops. The lights were bright, the music loud. The following Saturday those not invited to the bash – though they were the true reason for it – the shoppers, came in droves. Lines formed in Bourke Street from nine p.m. before the first day of trading, which saw 15,000 customers through the doors.

This whole queue-to-be-first-in thing is normal in Australia now, though I still can't get my head around it, even though I'm British (and we invented waiting in line, back in the days of bowler hats; 'After you, sir.' 'No, after you ...'). In my teens I queued for concert tickets, and I now queue in airports and banks, but the idea of bedding down in the gutter by choice for the chance to buy a $19 necklace seems bonkers to me.

Queues at new store openings form because brands succeed in creating that heady mix of desire, anticipation and panic. *What if someone else buys the last of those necklaces?* (#FirstWorldProblems) One way to create this fever is to hire an It girl (because make no mistake: 'brand ambassadors' are not just fans, they are on the corporate payroll) and get them to pose in front of a logo wall. Mostly the posing person is wearing a much more expensive brand (Balmain dress, Prada shoes) than the one holding the 'social event', and if we, the shoppers, think too hard about that it might make us feel cheated. But life's too short to worry, what with all this fuel being shovelled on the fires of our aspiration, so nine times out of ten we simply obey the call to shop. If we head to this place, so recently filled with famous people quaffing champers and laughing, their wonderful whitened teeth as bright as the flash bulbs, won't some of that glamour rub off on us?

The fast fashion queue is a trend created by marketing managers, and it started in London back in 2007 with a clever gimmick. Kate Moss had designed her first collection for Topshop (owned by Sir Philip Green's Arcadia Group). The sequined capes, floral tea dresses and versions of Mossy's favourite denim shorts would have sold if all she did were talk them up on breakfast radio. Instead, she donned a red dress based on a 1930s original from her personal wardrobe and posed in Topshop's Oxford Circus windows. It was like the 1980s movie *Mannequin*, only better. Remember this was a limited edition. #FOMO. On the preview night, for a four-hour period, shoppers were admitted in small groups, their browsing time limited to twenty minutes. Fans, crazed by queuing, lack of sleep and the tantalising promise that a dose of *bone fide* supermodel glamour could be theirs (for thirty quid), grabbed clothes without checking the sizes, let alone trying them on.

Too cheap?

Alas demand for a bargain does not usually result in better conditions for garment workers, who are mostly concentrated in the poorest nations on earth. Shortly after Moss's Topshop debut, the *Sunday Times* reported that agents for factories in Mauritius supplying Arcadia Group were recruiting workers from Bangladesh, India and Sri Lanka, promising to pay up to five times more than they ended up doing and charging workers hundreds of pounds for the privilege.

Nine-hundred kilometres off the coast of Madagascar, Mauritius is an island nation known for its physical beauty, so I'd probably cough up a few quid for a job there too, given the right sales pitch and a piña colada. But there were no sunset cocktails for these workers. Adrift in a strange land with no means to get home and isolated from their support networks, they reportedly received 40 per cent less than the average local wage, and no sick or holiday pay. Many worked fourteen-hour shifts six days a week, returning to on-site dormitories at eleven p.m.

In 2008 the island's minister of industry, Dr Rajesh Jeetah, told members of the International Textile Manufacturers Federation, 'I am convinced that "Made in Mauritius" will be a premium label shortly.' Five years later Mauritian textiles and apparel exports were worth nearly US$900 million. The industry employed 44,000 people, but the minimum wage for unskilled workers remained low – about $US20 per week.

This is a drop in the Indian Ocean in the grand scheme of things. China is the garment factory of the world – with textile and apparel exports worth $US288 *billion* in 2014. While wages in China have risen in recent years, and the rapidly expanding urban middle class is now a major consumer of Made in China fashion, official figures mask the reality for the migrant workers who keep the economy turning.

According to Ellen Ruppel Shell, author of *Cheap*, millions of workers, many of them migrants from remote rural areas, do not have formal employment contracts, 'leaving them completely vulnerable to exploitation and abuse. Without a written contract, Chinese labourers have no evidence they are employed, and employers can simply deny their existence.'[2] Meanwhile, as Chinese factories raise their prices, fashion brands are looking elsewhere for the most cost-effective production.

The second largest global exporter of ready-made garments is Bangladesh.

In April 2013 the Rana Plaza complex collapse in Savar, Dhaka, killed at least 1,133 people, injured more than 2,500 and orphaned an estimated 800 children. Built without proper permits, the buildings were designed to house offices, not factories, and had been illegally extended. There weren't enough exits, and many of these were habitually blocked. When the structure began to visibly crack, warnings were issued and some factories were temporarily closed, but others producing garments to deadline for big-name brands ordered workers back the following day with disastrous results. Brands that had placed recent orders with factories in Rana Plaza, or sold garments that were made there, include Italian staple Benetton (makers of the lambswool jumpers I prized highly as a teen), Mango, Walmart and Primark – though neither H&M nor Zara, both of which were among the first companies to sign the subsequent Accord on Fire and Building Safety in Bangladesh. By 2015, the accord had been signed by 200 apparel brands, retailers and exporters from over twenty countries – but there was still no resting easy in our $5 T-shirts. As I write this, labour rights groups are criticising brands, including H&M, for being 'painfully slow' to implement new safety measures.

Six months after Rana Plaza, CNN reported that things were running much as they were before the disaster for Bangladesh's four million garment workers – stupidly low pay, cramped, dangerous conditions and less-than-zero rights.

If you're shocked, ask yourself how your new jeans can possibly retail for twenty bucks after import, tax, marketing and store mark-ups. The big brands will tell you it's because of economies of scale, but they would say that wouldn't they?

On the second anniversary of the disaster, many victims were still waiting for compensation; it was only after sustained campaigning by human rights groups that compensation targets were finally met in June 2015. Meanwhile, worker protest marches in Dhaka have become a regular thing, often suppressed brutally by police. And the factory accidents keep coming – according to the *Guardian*, nearly 800 people were injured 'in scores of largely unreported fires in garment and textile factories' in Bangladesh in 2013.

In October 2013 *Toronto Star* journalist Raveena Aulakh's story about going undercover in a smaller Dhaka sweatshop was published. She described her experience of sitting on the floor for twelve-hour days snipping dangling threads from shirt collars and cuffs. Her 'boss' was nine years old. Younger workers, wrote Aulakh, are prized for their good eyesight and nimble fingers, and because they complain less.

Such travesties are not confined to the so-called developing world. In December 2013, this time in Prato, Italy, a fire killed seven sweatshop workers as they slept in a makeshift cardboard dormitory onsite. The city's mayor, Roberto Cenni, acknowledged there were only two government inspectors to cover the 5000-odd Chinese-run workshops that dot the area. Immigrants arrive on short-term tourist visas, he said, then disappear into the black economy; authorities estimate that up to two thirds of workers currently employed by factories in Prato are illegal immigrants ripe for exploitation.

In January 2014, when Cambodian garment workers protested in an industrial park outside Phnom Penh, demanding the right to a minimum wage, soldiers gunned them down. Two years later, the authorities were still using water cannons against striking garment workers.

It is precisely these sorts of chilling events that inspired Fashion Revolution Day, which marks the anniversary of the Rana Plaza disaster. The idea, established in London by sustainable fashion campaigners Carry Somers, Orsola de Castro and Lucy Siegle, with help from Livia Firth, is to raise greater awareness about fashion's supply chain issues. The first event, in 2014, encouraged shoppers to ask each other, and the brands they buy from, a seemingly simple question: Who made your clothes?

Liane Rossler sits on the Australian advisory committee for Fashion Revolution. When I interviewed her about it for a story for the *Australian* she said simply, 'No one *wants* to support modern slavery. I mean, are you going to feel glamorous in a new dress if you know someone suffered to make it?'

The idea that our fashion habits may be contributing to such misery and devastation doesn't bear thinking about, does it? The problem is that the sheer scale of all this encourages ostrich behaviour. I'm as bad as anyone. Worse, probably. At least I was when I started writing this book.

But I believe we are at a tipping point. The 'faster, bigger' ride is starting to sicken us. We are searching for ways to feel more grounded, more connected to the earth. What excites early adopters today are farmers' markets, upcycling, crafternoons. Chefs have made foraging cool. Designers are talking about 'cradle-to-cradle'. Everyone wants to 'meet the maker'. Small is beautiful again.

The food industry offers a good example. What not so long ago was a niche concern: obsessing over the origins of what we eat and drink – whether it's healthy, organic, low fat, gluten-free, grown locally, cooked slowly – has become normalised, at least in countries where food is plentiful. Increasingly, those of us who can afford to make our food-buying decisions along these lines, do so. We invest time, energy and money into seeking good health, from juice cleanses to yoga to what we eat for dinner. Not just the hippies and Pilates instructors of cliché, but rather your average mum, the woman in the street, her teenaged daughter; you and me. And that's just the female of the species. Men are in on the health kick too – and they're also buying fashion like never before; global menswear sales increased by 70 per cent from 1998 to 2014. If we define good health as 'being vigorous and free from disease', isn't it about time we applied that to our wardrobes too?

Slowly the fashion world is beginning to catch on, thanks in part to the increasingly visible work of people on the inside like Simone Cipriani from the UN's Ethical Fashion Initiative and Italian *Vogue* editor-in-chief Franca Sozzani, who works with Fashion 4 Development. Some established designers, such as Stella McCartney, Tomas Maier and Bruno Pieters, have good ethics in their DNA – and more are emerging, both big and small. In Australia, Kit Willow has reinvented herself with the ethical brand KITX. New Zealand's Kowtow uses only Fair Trade organic cotton and biodegradable cornstarch packaging. Movie star Rosario Dawson is part of a fashion project designed to help empower women's collectives in Ghana. Pharrell Williams and his partners from Bionic Yarn are trying to save the oceans one pair of G-Star jeans at a time. Surf legend Kelly Slater is behind sustainably produced menswear brand Outerknown. And luxury's first serious contenders based entirely on ethical production – Edun, Suno and Maiyet – are leading by example. At the big end of town, sustainability departments have become the norm.

Eco is no longer a dirty word. As public opinion swings, it is beginning to look like guzzling resources without thinking about the consequences for people and the planet might make crap business sense.

People in over fifty-five countries turned their clothes inside out on the first Fashion Revolution Day in 2014, and asked on social media: Who made your clothes? Who spun the threads? Who sewed them together? Who grew the fibres in the first place? The message to brands is: customers care.

Clare Press, May 2016

CHAPTER 1

Behind the Seams

Trash and treasure

I've decided to have the skirts made. At 10 a.m. Monday morning in Sydney's Kings Cross, the lights are off on the landmark Coke sign, and in the harsh sun the white letters that spell out 'Enjoy Coca-Cola' are the grey of grubby bra-straps. An empty can rolls past, and a man-mountain grins at me as he stops it with his foot. He has the Southern Cross inked on his neck above the collar of his nylon football shirt, the kind that takes forty years to degrade in landfill.

I turn down past the newsagent, which has a display of $8.95 caps out front. The original baseball caps were made in the 1840s from straw for the New York Knickerbockers; these are polyester with plastic trim. Polyester is made from ethylene, derived from petroleum; its production is energy intensive and heavy on the greenhouse gases. Aesthetically speaking, poly turns me right off – often shiny, always sweaty, it crackles with static best left to Boney M – but environmentally most cotton is no better. It takes up to 2,700 litres of water to make enough cotton for one T-shirt. Conventional cotton farming uses one quarter of the world's pesticides. Straw starts to sound like a pretty good idea.

I pass a gentrified pocket set back from the street, with a slick café, a gym, and a nightclub with a velvet rope – while it's smarter than the dives on the main drag, the female patrons still shriek and stumble in their too-high heels as they leave the club. I know; I've been one of them. I used to buy a new outfit every week for those Friday night shenanigans. I never thought about how it was made.

This end of the street lacks the pulse of further up. There's a greasy spoon and a drycleaner advertising 'Repairs, alterations, jeans patched,' with a sewing machine in the window I've never seen manned, and then a dead end. Only those on foot can snake down to the Gothic arches of the Jesuit-run St Canice's church. One Christmas, a woman turning into Roslyn Street after midnight mass was stabbed multiple times by a mugger. He escaped with small change – barely enough to buy a baseball cap.

Sometimes when I drive here, I approach the back way and park outside the church gates, where the homeless queue up for their free lunch. I feel guilty, ashamed that I make snap judgments based on how they look; but there's something about their enveloping layers I find threatening. What's under all those blankets and scarves? *Who* is under there? I know full well that they must wear those heavy coats in the sun or risk losing them because they don't have the luxury of a wardrobe, and that admitting this makes me sound like a caricature of a shallow fashion person, like Will Ferrell playing Mugatu in *Zoolander*: What's the vision behind your new 'Derelicte' collection, Mugatu? 'I'm inspired by the homeless, the vagrants, the crack whores!'

'Derelicte' is a parody of a fashion moment that actually happens – repeatedly. You can trace its origins back to the London punks who wore bin bags, and Sid Vicious holding his shredded pants together with safety pins. Jean Paul Gaultier had them in mind when he dreamt up his *robe sac poubelle* ('garbage-bag dress'). He was twenty-eight at the time, and fresh from learning his trade at Pierre Cardin, but the dress, made of draped black plastic, accessorised by bangles recycled from empty tin cans and a handbag made from an old ashtray, gave those who saw it a glimpse of the '*enfant terrible*' Gaultier was to become. It's a tag he doesn't like, but one that fits him rather well – even now he's of an age more suited to pottering around the garden.

Four years *après* Gaultier's garbage-bag frock debuted in Paris, John Galliano finished studying fashion at London's Saint Martin's School of Art and Design with a graduate collection titled 'Les Incroyables,' inspired by French revolutionaries (and perhaps Vivienne Westwood – she did it first).

Gibraltar-born Galliano was dark-eyed and dangerous, with the swagger of Rudolph Valentino. 'Les Incroyables' featured his clubbing friends as models, music by DJ Jeremy Healy, and fabrics begged and borrowed. One look in particular hinted at what was to come from Galliano down the track – it included a pair of reading glasses held together with sticking plaster.[1] Down-on-your-luck chic; it was a weird idea but it might just fly.

That first collection was a smash. It so impressed the retailer Joan Burstein that she bought every piece for her cult London boutique, Browns. 'I just thought, wow! How exciting, how marvellous, so unrestrained,' she told me. 'We bought the lot. There was no production, it was just the samples from the show, but we sold it very quickly, every piece.'[2]

With Burstein's stamp of approval, Galliano was anointed 'most promising one'. He was named British Fashion Designer of the Year four times. By 1989, he had secured serious backers and was showing in Paris. When, in 1995, the execs at Louis Vuitton Moët Hennessy were looking for young blood to revitalise the French couture house of Givenchy, they chose Galliano. Barely a year in he was moved to the top job at Dior.

In 1999, Galliano was working on his seventh couture collection for that venerable Paris house, by now a fashion legend in his own right, as famous as Mr Dior had been fifty years earlier. Paris, the city of Robespierre and the *sans-culottes*, teemed with inspiration but, like his peer Alexander McQueen, Galliano struggled with the stresses of fashion's relentless pace, and self-medicated with booze and drugs. When he wasn't battling a raging hangover, he jogged with his personal trainer along the Seine. That's where he first noticed the shadowy cliques of city's rough sleepers, *les clochards* (the literal translation is 'the ones who limp'). He was thinking of them, he said, when he draped his Spring 2000 couture models in newsprint-patterned silk, and hung their belts with empty liquor bottles tied with string. The press dubbed the collection 'hobo chic'.

'Some of these people are like impresarios, their coats worn over their shoulders and their hats worn at a certain angle,' said Galliano of les clochards. 'It's fantastic!' These people.

Charles Manning, who went on to become an editor at *Cosmopolitan*, was witness to Galliano's enthusiasm for hobo chic. In the 2000s, Manning was a young stylist assisting Mel Ottenberg, the New Yorker charged with organising Galliano's personal wardrobe (these days he's best known for dressing Rihanna).

Always a flamboyant dresser, Galliano took great care over the eccentric outfits he wore to strut out on the runway for his finale bows. For Dior's Resort 2009 show, Galliano briefed his team to make him look like the Artful Dodger from *Oliver Twist*.

So Manning and Ottenberg went shopping for oversized $2000 boots and thick woven pants worthy of a vagrant. On the way back to their office they passed a tramp rooting through a garbage bin, as Manning recalled in a nostalgic post for Cosmopolitan.com:

'That's the look. It's perfect. Ask him how much he
wants for it?' said Ottenberg.

'How much he wants for what?!'

'Everything! The coat, the shoes, those socks.
That's the look!'

I refused. I told Mel there wasn't time to clean it and
Galliano wouldn't want to wear something smelly. 'Besides,'
I said, 'where would he change? Here on the street?'

Ottenberg gave in, but instructed Manning to ensure 'the rest of
the outfit had that same feel and patina as what the homeless man
was wearing'. So Manning set about distressing the boots, throwing
paint at them, spraying them with vinegar then leaving them in the
road for cars to run over.[3]

Galliano's take on *haute* homelessness didn't go down so well with
the critics – at the *New York Times* Maureen Dowd took umbrage at
'Dior models who starve themselves posed as the starving' – but
maybe the old there's-no-such thing-as-bad-publicity idea proved
too big a pull, because Galliano was not the last designer to mine the
'edgy' possibilities of street-people style.

At Berlin fashion week in July 2009 Patrick Mohr, an avant-garde
German designer with a Wilf Lunn moustache, recruited homeless
people from local shelters to walk alongside the professional models
in his show.

Westwood found inspiration here too. According to the show
notes for her Autumn 2010 menswear collection: 'Perhaps the oddest
of heroes to emerge this season, Vivienne Westwood found inspiration in the roving vagrant whose daily get-up is a battle gear for the
harsh weather conditions ... Quilted bombers and snug hoodies also
work well in keeping the vagrant warm.'

I don't want to live in a bubble like these designers, to sound like Mugatu, see everything through the warped glass of fashion. I yank my prejudice back and twist it angrily off to the side, but I know it will slip back again when I'm not watching.

I write about clothes for a living. They are the first things I notice, and, by habit, the first thing I draw conclusions from; my grandmother's warning that we *never get a second chance on first impressions* taken to preposterous levels. I notice clothes and I remember them, imbuing them with meanings that are probably not there.

The old-fashioned approach

A girl in red ballet slippers hurries past. She is wearing scarlet lipstick and one of Melbourne label Gorman's amusing sweatshirts embroidered with vegetables (a big green and yellow corn on the cob). My heart leaps a little because her outfit looks so cheerful, although actually the girl's expression is grim. I think of something the writer Marion von Adlerstein told me once, that it is always pleasing to see a person who has made an effort: 'Dressing nicely helps the landscape.'

I am thinking about this, and the fine line between appreciating such things and being – or even just seeming to be – barmy enough to forget that there is more important stuff going on, as I reach the faded pink awning of Marisa Regozo's shopfront. It is sandwiched between a pharmacy and a backpacker hostel, and I note, as I always do, that this is a rum spot for a genteel dressmaker's.

Outside two female tourists perch on the curb smoking roll-up ciggies. They look like they should be in school, with pipe-cleaner legs in too-short shorts. One wears a singlet with a sparkly cat's face on it. There are pink marks on her shoulders where the straps of her rucksack have cut in.

Marisa's door is unlocked. I push it, which makes a bell on a velvet ribbon clang. 'Ai,' says Marisa, rounding into view. 'Those girls! I want to make them a proper skirt.'

'Me too,' I say, as Marisa takes my face in her hands and pats my cheeks. Gold rings, glinting with diamonds and sapphires, bisect her swollen fingers. I think about muggers and decide this is jewellery that won't easily slip off. Then I think about places where they'd chop off your fingers for less, and I remember that Australia is a lucky country.

There is a flicker of disappointment as Marisa glances at my belly; she longs for me to be pregnant. Her grandson Maxim is on the other side of the world in Madrid. Photographs of him fight for space on a corkboard. There is Mozart on the radio, Symphony No. 35 in D. 'I know this one,' I say. 'We have the CD.'

'Mozart is the most beautiful music in the world,' says Marisa. Her son, Maxim's father, is a concert violinist.

'Look at this!' she says, leading me to the half-height divider wall that sections off the workroom from the front parlour. Along it hang a nearly-made print jacket, two dresses and a blouse with a pie-crust collar. 'Isn't it?'

Isn't it? (*eez-un-eet*) is a catchphrase for Marisa, which reminds me that English is her second language. She grew up in Ferrol, Galicia (where General Franco was born) and first came to Australia 'with a boatload of other Spanish girls' looking for work in 1962. She studied in Germany and worked in Paris before moving to Sydney for good in 1968. Marisa says 'isn't it?' to mean both 'isn't it wonderful?' and 'isn't it dreadful?'; sometimes it is not a question but a statement, and she says it apropos of nothing at all.

'Hello!'

'Isn't it?'

'Isn't it, what?' It doesn't matter. Today she means, isn't it beauti-ful? And the answer is yes. It's vegetables again. The jacket is made from thick cotton piqué, with a wild design of painted eggplants.

'This fabric! Dolce and Gabbana,' she claps. She buys it from a supplier in Brisbane that stocks European designer surplus. She's recycling, although she doesn't know it.

Marisa's own jacket today is sunflower yellow linen. It's from the 1980s, but Marisa wouldn't think to call it vintage. It is simply old, and was built – by her – to last. She has teamed it with a powder-blue blouse, a brooch shaped like an Alexander Calder mobile pinned to the lapel. It must be thirty degrees out, but Marisa is wear-ing tan stockings. She looks like a socialite on her way to lunch in a smart hotel, and I'm reminded of my grandmother, the one so keen on first impressions, with her Bally handbags and endless Prin-gle of Scotland knits; she was on first name terms with the department store ladies in the northern English town where we lived – the Peggys and the Reenies who sold her cashmere sweaters, one in every colour.

My grandmother was too busy shopping and having her nails done to cook dinner. She was what used to be known as *clothesy* (a word used most effectively while raising one eyebrow). She grew up in a flat above a lolly shop, with her mother and a cranky old aunt. She sewed her own clothes back then, and there weren't many of those. Her mother made her leave school early and work in the shop, and later in a pub, and my grandmother squirrelled away extra pen-nies until she had a secret nest egg. One day, she went out and blew the lot on bottle-blonde hairdo and a pair of silver high-heeled san-dals. She married up, so that she never had to work – or sew – again, and she set about collecting those sweaters and silk dresses, wool coats, and brooches she'd pretend were by Cartier, like the Duchess of Windsor's. But try as she might she couldn't expunge the thrifty gene, and despite the summers she spent in the South of France ordering people to bring her gin and tonics in her fake-posh voice, she still saved the tiny bits of soap from the end of the bar. Once she had a whole bunch, she'd squidge them all together to make a new one. Her entire life she never threw out a pair of tights out when they first laddered. She'd cut off the spoiled leg at the thigh, then wait patiently for her chance to match the pair.

'Isn't it uncomfy, doubling up the tops like that?' I asked her once.

She tutted, and said, 'You never lived through a war.' But it wasn't that really; it was the lolly shop.

I'd lay money on the fact that my grandmother never thought about the people who made the fashion items she valued so highly. She thought about how much they cost, and how much she had saved in the sale, and the precise shade of pea green Audrey Fullerton would go when she saw them.

I ask Marisa if she cooks. She surely hasn't time. 'Of course I do,' she grins. 'I cook with herbs and spices, with love! I do not understand how people, they will buy their meals from a take-out shop. People want everything instant, instant. I don't like.'

Marisa, at the time of telling, is seventy-four years old, and she works five days a week, fitting, sewing and cutting to order. Many of the outfits she makes are for special occasions, and over the years more than a few of them have been wedding dresses. Making these kind of clothes comes with added pressure. The best dress, the memory dress; the dress you spend a month's salary on.

Marisa can remember when most women owned clothes made by people like her. When I say 'like her' I'm talking not about Marisa's mannerly tastes and her Spanish accent, but her process: Marisa makes a garment from start to finish.

Fashion remains one of the most labour-intensive industries on earth, and humans, not robots, still cut and stitch our clothes. Globally, these workers number more than sixty million. But these days the overwhelming majority of them work on a factory line, focusing on just one tiny part of the whole. A seamstress might sew only the back pocket on a pair of jeans, or only a buttonhole, a hundred times a day, six-and-a-half days a week. This is something we know but we don't dwell upon, like the reason for saving the laddered tights. Only easier than that, because we almost never have to see any evidence of the fact – the factories are tucked away conveniently on the other side of the world.

Sometimes it seems as if our clothes appear by magic in the sparkling shops that fill our cities and malls. As if nobody makes them at all; they simply spring, fully formed, from the ether – like alien mushrooms out of *Dr Who*. Alien mushrooms with random price tags. Some of the clothes seem mighty cheap, some expensive – but who knows really? It's impossible to determine the true value of something when you don't know how it came to be, or what it means. My grandmother's silver sandals meant freedom – what does your seventh pair of jeans mean?

Marisa has brought me an article clipped from a 1960s magazine, with a picture of her younger self pinning the hem on 'a cowl-necked, sleeveless dress in a Ben Shearer fabric'; it cost $58. That's the equivalent of $380 today.

'Wowee!' I say. Marisa was never about cheap and cheerful. She gives me *a look*.

'Why should I be?' she says. Marisa is an artist.

In 1969 she operated out of Aladdin Gallery, an arty, buzzy space a couple of blocks away on Elizabeth Bay Road. Not that we're talking Swinging London here; Sydney in the sixties was conservative, and young Australians were still leaving for Europe by the boatload. But the Aladdin was a hot thing for a certain type: *clothesy* ladies, who came to choose fabric from the exotic stock – silk-screened velvets, imported batiks – then commissioned Marisa to make them bespoke outfits. I imagine there were a lot of caftans being made, worn to drinks parties with jewelled mules, hair set in Carmen rollers, and henpecked husbands in sports coats with leather patches on their elbows.

Marisa says the Aladdin Gallery arrangement suited her better than working in Paris, although her first job in that city was at the famous house of Nina Ricci. 'I always had ambition,' she says. 'As a girl I used to take our donkey down to the beach and sell drinks to the holidaymakers.' Both her mother and grandmother were dressmakers. 'I always understood about clothes. I made them for myself, I made them for other people. I moved to Paris to follow my dream. But when I arrived, it wasn't for me.'

The House of Nina Ricci occupied elegant premises at 20 Rue des Capucines. Maria 'Nina' Ricci was an Italian. Born in Turin, her family moved to Paris when she was twelve and the young Nina was apprenticed to a city seamstress. She scored her first job in a couture atelier at sixteen. She made a name for herself with her clever, feminine draping, but it's hard to imagine Ricci had huge entrepreneurial ambitions – she stayed two decades at maison Raffin (big in the '20s, now forgotten) and was forty-nine in 1932 when she finally set out on her own. It was her son Robert who talked her into it. He became her business partner, and he was the one who made the house's name with his canny development of perfumes like L'Air du Temps in its Lalique-designed bottle – another status symbol my grandmother held dear.

Robert Ricci had no cause to speak to Marisa, and his crotchety beturbaned mother, by now well into her eighties, was a distant figure by the time Marisa arrived at the house. She reported to the formidable atelier *première*, who treated the girls like students at a strict convent school.

Marisa was too independent-minded for the couture atelier, and she bristled at the idea of working on 'only the collar of a dress, or only the sleeve'.

'Like a production line!' I say.

'Not quite, but it's true that we were not encouraged to be creative,' she says. 'We did as we were told. And they picked a bit from here, a bit from there.' Too often, insists Marisa, the results were 'just a hotchpotch with a pretty label'. Worse still was the rivalry between the girls: 'Everybody copies your work.' And as for the wages: 'Terrible money. I can barely afford to eat.'

While Marisa was wondering what to do next, a cousin in Sydney provided the answer. There was a broken love affair, or perhaps this cousin fell ill, anyway Marisa came back to comfort her. It's been a while since Marisa told me this story, and I can't remember the details, but when I ask her again, she shuts me down. 'You don't want to know about all that,' she says, steering me into the kitchen, and taking out a fruitcake. 'Cut this please. Ah, now Bruna is here.'

Bruna has been working with Marisa 'for so long, we are like family'. The two of them squeeze into the small sewing room, with two elderly sewing machines and an overlocker. There's the ironing board, its metal iron perpetually turned on, which on days like today makes the windows steam up. There's a cutting table, and underneath are boxes of buttons, zips and trims that look like Andy Warhol's Time Capsules. The radio is the kind with a manual dial and extendable aerial. The rest of the table is strewn with just-cut parts of a pink and yellow striped shirt. At the back of the shop is the kitchenette from which the ladies brew endless cups of tea.

A few years ago a local designer talked Marisa into sewing some feathered skirts for a runway show, because the skirts were tricky to fathom in the sampling stage and the designer didn't trust sending them overseas. And because Marisa and Bruna have ninety years' dressmaking experience between them, and make the hardest jobs look simple. They put their regular customers off and stayed back late to finish the order on time. But the feather quills were thick and tough and broke one of Marisa's geriatric Singers. It was, the designer told me, 'a nightmare'; the pressures of the deadline and the stressed machines upset everybody.

When he came to make the skirts for production to deliver to retail stores, the designer sent them to Guangzhou, the massive Chinese garment production hub, where he paid a fraction of the price charged in Sydney. Who wouldn't? Business is about turning a profit, and it is increasingly hard to do that by manufacturing any product in Australia, or indeed in Britain, the US or France. These are post-post industrial countries, where all we make is skinny lattes and cold-pressed juice – and trouble for the rest of the world.

The feather-skirt designer went out of business despite his cost-cuttings, and he never paid Marisa for her samples. I wish this wasn't a familiar story, but it is. Marisa and I talk about this often.

'I am disappointed,' she says. 'We sew with love.'

My own skirts will be exquisite, with French seams, thirteen stitches per inch, and hand-sewn hems. They are costing me $250 each (and that doesn't include the fabric, which I supplied myself). Expensive. As they should be – I have no intention of throwing them away.

'So,' I urge, as I hand over my hefty wad of cash, 'when will you buy a new machine? Shall I ask my husband to help move the broken one?'

'Isn't it?' she says, and we both understand that she is saying it is too late. I have asked her before why she has no apprentice, and she says she trialled a few fashion students, but they weren't interested in the craft of making clothes, only in fashion's associated trappings; they wanted, she said, to be famous (I don't think she's heard of the blogger phenomenon, but that's the subtext; it's instant gratification they are after, and perhaps a shampoo campaign). Some of Marisa's students feigned a passing interest in the art of setting a sleeve. None wanted to learn to sew a buttonhole by hand. Yes, Marisa could probably afford to invest in new equipment, but she won't go on making clothes here forever. Maybe not past next year.

The next time I visit, there are roadworks outside. The air is thick with tar. Six blokes in fluorescent jackets are shooting the breeze, dropping stray chips from McDonalds bags onto the treacly ground. A ginger kid in a hard hat is the only one working – she twirls her lollypop sign when she sees me, from SLOW to STOP.

I complain to Marisa that it's disruptive, that half the parking spots have disappeared.

'It is good,' she says, 'they will make a garden at the bottom there, they are fixing it up.'

'It needs it,' I tell her, and then I ask something I've often wondered about: Why did she choose this down-at-heel bit of Kings Cross to set up shop? Why not one of the chic arcades in the city, or a leafy street in the suburbs?

'But this is always the smart place, isn't it?' she says. 'All the fashion was on Macleay Street.'

CHAPTER 2

The Couture Effect

Who used to run the fashion system?

In the Jazz Age, stylish enclaves were springing up in Sydney's Kings Cross and Potts Point. Where flappers and bohemians met, fashion followed and by the 1930s there were three frock shops and at least six upscale dressmakers around Macleay Street, just up the road from where Marisa is now.

Beril Jents, Australia's most famous postwar designer and self-styled 'Queen of Couture,' got her start here. In 1933, at the age of fifteen, she applied for a position with an expat-French dressmaker named Madame Gallet, who ran an atelier on neighbouring Orwell Street. Then, as now, to put the word French before the word fashion was to add cachet. If you were Paris-trained, you must be chic. If you were clever, you might market yourself as the next best thing to Chanel.

Back then the top dressmakers wielded their scissors without the need of a pattern. The art of cutting was all. As Gabrielle 'Coco' Chanel said, 'A sketch, a drawing – that's not the body, I don't sell bits of paper.'[1] Chanel cut for hours on end on a house model (fidgeters were fired), obsessing in particular over the set of her sleeves, which she would frequently yank out, re-cut and re-pin, sometimes drawing blood.

Chanel was born in 1883 in the Loire Valley, France. At the age Jents got her start, Chanel was living in an orphanage. Her mother had died of 'poverty, pregnancy and pneumonia'[2] and her father had abandoned her. At eighteen she was working as a shop assistant by day and singing in rowdy bars full of military men by night. When a rich bloke offered her a way out, Chanel went to live with him. His name was Étienne Balsan, and his family had made their money in army uniforms. Balsan played polo, drank like a fish and lived in a chateau; Chanel loafed around his house and learned to ride his horses, and planned her next move – although it has to be said she took her time. She was twenty-six when she opened her fashion business. Initially she sold only hats: funny, plain little straw boaters, the complete opposite of the frou-frou, net-swathed confections that were popular at the time. Money for the venture came from Balsan and Chanel's next love interest, Arthur 'Boy' Capel.

In 1910, Chanel opened her atelier at 21 Rue Cambon – acquiring larger premises at number 31 eight years later (still the address of Chanel HQ today). By the mid-1920s, she had converted *le tout* Paris to her simple black dresses, costume jewellery and jersey suits. Destined to become an iconic figure, between the wars 'she was dressing the world, not only from her couture house but through the millions of copies that were made of her clothes.'[3] We'll come to how that worked in a minute.

To reach Chanel's heights, the teenaged Jents had a way to go. Though proficient enough to make her sister's wedding dress from scratch, she had exaggerated her skills to Madame Gallet. Jents writes in her memoir that, 'At nights, I would cut out the next day's work in newspaper because Madame was using very expensive material – crepe de Chine, chiffons, silks.'[4] She was soon found out. But Gallet, recognising a budding talent, decided to teach rather than fire her. 'As well as the finer points of cutting,' Gallet taught Jents 'about quality – how to appreciate and flow with the cloth.'

It was the era for caring about such things. The anything-goes flair of the '20s died with the Wall Street Crash, and in the '30s formality came back in fashion. In Sydney, as in Paris, London and New York, separate outfits were worn for town and home, day and evening. Hemlines dropped, matching bags and shoes were in vogue and any woman concerned with looking classy, be she in a big city or a country town, wore a hat and gloves in public.

It wasn't just society dames who spoke of 'my dressmaker' – ready-to-wear fashion in specific sizes was a relatively recent invention, and most clothes were still handmade. Girls, rich or poor, learned to sew, darn and knit.

When the Second World War broke out these skills were doubly useful. Everyone had to make do and mend. On the home fronts, there were shortages of men, petrol, metal and food, but restrictions also affected less obviously important things. In the UK, rationing extended to household linens and children's socks, and the austerity rules restricted how much cloth a garment could legally use, as well as quantities of buttons, skirt pleats and even pyjama pockets. Lace and embroidery were banned. Magazines carried advertisements describing 'Useful jobs that girls can do to help win the war!', which detailed things like how to make a pair of house slippers from an old felt hat. Women lucky enough to have stockings didn't chuck them out when they laddered. Clothing rations weren't phased out in Britain until 1949.

Australians had a slightly easier time of it, but still required coupons to buy clothes – those caught flouting the rules (or buying luxuries on the black market) faced fines of up to $100 or a prison stint. In its own nod to the austerity trend, Australia outlawed the long evening dress in 1943.

Party clothes were in short supply in Paris too. Leading couturiers, including Chanel, the surrealist Italian Elsa Schiaparelli and the brilliant bias-cutter Madeleine Vionnet, shut down or fled the city after 1940 when the occupying German forces moved in. Chanel moved to Switzerland, Schiaparelli sailed to New York. Lucien Lelong was one of the few who remained, proclaiming: 'If Paris fashion must die – let it die in France!'[5] No wonder when peace came women yearned to kick up their heels – preferably pretty ones, worn with shockingly extravagant skirts.

The time was ripe for Dior's New Look, something even Jents, a creative designer who generally avoided copying, admits she referenced – at one point knocking off a Dior dress at the request of Mary Hordern, then fashion editor of the *Australian Women's Weekly*.

Christian Dior did not have his own couture house before the war. He was raised in Granville on France's coastal northwest, where his father Maurice co-owned a fertiliser factory. The Diors had money, and when twenty-three-year-old Christian decided on setting up an art gallery in Paris, daddy provided funding. Back then Dior also fancied himself as a composer like Erik Satie, and hung out at Le Boeuf sur le Toit with Jean Cocteau. But he didn't have the musical gift, so he and his friend Jacques Bonjean exhibited works by Cocteau, Max Ernst and Paul Klee. Soon, they joined forces with a third man, Pierre Colle, to show surprising new work by Salvador Dalí, Alberto Giacometti and Alexander Calder. For a while the gallery looked like succeeding, but the bottom fell out of the modern art market at the end of the '20s, just as Maurice Dior's investment portfolio plummeted. Shares worth a pile one night were worthless by morning, and all sorts of people went bust in spectacular fashion. Christian Dior found himself suddenly broke and driven to eke out a living as a freelance illustrator, mostly selling sketches of hats.

He had none of the technical skills of Chanel or Jents. Dior did not sew or cut or make patterns, but he did have ideas – and connections. In 1938 he talked Robert Piguet into hiring him, then later moved to Lelong, where his designs attracted increasing attention.

In 1946 Dior – now forty-one, balding and a little tubby; in pictures he looks less like the sort of man who partied with Cocteau, more like a small town bank manager – consulted his beloved astrologer. The stars were on Dior's side when he accepted investment from textiles manufacturer Marcel Boussac to set up premises of his own on Avenue Montaigne. The very first Christian Dior collection was shown the following year.

Vogue pronounced it 'fresh and put over with great authority'. Ernestine Carter, then newly installed fashion editor at *Harper's Bazaar* in New York, declared that Dior's 'vast skirts, the soft shoulders, the tight bodices, the wasp waists' offered 'a new softness that was positively voluptuous'. It was Carter's boss, the fierce Irish-born editor Carmel Snow, who dubbed the collection 'The New Look'.

Others talked of a fashion revolution, and a return to pleasure; of the thrill, so pronounced after years of going without, of the yards of fabric Dior used – twenty-eight in a single skirt. A snippy few noted that, in fact, Cristóbal Balenciaga had pioneered this silhouette before the war, but Balenciaga was always ahead of his time. Dior's fashion genius was being right on the exact moment.

In his own words, he had 'designed clothes for flower-like women'.[6] 'The style which was being universally hailed as new and original, was nothing but the sincere and natural expression of fashion, which I had always sought to achieve ... It happened that my own inclinations coincided with the tendency of the times.' Dior himself saw that he had 'brought back the neglected art of pleasing'.

Not everyone was happy though. In Paris one morning, ladies who had fought hard for their right to wear short skirts set upon models wearing Dior's designs and tore their dresses to shreds. When the designer travelled to New York, he was ambushed on Park Avenue by a group of women with placards yelling 'DIOR GO HOME!' and 'ONLY SHORT SKIRTS'. In Chicago it happened again, with housewives chanting, 'Mr Dior, we abhor dresses to the floor!' It was fashion against feminism they thought; fashion as a tool of control, reducing women to the purely decorative.

It didn't matter. Dior's New Look would dominate fashion for the next decade, sold in stores as far away as Sydney, and referenced by the likes of Jents and Marisa Regozo the world over. The way that happened was via a handy little thing called the couture caution system, which allowed mass reproduction of Paris designs through official channels.

Cautionary tale

This is how it worked: to gain access to a Paris couture collection show, professionals (store buyers and secondary manufacturers) were required to pay a deposit, known as a 'caution fee', to the house. Think of it like an insurance policy, a payment against which they placed orders for particular models. (Use of the word 'model' is confusing, given its most common meaning today, i.e. pretty girls who get paid wear fashion on the runway. The term 'models' in the couture context refers to the outfits; until the 1960s, the girls who paraded the clothes were called 'mannequins'.)

Pay up, and the couturier granted you permission to reproduce your chosen models in specific territories, or for particular shops.

This is how the department stores Bonwit Teller or Lord & Taylor in New York, for example, could market Dior copies to their American customers.

Most official copies were made up from inferior fabric, which helped bring costs down, although a handful bought by the swankiest department stores might be sewn from imported European fabrics of the same quality used on the original.

A season or so after the legitimate models were displayed in the stores, unlicensed manufacturers would begin to knock them off for the cheaper end of the market – by which time there was nothing the couturier could do about it. At-home dressmakers followed suit. And lo, a trend was born.

At the start of the process designs were fiercely guarded secrets, with paranoid couturiers desperate to keep unscrupulous sketchers out of the collection shows. There are stories of people posing as private buyers, sitting through the presentations poker-faced, then running back to their hotel rooms to sketch from memory what they'd seen, down to the last dart and bow. It's hard to imagine this now, in the Instagram era.

The caution system's origins date back to 1868 when Charles Frederick Worth set up the first modern couture union, the mouthful that was the *Chambre Syndicale de la confection et de la couture pour dames et fillettes*. Its primary purpose was to lobby on behalf of its members on labour and tax issues, but it was also a bid to stop unauthorised copying.

Oh Lord!

Lord & Taylor on 5th Avenue in New York produced the first known official Worth copies in 1874, advertising the fact in *Harper's Bazaar*. At that time, there was no formal distinction made between the top couturiers like Worth, who catered to royalty and the über rich, and the more basic dressmakers further down the ladder. So in 1910, the union marked the difference out in black and white, reserving the term 'Haute Couture' for the select few and binding them by strict rules of operation. The Chambre Syndicale de la Haute Couture Parisienne was born.

Now retailers across the world could buy models under the caution system. In 1946 Mary Hordern had helped the David Jones department store stage Australia's first 'French Fashion Parades'. She attended the Paris collections and selected models by Lucien Lelong, Pierre Balmain and Jacques Fath to be shown on the catwalk locally; in Sydney at David Jones, in Melbourne and Adelaide at Myer, and in Brisbane at Finney, Isles & Co.

In 1947, Hordern did it again with the New Look, and the parades of July 1948 included fifty Dior originals. To talk them up, Christian Dior himself gave an interview to the *Sydney Morning Herald*, in which he enthused, 'Australians have a cleaner, brighter outlook and are more receptive to new ideas than the tired people of European countries.'

For many years David Jones produced official Dior copies. One 1960s advertisement shows a smartly clad women stepping out in Sydney's Hyde Park, and reads: 'Christian Dior has a feeling for wool expressed in this two-piece belted suit with blouse. We purchased the original in Paris and faithfully copied it in pure new wool – part of our exclusive collection of line-for-line copies of the French couture at prices you can afford. Sizes 12 – 14. Colours grey/fuchsia, grey/red, grey/emerald. The original (at left) A$2500. The perfect copy (at right) A$160.'

That Hordern, one of the key figures working under the caution system in Australia, flouted it by asking Jents to run her up an unofficial knock-off is quite funny, isn't it? Before we complain about fast fashion's designer copying culture today, we might remember that it's been going on for donkey's.

Whether clad in official Dior copies or naughty knock-offs, fashionable Australian women of the late 1940s and early '50s were once again braving the hot summers in giant skirts and heavy corsets. Chanel, by the way, had fallen from favour – her sporty, straight-skirted aesthetic did not chime with the times.

Jents remembers the big skirt brigade from Kings Cross – where, before she took over her famously grand rooms in the CBD, she'd rented 'a modern shop' behind Macleay Street opposite the Roosevelt nightclub, a stone's throw from Marisa Regozo's place. The Roosevelt was popular with the horseracing crowd – and the races were then, as now, prime fashion peacocking territory. The women, writes Jents, 'would meet after the races wearing elaborate clothes with exotic hats, all jewelled and feathered'[7] – many of them made by her. Fashion as glamour, as status. Some things never change. Locations do, though.

The newest look

I am walking down Macleay Street, looking for any last vestiges of serious fashion. The frock shops are gone. The nightclubs have relaxed their dress codes, to allow tank tops and jeans. Today, most of the area's *chic* comes from restaurants. I'm about to give up when I see it: Paws Point Boutique, with a 'world-class range' of fashion-forward coats.

For dogs.

The 'Duke' is a lightweight rayon duffel style; the 'Harley Leather Look' boasts 'great zipper details' and a biker-inspired eagle appliqué on the back. I'm drawn to the 'Madonna' (pink patent), but the winner for me is the 'Whistler Puffy'. It comes in two sophisticated colours (chocolate and champagne) trimmed generously with faux fur. It costs the princely sum of $54.

Such riches before you even reach the special occasion department. At Paws Point, you can buy a tuxedo for a bulldog, a ladybird costume for a chihuahua. When I visit it's Easter, and there's the full Playboy bunny ensemble in the window for your canine dress-up fan, complete with pink rabbit ears and a tie-on pompom tail.

'Do people actually buy this stuff?' I ask the girl behind the counter.

'Yeah,' she says. 'You got a dog?'

'Sure,' I lie. 'I'm very interested in this Kermit the Dog outfit. How does the hood work? Do the googly eyes go over his ears?'

'Uh-huh,' she nods. 'Some dogs don't like it though; try to scratch them off. S'not our fault. Depends on the dog.'

'Where's it made?' I say.

'What?'

'Where is this garment made? Are they made in Australia or offshore?'

'Dunno,' she says. 'Sorry, excuse me.' The phone is ringing and I make a run for it.

Canine apparel is now a booming fashion category in its own right. PetsPyjamas, a kind of Net-A-Porter for the doggie-duds world based in Shoreditch, offers 'more than 10,000 pet accessories', curated by a team of in-house pet stylists. Elsewhere, the smart hound may sport a raincoat by British heritage brand Mulberry that matches mummy's, or make like a rock star in a collar set with Swarovski crystals. Milanese leather goods house Valextra sells swanky dog leads, and a purse designed to house the placky bags you take on walkies for scooping up poo. Spoilt bitches, though, insist on Louis Vuitton, where a monogramed leather dog carrier will set you back three grand or more.

The market has even exploded in China, which is weird because you can still order dog for dinner in certain Beijing eateries.

According to the Humane Society, restaurants in Yulin in Guangxi province down south serve up 10,000 dogs over the annual summer solstice festival. That's happening even as sleek Shanghainese urbanites are elevating pugs to celebrity status.

In 2013, Glamour-Sales, an online fashion retailer based in Shanghai, hired an 'über fashionable dog with a glamorous attitude to match' to star in its campaign. They named him Little Glam. When a bunch of look-a-like mutts took to the Glamour-Sales runway modelling sunglasses, necklaces and hair bows, human fans waved pug-shaped balloons and screamed like Beatlemaniacs. A video of the show scored 2.6 million views online, proving so *pup*ular that sales spiked 47 per cent.

CHAPTER 3

More Please, Sir

Want fries with that?

Look, I don't want to risk alienating you and your pug in his bespoke pyjamas, but fashion for dogs is insane. It's just one example of an apparel industry that is out of control, producing way too much: things we don't need and wouldn't want if we weren't so brainwashed by advertising and celebrities who never wear the same thing twice.

Indeed, so used are we to that last concept that back in 2012, when the Duchess of Cambridge wore a pale pink frock to two events, she made headlines: 'Kate Wears Same Dress Twice in 11 days!' Said dress was by the London-based New Zealander Emilia Wickstead and retailed at more than £2,000, so Kate would have to wear it many more times to get a reasonable cost per wear – but that was beside the point. It's impossible to imagine the equivalent of Dior's New Look being 'in' for an entire decade today. Our current definition of glamour is based on rapid trend turnover. You're nobody unless your outfit is brand spanking new.

Fretting about wearing a party dress twice in case the repeat performance turns up on social media and makes you feel like a C-lister, is now an ordinary person thing. Most of us aren't so rich that we don't have to think before we splurge, but then again most of the garments we purchase aren't in Wickstead's price range.

According to the *Wall Street Journal*, American shoppers bought an average of sixty-three-and-a-bit garments per person in 2013, but spent only $907 in total. Take the socks and jocks out of that equation and you're still left with a shockingly cheap average garment price of less than $15. Meanwhile 40 per cent of our in-store purchases are unplanned.

We shop on whim because we are told to ('Hurry, sale ends this weekend!'). We shop for the thrill of it, out of habit, as a leisure pursuit. We shop because it's easy to do so, and sometimes because we are bored, lonely, insecure or heartbroken.

We tell ourselves, as Madame Bovary did, that we deserve it, and that a treat will make us feel better. Little has changed since Gustave Flaubert was writing about his doomed heroine, except that such behaviour has gained a name: 'retail therapy'. We are encouraged to do it to heal our psychological ills, to sate some yawning emotional void within us; but too often this is bad medicine.

Back in 2001, a British study by Publicis found that, far from being a salve, the act of shopping can actually cause depressed feelings. That same year, the *Guardian* reported the results of a European Union survey into addictive spending. 'Thirty-three per cent of consumers displayed a high level of addiction to rash or unnecessary consumption.'[1] The formal name for this affliction is oniomania – but even as doctors treat it as an addiction, with similar drivers to alcoholism or drug dependency (low self-esteem, a substitute for love, the urge to appease feelings of deprivation with 'things'), rather than stigmatise it, we seem to think it's cute. Hence Sophie Kinsella's *Shopaholic* novels are bestsellers.

In 2015, American households owed an average of $15,609 on their credit cards. The collective British credit card debt was nearly £63 billion; in Australia it was $51 billion. Analysts predict the current generation of teenagers won't even try to pay it off. We risk becoming insecure shopping addicts, buying a lot of rubbish on impulse to wear once, spending beyond our means for no good reason.

According to Livia Firth, who is trying to get us to slow down and shop for fashion more sustainably by way of her Green Carpet Challenge, eighty billion garments are produced globally each year. 'Just imagine the resources this requires,' says Firth.[2] 'And underneath it all we have an army of millions of humans, tilling the soil and picking the cotton; ginning, weaving, dyeing; working looms, sewing embellishments and sequins and buttons in huge factories.' Only we don't often remember that, when buying a seven-pack of knickers with the days of the week embroidered on them. Or a silly yellow jumper that's too small but never mind because it's cashmere, AND A CRAZY BARGAIN WE ARE POWERLESS TO RESIST.

Are we really such dopes? If the fashion industry is having a laugh at our expense, is it not our own fault?

In 2013 the Kansas-bred boundary-pusher Jeremy Scott was named creative director of the Italian house of Moschino, the one celebrated in the '80s for its kitsch irreverence. Scott's first Moschino runway collection, ready-to-wear Autumn '14, was inspired by McDonald's and the cartoon character Spongebob Squarepants. There were red skirt-suits trimmed with yellow plastic chain trims, handbags carried on fast food trays and gowns of draped silk printed to resemble junk-food packaging. It was bedazzled with Scott's take on the iconic Golden Arches, morphed into a Moschino 'M'. He splashed this logo on everything from shoes and sweatshirts to fur coats – and an iPhone case shaped like a packet of fries.

Scott claimed his aim was simply to make people smile[3] – he enjoys a joke; his eau de toilette, Moschino Fresh Couture, is bright blue and comes in a bottle designed to look like window cleaner – but it was impossible not to make the fast-fashion connection, or see the whole thing as either comment on, or part of, the cynical commodification of self-expression through style.

It was the season for it.

Supermarket sweep

In London, the week before that Moschino show, accessories designer Anya Hindmarch presented her vision for Autumn '14 on a moving catwalk-conveyer-belt against a backdrop of barcodes. Hindmarch doesn't make clothes, so all the models wore the same white dresses, the better to show off their handbags, which this season featured ads for branded household groceries. There were clutches made to look like boxes of Swan Vestas matches and Ariel washing power, canister-shapes like packets of McVitie's Digestives biscuits, and satchels and totes embossed with vintage Kellogg's graphics, including Tony the Frosties Tiger.

The show, titled 'Counter Culture' and attended by the actor Richard E. Grant (because, why not?) was sponsored by Kellogg's, which launched a limited edition range of Anya Hindmarch cereal packets to promote it. Cornflakes were temporarily renamed Handbags At Dawn Flakes (RRP £3) and sold through Hindmarch's London stores, Harvey Nichols and Waitrose supermarkets. Fans were encouraged to use the hashtag #cerealshopper on social media for the chance to win an electric-blue leather tote emblazoned with Tony the Tiger's lipsmacking grin (RRP £1,350).

Like Moschino's, this collection was either a lot of fun, deeply Warholian, a wry comment on consumer culture, or a gloom-inducing example of fashion reduced to an Instagram joke – depending on your point of view.

Hindmarch is an extraordinary woman; mother to five kids, she is an MBE, a UK trade ambassador, and the recipient of many fashion gongs. She designed her first bag, referencing a vintage sample she'd found in Florence, a year after leaving high school – and received 500 orders before she'd even gone into production. By the time those models with their shopping trolleys were gliding down her runway, Hindmarch had her name on more than forty stores in Europe, the US, Asia and the Middle East.

What would it take to upstage her? Try the mighty Chanel Shopping Centre. It didn't matter that Hindmarch had gotten in first with the ironic supermarket concept – when the Paris shows swung around at the end of the month, Karl Lagerfeld's checkout chic was all anyone was talking about.

Lagerfeld is arguably the most famous designer of our times, maybe more famous than Chanel herself. When, in 1971, Coco died in her private apartments at the Ritz, aged eighty-seven, she left behind a house that many dismissed as past its prime – Chanel's clients, like her silhouettes, were getting old. Her former assistant designers took over and the house limped along until 1983, when its co-owner Alain Wertheimer poached a gun designer from another Paris house: Chloé.

Karl Lagerfeld was then forty-nine years old, known for his rivalry with Yves Saint Laurent and his love of eighteenth-century antiques. He was a collector of grand houses, who tied his ponytail back with a ribbon and carried a signature fan (he used it to waft cigarette smoke out of his eyes in nightclubs). Few could have predicted that Lagerfeld would still be in the top Chanel job thirty years later, heading a company worth US\$7 billion – Alain and his brother

Gérard are also still around, although quietly behind the scenes; they are the grandsons of the man who financed Chanel No. 5 perfume in 1924 – but there indeed he was, masterminding a *Stepford Wives* dreamscape of joke-grocery-stuffed aisles inside the historic Grand Palais on the Champs-Élysées.

Inside this surreal installation, models shopped for over 500 different novelty items, including Chanel-branded eggs and milk. There was Chanel bottled water (Eau de Chanel No. 0), Chanel pasta, a Chanel cheese counter, a hardware department stocking Chanel chainsaws. As for the clothes, Lagerfeld had re-invented bourgeois tweed (again), adding volume and playing with proportion – there were round-shouldered coats, baggy flying suits and abbreviated blouson jackets, layered spliced skirts and shorts and shrunken leather corset belts. The mood was kept *real* with the addition of sneakers – 'If you want to look really ridiculous, you go in stilettos to the supermarket,' Lagerfeld told Style.com – and the hole-ridden long johns worn by Cara Delevingne that seemed to have been attacked by hungry goats.

American model Ondria Hardin slouched on set in a sporty panelled tweed dress of lemon yellow and pink worn with knee-high white basketball boots, the quilted bag slung over her shoulder encased in a polystyrene meat tray and slapped with a sticker that read '100% agneau' – *agneau* is French for lamb.

After the show, Lagerfeld explained it all in Orwellian double-think, or was it nonsense poetry? 'We did an art gallery,' he said, referring to the fake museum he'd conjured the previous season (complete with seventy-five fake art works – every one of them designed by him) 'and an art gallery is essentially a supermarket of paintings for rich people, so [this time] we decided to return to the real world, because people who go to an art gallery also go to the supermarket. But we have to break away from this exclusive, luxurious side.'[4]

That explains why Lagerfeld's metal shopping baskets were strung with leather-threaded chains, like those used on Chanel's iconic 2.55 quilted leather bags. Fancy taking one to Waitrose to pick up your Handbags at Dawn Flakes? Six months later, those baskets were commercially produced – they retailed for £7,190. If only getting the rest of the joke were half so easy: after the show, when editors tried to shoplift those witty packets of Little Black Tea and Jambon Cambon (which they did, in their scores), they were stopped by security guards. The Chanel-stamped items were auctioned off for charity. No word on what happened to the meat trays.

In real life, that won't happen. No burly bloke will stand in your way. Whatever your fashionable heart desires is there for the taking, at all hours.

Vending machines in Tokyo spew out tailored suits for businessmen who've been out all night. At airports, you can buy luxury leather goods that cost more than your plane ticket. You can shop on your tablet while pretending to pay bills, or on your phone while your spouse thinks you're talking to the in-laws. While the much-admired fashion critic Suzy Menkes has said she thinks 'we need to realise that it's morally wrong to buy a bikini for the same price as a cappuccino',[5] that doesn't seem to be happening. In today's click-to-buy culture, saving up for some coveted thing, dreaming, waiting or – heaven forbid – denying are things of the past. It's not just fantasy supermarkets selling clothes; real ones do too.

The first grocery store to introduce a fast-fashion line was Asda, the British chain, owned by the American giant Walmart. The George at Asda range launched in 1990, named after its designer-for-hire. George Davies, the son of a Liverpool sausage-maker, is also the man behind high street chain Next, and after Asda he came up with Per Una (which he subsequently sold to Marks & Spencer for £125 million) but George is the one of his brands that changed the retail landscape most drastically.

According to a 2014 report in the *Financial Times*, 'apparel is growing rapidly in UK food retail'. The shop floor space allocated to non-food items may be smaller, but the profit margins on them are way bigger. No wonder there's a rush to market apparel as if it were fruit and veg.

In the UK, Tesco and Sainsbury's soon followed Asda's lead. Men can buy a tie from Sainsbury's Tu collection for £5, or a puffa coat for a few quid more; women can shop for Tu ankle boots and swimwear as they're picking up their loo rolls and dog food. In Australia, Collette Dinnigan, once known for her luxurious lace ladies' wear, did a kids' collection for the discount supermarket chain Aldi, while over at Coles, prices for Mix brand womenswear start at $8. I'm hard pushed to think of anything more depressing – because someone always pays the price for too cheap.

UK supermarket clothing brands and US discounters have eclipsed the fast fashion giants as key players in the hideous devaluing of cashmere. Once a true luxury fibre, it's now an over-produced environmental nightmare that has grazed the grasslands of the Alashan Plateau 'down to a moonscape'.[6] To find out how this happened, you can't beat Lucy Siegle's account in *To Die For*; suffice to say that cashmere sweaters used to cost many hundreds of dollars and were designed to last a lifetime; in 2006 George at Asda was flogging them for £22. You need a lot more goats than the wilds of Mongolia can sustain to produce economies on that sort of scale.

The day after Chanel's Autumn '14 show, Asda execs saw a smart promo op, and staged a fashion happening in the 'five for 4' juice aisle at their Park Royal branch (near Wembley) 'with the looks and models to compete with the Parisian catwalks'.[7] Well, kinda. Cara Delevingne was conspicuous in her absence, but at least you could buy the frozen peas in the models' trolleys. Probably if you tried to nick them, the security reaction would be the same as at the Grand Palais.

'If Chanel can do it, so can George,' said the latter's then head of design, Helen Low, of the Park Royal event. 'After all, we bring the latest trends straight from the catwalk to our customers every single day at a fraction of the designer price tag.'

The George brand bought fabric from one of the factories based at Rana Plaza. In the aftermath of the disaster, George – and Walmart – refused to sign the Accord on Fire and Building Safety in Bangladesh. Six months later, when fire devastated the Aswad Composite Mills in Dakha, killing nine people, George was a client again.[8] The Accord is a five-year contract between brands, factories and local trade unions that makes safety inspections compulsory. In the UK, Asda's competitors Sainsbury's, Tesco and Morrisons are signatories – at the time of writing Walmart and Asda still are not.

Stuff and nonsense

New clothes have become so instantly available we've lost that connection, once so deep, to how the things we wear are made. When this happens, fashion becomes unmoored from reality: its beauty is diluted because it has no soul. It's just a quick fix of instant gratification – empty calories.

But there is no escaping it. Commercial fashion is everywhere we look. Retail stores are presented as cultural institutions, and designers have become celebrities. Red carpet coverage has taken over awards shows while style-obsessed reality TV – *Next Top Model* and *Project Runway* – scores monster ratings. Since *The Devil Wears Prada*, the fashion film has become mainstream and museums are mounting fashion exhibitions like never before. There are more students on fashion courses, and more colleges offering them. In 2013 the publishers of *Vogue* opened their own school in the UK – if you can make it through the rigorous selection process and find the tuition fees, you can take a year-long diploma at the Condé Nast College of Fashion & Design in Soho.

By the time you graduate, there will be even more ways to market and shop for clothes. Already we are seeing shopable runways, led by Topshop and Burberry's click-to-buy livestreams, which is surely the death knell for those endless seasonal lead times. Jeremy Scott's Spring '15 Moschino show was Barbie-themed, with a capsule collection of candy-pink doll clothes for adult humans for sale the very next day.

CHAPTER 4

Status Anxiety

Them and us

So how did we get here? Conspicuous consumption is as old as the hills, but for most of human history it has been the preserve of the select few. Luxury goods were a tool used by the ruling classes to show the hoi polloi they meant business.

Egyptian queens were gadding about in their jewelled collars while their lowly female subjects who worked in the fields wore nothing but white kilts. Dancing girls wore nothing at all.

The Romans passed the first sumptuary laws to prevent the *nouveau riche* from dressing above their station – true excess was for emperors (and their womenfolk). Legend has it Caligula plaited the tail of his horse with gems, and Antonia Minor, the youngest daughter of Marc Antony, ordered her fish bejewelled so they might glitter more brightly as they swam.

In sixteenth-century England, Queen Elizabeth I decreed that only royals could wear clothes of purple silk or velvet of any colour, although she allowed 'dukes, marquises, and earls' and their wives to dabble in these fabrics as linings and trims. The Statutes of Apparel also forbade those of lesser rank from frocking up in 'cloth mixed or embroidered with any gold or silver'. STEP AWAY FROM THE PRE-CIOUS METAL. Commoners must keep their dirty mitts off 'cowls, sleeves, partlets, and linings, trimmed with spangles or pearls', and leave the 'fur of leopards' well alone too. Because what is luxury if every WAG has it?

Elizabeth had over 3,000 gowns, many trimmed with another restricted fabric, ermine fur, which represented purity because it was believed the fastidious critter would rather die than soil its fur. Eliz-abeth's wigs numbered more than eighty and were sewn, in Liberace proportions, with pearls. Her ruffs were festooned with the finest lace. Her farthingales stiffened with whalebone. Bess was the boss, and she dressed like it. Clothes announce who we are – or who we want to be.

Perhaps the most famous royal showoff was Marie Antoinette, she of the three-foot-high hair. Known as *poufs au sentiments*, these wigs were designed by the woman snidely referred to as the Minister of Fash-ion, Rose Bertin, and styled by the first celebrity hairdresser, Léonard Autié. They contained miniature gardens, street scenes, and most famously, in the summer of 1788, an exact replica of the victorious French battleship *La Belle Poule*. Marie Antoinette's standing kid-glove order ran to eighteen pairs a week, and she had two yards of new taffeta delivered daily, just to cover the basket they were carried in.

The French queen's sartorial extremes continue to inspire art and gossip today. In 2010 shoe designer Christian Louboutin released his 'Marie' heels, which came in a box shaped like a Fabergé egg – and cost US$6,295. They were embroidered by couture atelier Lesage with a likeness of the doomed one's ship hairstyle. Dita Von Teese has a pair; I saw them when she let me poke my nose into her walk-in clos-ets – she has two, each filling an entire room, with custom-built shelves in Chinoiserie red. There are hundreds of pairs of shoes in there. That Marie Antoinette has a lot to answer for – still inspiring fashion maniacs today.

In fact it was the 'Sun King', Louis XIV, and his finance minister, Jean-Baptiste Colbert, who brought the passion for fashion to the French court – a good century before Marie Antoinette was born.

The couturiers' guild, great-granddaddy of today's Chambre Syndicale, was established on Coulbert's watch in the 1640s, and the city swelled with embroiderers, lace-makers, haberdashers, milliners. Fashion fans pored over increasingly elaborate 'fashion plates' – detailed engravings of society figures, printed, from the 1670s, in popular magazines like *Mercure Galant*. It was said that Colbert encouraged fashion in order to quash political intrigue – courtiers vying to outdo each other's supremely camp outfits would be too busy trying to avoid bankruptcy to plot against the King.

Louis XIV also had his sumptuary laws – he decreed that only the nobility could sport red shoe-heels. When anyone raised the subject of sartorial excess, he is said to have shrugged, 'Fashion is the mirror of history.'

Paris continues to rule fashion. For all the talk of Shanghai and Mumbai as the centres of the future, the city still occupies a special place in the style vernacular, being the only legitimate home of haute couture.

Worldwide, today's couture customers are estimated to number less than 4,000 people. The couture houses do not release prices to the public (perhaps not even to their clients; if you have to ask, you can't afford it), but according to Valerie Steele, director of the Museum at the Fashion Institute of Technology, New York, a pair of haute couture pants might cost $50,000, and gowns up to $300,000. In theory there is no ceiling on price. Should you wish for that runway look fancied up with real diamonds or embroidered with detail from *La Belle Poule*, it's unlikely anyone is going to say no.

Often misused, the term 'couture' refers to made-to-order clothes created by a few officially recognised ateliers, which must be members of the Chambre Syndicale. Beryl Jents was no more 'queen of couture' than I am. Dior and Chanel are couture houses. Jean Paul Gaultier is one, Givenchy another. Christian Lacroix was a couturier before he went belly up. Those on the 'in' list must conform to strict rules, governing, for instance, the atelier's number of full-time, Paris-based employees (at least twenty), and the number of designs presented each year (at least seventy-five). The Syndicale allows a select few 'foreign members' including Valentino, which is based in Rome. Giorgio Armani is a newish recruit (Armani Privé launched in 2005).

Despite those exorbitant prices, the couture industry today is a loss-making dinosaur, fashion's ultimate indulgence. That's partly because there are no economies of scale – the surprising maternity bridal gown of ivory neoprene with matching embroidered cape that closed Chanel's Spring '14 Couture show, for example, took 933 hours to make.[1] Most designs are never produced, especially not if the sample has been lent to a celebrity to wear to an awards show – *quelle horreur!* Couture's clients are famously discreet.

And yet while most of us will never wear, or even see up close, a piece of haute couture fashion, the idea of it is embedded in popular culture. When we think Fashion (with a capital 'F') we think Paris, *non?* It is Audrey Hepburn in *Sabrina*, dressed by Hubert de Givenchy and sighing, 'Paris is always a good idea.' It is Christian Dior and his New Look. It's Coco Chanel's apartment and Yves Saint Laurent's Le Smoking. It's leather goods by Louis Vuitton and Hermès, jewels from Cartier and Boucheron – Paris is inextricably linked to the top names of luxury fashion.

When, in the 1920s, the socialite Rita Lydig made her annual voyage to the city from New York, she travelled with forty Louis Vuitton trunks.[2]

In 1835, Louis Vuitton was a thirteen-year-old boy setting out from his village in the Jura mountains to seek his fortune. It took him two years to reach Paris. There, just as the first ocean liners were about to make their debut Atlantic crossings, Vuitton found work with a travel trunk-maker (name of Maréchal, case you're wondering) – and stayed for seventeen years. In 1854, newly married and keen to take his place as a man of substance in the world, Vuitton struck out on his own. His big idea was to modify the traditional trunk, flattening the lid to make it stackable and replacing the leather that was prone to cracking with a flexible, lightweight canvas. Later, he monogrammed this to foil copycats, and that simple act made this thickset gentleman with the intense stare and groucho moustache an unwitting founding father of today's designer logo culture.

By the time Lydig was a big spender, Louis Vuitton, the man, was dead, but his company was known for making the most luxurious luggage in the world. Still is.

Lydig ordered her umbrellas from Cartier, complete with platinum handles and diamond tops. Cartier is quintessentially Parisian too.

In 1847, Louis-Francois Cartier took over the Rue Montorgueil premises of his one-time boss, the jeweller Adolphe Picard. Monsieur Cartier was the consummate networker and had soon scored his first royal client. His sons and grandsons became jewellers and inherited this flair for wooing VIPs. Louis-Francois's son Alfred had big ambitions for global expansion. He in turn sent his son Pierre to Russia to study with Fabergé, then to New York to butter up the Vanderbilts and Rockefellers. Pierre's brother Louis married a Hungarian countess, branched into men's wristwatches and hired the designer Jeanne

Toussaint – who created the Duchess of Windsor's panther brooches (the ones my grandmother aspired to). By the early 1900s the house of Cartier was established as the go-to tiara joint for European royals.

Lydig's shoes – at least 300 pairs of them – were made bespoke by Pietro Yantorny. An Italian émigré from Calabria, like Vuitton he moved to Paris to make his fortune. Yantorny was blessed with Clarke Gable looks and plenty of chutzpah – he displayed a sign in the window of his Place Vendôme shop proclaiming himself 'the most expensive shoemaker in the world'. Perhaps he started the rumours that his insteps were fashioned from the wood of antique Stradivarius violins – they weren't, but the idea added to his glamour. A single pair of Yantorny custom-made slippers might take six months to make and, in 1914, cost the client 25,000 francs[3] – more than $100,000 in today's money.

Mouna Ayoub is the equivalent of Rita Lydig today – although Lydig was descended from Spanish dukes, and Ayoub has more humble origins. She was a waitress when she met her future husband Nasser Al-Rashid, an adviser to the Saudi royal family, in Paris. They married in 1978 and she moved to Riyadh, but made regular trips back to Paris for the couture shows. By 2014 she had amassed 1,598 couture purchases 'plus or minus two, I have to redo the math'.[4] Now divorced and living in Monaco, Ayoub wears couture every time she goes out. She wears each outfit just once before retiring it to storage, either in the second apartment she bought in Monaco explicitly for that purpose, or the high-security storage facility she maintains near the French city of Tours.[5]

The rich have always known how to throw their cash around – luxury was created for that very purpose. *But what the Chanel has that got to do with us?*

CHAPTER 5

Because You're Worth It

Strata titles

My dictionary defines luxury as 'something considered an indulgence rather than a necessity', but that might apply to a bubble bath as well as a couture gown.

Today we use the word to categorise fashion in terms of how expensive it is, *or appears to be*: a coat from a top brand might be luxuriously priced, but that brand also sells trinkets that aren't worth much at all, in real terms – although they make a tidy profit. A silicone phone case is just that, whatever the name attached. Logo-bearing key fobs can be knocked out on Chinese assembly lines for peanuts. Designer lipsticks and perfumes carry substantial mark-ups and sell in far greater numbers than clothes.

If we can't always identify a luxury brand by its products, we can recognise its image – for these are the storied houses, those at the top of the pyramid, helmed by high-profile names such as Lagerfeld and Scott, Riccardo Tisci (at Givenchy) or Francisco Costa (at Calvin Klein), and the superstar brand builders like Tom Ford and Marc Jacobs who run their own shows.

Midmarket is a crowded space, occupied by all the stuff that is a little bit expensive, but not bank-breakingly so, and mostly designed by people we've never heard of. It includes the Jigsaws and J.Crews of the world as well as 'contemporary' brands like Maje and Sandro.

Also in this space are diffusion brands, designer spin-offs at friendlier price-points – Armani Exchange, for example. Remember D&G? It merged with the main Dolce and Gabbana line in 2012 – a sign of the times. This middle sector is contracting, which is a shame because, traditionally, brands that charged a sensible amount for the garments they produced had more ethical supply chains than those lower down.

At the bottom is cheap fashion, aka 'mass market' or 'high street' – terms that have in the last fifteen years become interchangeable with 'fast fashion' – although, increasingly, brands are trying to distance themselves from that. Here lies your $25 party frock, your supermarket cashmere and your jumpsuit that's kind of like the Gucci one only creases like a bastard.

Once upon a time we all knew where we belonged. As a Yorkshire teenager, I shopped at Etam, Dorothy Perkins and Miss Selfridge – I bought leggings and off-the-shoulder T-shirts and lace fingerless gloves that made me feel like Madonna, but I didn't buy them every week: I bought them on high days and holidays (or when I got paid from my Saturday job). I shopped at Topshop too – but it wasn't the beacon of fashion-forward excitement it is today. I'd have no more aspired to a Louis Vuitton bag (or key fob) than I would a spaceship – it simply wasn't on my radar.

Back then in '80s and '90s Britain, recent uni grads shopped at Oasis and Warehouse, solicitors' wives at Jaeger, average mums at M&S. Artists, music and fashion people either made their own clothes, or kept the likes of Vivienne Westwood in business. The sorts of women who partied at Annabel's and holidayed in St Barts shopped at Chanel. No one crossed over unless they won the Football Pools, or lost their house.

Simple. The end.

But knowing your place is so last century. As we approached the millennium, the system sprung leaks. We became the L'Oréal generation. Fed on Beyoncé telling us 'we're worth it', we were no longer content to look up at society's doyennes of fashion; we wanted to join them. And for those of us who hadn't thought of that yet, there was *Sex and the City*.

The HBO TV show about the lives of four Manhattan career girls was a total fashion game-changer, watched by millions of women across the globe from 1998 to 2004. Sarah Jessica Parker played Carrie Bradshaw, a woman whose worldview can be summed up by the recorded greeting on her answer machine: 'I'm not here but my shoes are so leave them a message.'

Carrie was a girl for the age: Single Income No Kids, she worshiped at the Church of Saint Manolo of Blahnik and was obsessed with *Vogue*. 'I've spent $40,000 on shoes and I have no place to live? I will literally be the old woman who lived in her shoes,' she said, when threatened with the loss of her rent-controlled apartment. And 'I'm homeless! I'm gonna be a bag lady! A Fendi bag lady, but a bag lady.' By that time we all knew a Baguette wasn't bread.

When Fendi lent SATC's stylist Patricia Field its now-iconic squashy oblong handbag, it promptly sold out. As Parker recalled, 'At this time, things were inaccessible and out of reach [for us]; Fendi was really the first important design house to loan us items.' Field had been combing thrift stores for designer bargains, so 'having the Fendi Baguette was a very big deal, and the gateway to everything else.'[1]

SATC was nominated for fifty-four Emmys; you couldn't open a paper without reading about it, or move in the subway for grown women in tutus. Thanks to Carrie, it was now socially acceptable to live beyond your means, spending silly money on wild luxury fashion. We all wanted to be the woman who lived in her shoes! The Baguette begat the 'It' bag phenomenon (try saying that after three Appletinis), as contenders from rival houses tried to top its cult status with hit designs of their own. Mrs Prada had done her first nylon backpacks in the '80s, and Louis Vuitton had its Sprouse and Murakami moments, but now the designer bag craze exploded: we went berserk over Chloé's Paddington and Balenciaga's Lariat styles. We learned to call metal studs and locks 'hardware' and spot the right ones. Nerdy bag names (Chanel's 2.55) and facts about the minor celebs who carried them (Mischa Barton from *The O.C.*!) passed into pop culture lore.

Meanwhile, the once-boring British leather goods brand Mulberry – founded by a man called Roger and known for its nice, reliable belts – received a cash injection from Asia, and was suddenly totally cool. Luella Bartley came up with Mulberry's first It bag in 2002. The Gisele was named after model Gisele Bündchen, and featured harness strapping and dangling leather heart charms. It was an instant hit. I remember trying to buy that $1500 bag a few years ago, and the embarrassing moment when I handed over my credit card to be told it was declined. Mulberry also had big hits with bags named after Alexa Chung and Lana Del Ray. I couldn't afford those either.

She's got it

The French house of Hermès was the first to sell a handbag named in an It girl's honour – but it wasn't created especially for her. In 1955 Grace Kelly appeared at the Cannes film festival with an oversized leather top-handle Hermès bag. She carried the same style again when her engagement to Prince Rainier of Monaco was announced, and was snapped a little later holding one protectively across her possibly-preggers belly. The bag was a 1935 design introduced by Robert Dumas, son-in-law of Émile-Maurice Hermès, the third generation family member who'd expanded the business in the 1920s. No one knows exactly who started calling that bag 'the Kelly' after the Grace sightings – but these days it is as much an icon as the movie star royal.

'It is still the number two best selling bag we have,'[2] Dumas's grandson Guillaume de Seynes told me one breezy Sydney day down by the Opera House. De Seynes, a managing director of Hermès, was in town with the travelling Festival des Métiers, which had set up shop in the Museum of Contemporary Art. I say shop, but that was really beside the point. You couldn't buy any of the truly luxurious items showcased – it was about the processes, from bag and watch making to silk scarf printing. 'The reason we come is to communicate what we mean by "contemporary craftsmanship",' said de Seynes.

At the exhibition, silk printer Kamel Hamadou explained how he fell 'hopelessly in love' with the scarf-making process when he joined Hermès. His contract was for one month; he stayed twenty-eight years. I asked him to write his details in my notebook and under 'job title' he put 'storyteller'. He said, 'For me, when I touch the silk it's like a baby with the mother, the contact. You know what I mean? It's *quelque chose en plus*, more sensation. It's not only a scarf we produce; it's an *objet*. First you have to select the best raw material.'

Hermès owns silk farms in Brazil, and weaves its own cloth in Lyons, home of the French silk industry since the eighteenth century. The brand's *carrés* (squares) are also made in Lyons, in Hermès-owned workshops, where they are printed and cut, and their edges hand-rolled. 'You take time with your tools, your knowledge and your heart to transform it,' continued Hamadou. 'You make it by yourself but *for someone*. You might not know who that person is, but you know they care about it.'[3]

I watched a woman named Laurence hand-stitch a bag with beeswax-coated linen thread. She makes each one from start to finish, from leather produced in Hermès-owned tanneries to ensure quality (there are Hermès tanneries in France, Italy and the US, and a croc farm in Australia). 'Every time it's different,' she said. 'I do feel these bags have a soul.'

The first Festival des Métiers was held in Seattle, where Hermès had a new store to promote. Visitor reactions were so positive that they kept on going. By the time it came to Sydney, it had toured the world. 'For us craftsmanship is a living reality,' said de Seynes. 'It's not just for the show. It's our every day. We have 2,300 people in our leather ateliers working like this.' They make wallets and belts, as well as the famed Cavale saddles, the Calèche travel bags and the Kellys and Birkins.

In 1981 the singer Jane Birkin sat next to Jean-Louis Dumas (son of Robert) on a Paris flight. She was carrying a ratty straw bag and the story goes that when she shoved it in the overhead locker its contents spilled out. Jean-Louis was inspired. The Hermès atelier made her a bespoke leather weekender and the Birkin bag was born. If you want one today you must get your name on the waitlist. The official line is that you need not have a pre-existing relationship with Hermès, but everybody knows it helps.

These bags weren't designed to be easily available or to spark high-turnover trends. As de Seynes said, 'I always like that sentence my great-grandfather Emile Hermès was so fond of: "A luxury object is one that you can repair". That says a lot to me about the real significance of purchasing a well-made object. We see this every day at

Hermès. After thirty, even forty years people bring us their bags [to repair]; maybe they belonged to their mothers, their fathers. They have become companion objects, imbued with a special magic. Important CEOs come to us and say, "Please can you repair the brief-case? Because each time I have been successful I have used it."'

'It's giving the object personality?' I said.

'Okay, yes,' he said slowly, cocking his head. Then he pushed me gently back on track: because for de Seynes the point of luxury is nothing so cute as *personality*; it's longevity. A little something in leather by Hermès is designed to last, and to be fixed when necessary, so it can last some more. 'That's absolutely essential because it goes back to our roots, when we were equestrian harness makers – a harness is a functional object made to use for years. It's not like we were born as couturiers, where you imagine a dress for one evening,' he said.

De Seynes and I didn't discuss Michael Tonello; it would have been *not very Hermès of me* to bring up that particular gentleman. Tonello is former makeup artist from Massachusetts turned eBay reseller, and author of the book *Bringing Home the Birkin*. It's seismic stuff. Outsmarting the waitlist system, he made it his mission to de-mystify Hermès, zipping all over the globe disguised as a well-heeled customer in order to buy Hermès items to re-sell online for a profit. In doing so, Tonello was tearing down the idea of us and them. In his brazen new world: you wanted the bag, you had the money, you got it. No sumptuary laws for him. Although it did help that, in the early 2000s when all this was happening, Hermès didn't have its own etail.[4]

And yet despite Tonello's best intentions to drag Hermès out of the exclusive realm, it didn't really work. Hermès remains one of the few genuinely exclusive luxury brands. The waitlists continue. Although they have online shopping now, they still work slowly; still produce goods entirely by artisanal hand, in France; still make it virtually impossible to get your hands on certain pieces. Hermès doesn't run on built-in obsolescence. Their bags never go on sale. 'We transcend fashion I think,' said de Seynes, 'we are active in the fashion space, but we are not a fashion brand.' There is no Hermès diffusion line – 'It would not be possible to imagine. We don't know what it means.'

If anything, they've gone the other way. The starting price for a Kelly in 2000 was US$4,800. By 2013 it was $7,600.[5] Times that by ten if you want croc. I asked de Seynes why the price-hike, and he shrugged. 'We don't do marketing prices. We look at our costs.'

Elsewhere, it was inevitable that the It bag would be replaced by the It shoe. Stefano Pilati at Yves Saint Laurent won the people's prize with his Tribute design. Around 2009 its drag-queen-worthy plat-form and 10.5 centimetre heel became ubiquitous. Rumour has it Pilati's replacement, Hedi Slimane, loathes the Tribute, but has to keep it in the product mix for his reconfigured Saint Laurent Paris because demand won't die. I often see a tribute to the Tribute totter-ing down the street, no matter, it seems, that it's crazy uncomfy and impractical. Fashion is weird like that.

Still, those in the know wouldn't touch a Tribute with a barge pole these days (over, sorry). Actually those in the know dropped it three months after it came out and moved onto the next thing. I remem-ber writing a story for *Vogue* about the 'trophy jacket'. Then came the 'statement necklace' and the 'hero sweater'. What now? Drama dress/wardrobe-refreshing mini kilt/stealth coat/beaded fruit-shaped key chain of the season?

The quest for the latest It item isn't just expensive; it's exhausting. Silent movie star Clara Bow was the first It girl (she starred in the 1927 Paramount movie, *It*, based on Elinor Glyn's novel about a fascinat-ing flapper) but if you fancy blaming a single person for our current – and by all accounts terminal – case of It-itis, I nominate SJP.

Weasel words: masstige and accessible luxury

Management consultancy Bain & Company track growth and trends with their annual Global Luxury Study. In 2013, it described 10 per cent year-on-year growth in the luxury sector, noting, 'each year, more "HENRYs" (High Earnings, Not Rich Yet) become potential customers, with ten times as many HENRYs as ultra-affluent individuals.' Alas poor Henry is not the smartest boy in the class – he might earn a bit but he regularly blows dough he can't afford on luxury status symbols. Henry's significant other is Carrie Bradshaw.

In *Deluxe: How Luxury Lost its Lustre*, Dana Thomas tells how the process began in the 1980s with the rise of the American meritocracy, which meant that: 'Anyone and everyone could move up the economic and social ladder and indulge in the trappings of luxury.'[6] Family-owned luxury businesses began selling out to big corporations, and rapid expansion ensued.

The luxury market is now dominated by three giant multi-brand corporations: Louis Vuitton Moët Hennessy, Kering (formerly PPR), and Compagnie Financière Richemont SA.

LVMH owns luxury fashion and leather goods brands, including Louis Vuitton, Christian Dior, Céline, Givenchy, Marc Jacobs, Fendi, Donna Karan and Edun. There are jewellery and watch brands in its portfolio including Bulgari, TAG Heuer and De Beers, and it also owns perfume and cosmetics brands, wines and spirits brands, the DFS duty free stores, media interests, factories and tanneries.

Kering owns both luxury and mass-market brands from Gucci, Balenciaga, Stella McCartney and Saint Laurent, to Puma and surfwear brand Volcom.

Richemont bought Net-A-Porter in 2010 before offloading it in 2015. Its stable includes Chloé, Azzedine Alaïa, and a bunch of fine jewellery and watch brands including Cartier.

Hermès remains independent. Chanel is the other major player that's not part of a group – it has been privately owned by the Wertheimers since the 1950s. Miuccia Prada is the only designer in this league to own her own show, Prada Group, with her husband Patrizio Bertelli. They also own Miu Miu and control British shoe brand Churches.

The big luxury fashion brands now have flagship stores in most major cities, their ground floors filled with perfumes and small accessories, with the real luxury products hidden away upstairs. Their corporate bosses, writes Thomas, have 'turned their sights on a new target audience: the middle market, that broad socioeconomic demographic that includes everyone from teachers and sales executives to high-tech entrepreneurs, McMansion suburbanites, the ghetto fabulous, even the criminally wealthy. The idea, luxury executives explained, was to "democratise" luxury, to make luxury "accessible" … But it wasn't. It was as capitalist as could be: the goal, plain and simple, was to make as much money as heavenly possible.'

What do the rich, the so-called '1 per cent', do when true luxury is diluted? They keep on ordering bespoke, and buying the best stuff that is still made for their consumption. But in recent years, they've been flirting with a bit of rough too – having been given the okay to shop downmarket by glossy lifestyle magazines and designer endorsements.

Recognising this, big brands across all levels now seek to smudge the old distinctions in order to attract new types of customer.

Karen Walker has noticed this. She sits in the mid-market range but, being independent with plenty of cred (based in Auckland, shows in New York, original point of view), she avoids the fate of being ignored by the media. 'Fashion is about rewiring what we already know, which happens most obviously at the product level,' she says. 'So we change the silhouette – last season was about maximalism, so now it's about minimalism – or we say, "You've already got a wardrobe full of florals, guess what? It's going to be about no prints now!" That's the fashion system, right? There's no use denying it. But at a deeper level the smartest brands are constantly looking to rewire the process too. So you see the high street redefining itself, in terms of where it sits.'[7]

Style magazines now advocate 'the high-low mix'; they advise picking up a bargain at Zara and 'working it back' with Céline. Savvy shopping on the newly fashionable high street has become something to brag about, especially now that so many of those blockbuster names from the top of the pyramid have been hanging out there. Top designers can earn fees of $1 million and more for putting their name to one-off collections for fast fashion retailers.

CHAPTER 6

What's in a Name?

The rise and rise of the designer collab

Target in the US started the 'designer collaboration' trend in 2002 by hiring the superstar American designer Isaac Mizrahi to create a 'cheap-chic' range. The partnership lasted six years, extending from womenswear to homewares and kids' clothes, and, according to the *New York Times*, generating sales of $300 million each year.

Karl Lagerfeld was next. His 2004 capsule collection for H&M sold out within hours, and prompted him to say he'd never do it again: 'They did not make the clothes in sufficient quantities. I find it embarrassing that H&M let down so many people ... I don't think that is very kind, especially for people in small towns and countries in Eastern Europe. It is snobbery created by anti-snobbery.'[1]

Luckily, time is the great healer everyone says it is, because Lagerfeld is now the king of the collab. He's popped his image on special cans of Diet Coke and T-shirts for Macy's, worked with Brazilian shoe label Melissa, and created a boxer's punching bag for Louis Vuitton. Even his cat is in on it. In 2014 Choupette, the pampered feline with her own Twitter account and coffee-table book, hooked up with Shu

Uemura to create a makeup line. Clever kitty. Around the same time Mattel launched a Karl Lagerfeld Barbie doll, endorsed by the man himself. A limited edition of 999 units sold out on Net-A-Porter – only to appear on eBay the following week at ten times the price.

H&M was also undeterred by early bumps in the road. Subsequent designer couplings with high-end designers and luxury houses (including Lanvin, Versace, Balmain and Alexander Wang) have proved stellar marketing opportunities for the Swedish leader – although the jury's out on whether they do much for the bottom line in terms of direct sales. Who cares, though? You couldn't buy better advertising.

Wang is the Taiwanese-American known for his cool take on urban sportswear. In 2012, just shy of his twenty-ninth birthday, Wang was named creative director at Balenciaga. He announced his H&M line two years later via Instagram (presumably a fair whack of the 12,000 fans who clicked 'like' became customers). Focused on athletic silhouettes, the collection was chic but not particularly cheap: prices climbed to more than US$349 for a hooded top. At the range's celebrity-packed New York launch, Wang said, 'It doesn't matter if you're a luxury customer or a mass customer. Everyone, at least that I know, works out, is always running around, and has a use for these clothes.'

Usefulness is one thing; hype is another. Like sex, star power sells. There was a reason Kate Bosworth turned up at Coachella in 2013 in the scalloped shorts and matching tank top from her first collection for Topshop – several weeks before they hit stores. It was surely the same reason that Philip Green was telling the press about his deal to produce athletic wear with Beyoncé – 'one of the most hardworking and talented people in the world, who spends many hours of her life dancing, rehearsing and training' – a full ten months before the finished product was available, but only four weeks before tickets went on sale for the *Fifty Shades of Grey* movie. Beyoncé provided a 'sexed-up version' of 'Crazy in Love' for the soundtrack.

There's a sophisticated marketing machine behind the fast fashion boom: we didn't just wake up one morning in the '90s and think *I wish four times as many clothes would be produced and sold.*

I interviewed Bosworth for a magazine around the time her second Topshop range dropped, and she told me she was driven by her personal wish 'to understand the design of apparel better'. She explained that her father was employed in the retail industry [as a US-based exec with luxury Italian menswear company Ermenegildo Zegna], as was her grandfather before him.

'Fabrics and textures have always been around me, even before I had the access to fashion as an actress,' she said. She loves clothes, and was interested to know how to make them. And she didn't want the Topshop stuff to be thrown away after a couple of wears. 'This design is about classic, luxurious pieces. Ones that are not disposable, but will remain in your closet for years.' It all sounded fair enough, like it came from a good place – but how much did Bosworth really know about how the clothes with her name on them were made? How much does anyone know, including Topshop's owners Arcadia Group?

'We don't own the factories that produce our merchandise so we do not employ the factory workers directly,' they say.[2] 'Arcadia supports the position that all workers in our supply chain, including piece rate, subcontracted, informal, home and migrant workers, should always receive enough wages to meet their needs for nutritious food, clean water and other needs (shelter, transport etc.) as well as a discretionary income, which is now a generally well accepted definition of a living wage. The challenge is how to measure and then implement it.'

Like all their competitors with complex supply chains, Arcadia relies on auditors to check that its codes of conduct are being respected. Inevitably, sometimes they are not.

In 2010, a Channel 4 *Dispatches* doco sent a reporter undercover to work in factories producing garments for British high street chains, including the Arcadia-owned BHS.[3] In one instance, the reporter was paid half the minimum wage, cash in hand. He told of unsafe equipment, of poorly ventilated basement units with blocked fire exits, and of being threatened with the sack if he didn't work faster. And where were these sweatshops? Some unregulated developing economy, known for its human rights abuses? Nope. In Leicester, England – the sleepy East Midlands town, home to Walker's crisps and Adrian Mole.

Buck-passing is a standard response from many fast fashion retailers (and a fair few luxury ones too) when asked about working conditions, or about the environmental impact of producing and dyeing fabrics, or tanning leathers. The only way we will get better answers is by asking better questions – and more of them. I'd love to know how many celebrities, or collaborating designers, ask about the manufacture of the fast fashion clothing they promote. How many of them ask to visit the factories? Or read about the pesticides sprayed on the cotton fields? Or demand to know exactly how the leather used on those cute shoes was made? I'm going to make a wild, unsubstantiated guess at none.

Crazy in love

'Democratising fashion' was a term we heard a lot when Target Australia first hooked up with Stella McCartney in 2007 to produce a range of dresses, trenches and peacoats which, in some stores, sold out in forty-five seconds. Fans stripped down to their undies on the shop floor when change rooms filled up, they pushed, shoved and swore at each other. A fight broke out in Melbourne's Chadstone mall, while 400 people queued outside the Target store there. 'McCartney's designs are beautiful and that's why people are willing to put up with this,' said one fan. 'Most women look at each other and they know it is crazy but it's worth it.'[4]

Let's define 'worth'. The promise of 'designer bargains at a fraction of the price of the real thing' might be enticing but it's also disingenuous. The idea that a 'cheap-chic' dress has much in common with the real designer garment is rubbish – whoever signs off on the sketch, be it Lagerfeld, McCartney or some faceless in-house designer. The problem is we believe the hype. And I confess that I've often perpetuated it. I've written glowing articles about Bosworth's Topshop collections and Dion Lee for Target. But the more I learn about how it all works, the more I question it. We know that fast fashion is not designed to last, yet we're surprised when it falls apart at the seams – there are masses of chat-room feeds and blog posts dedicated to the fact.

Peter Pilotto is a high-end British brand known for its innovative prints and textures. Actually designed by two people, Pilotto himself and his creative partner Christopher de Vos, it is sold by prestige stores; as I write, there's an embellished wool crepe mini dress of theirs on Net-A-Porter for $3,567.

In 2014 they designed a collection for Target US and most of it retailed for under US$60. As it hit stores, journalist Daisy Buchanan mused in the *Guardian*: 'We don't have enough disposable income to buy something new every week or month, but we do want to participate in fashion.' But, she said, 'there's something quietly awful about these low-end collections that are created to make us feel as if we have been tossed a bone.'[5]

Quietly awful or no, consumers voted with their wallets in favour of access to one of fashion's cult-insider names: the Peter Pilotto for Target line broke records.

And so the collabs keep coming: Jean Paul Gaultier for Target, Kanye West for Adidas, Christophe Lemaire (once artistic director for Hermès womenswear) for cheapie Japanese chain Uniqlo. It would be nice if one of these brilliant designers – McCartney, for example, who refuses to work with leather for ethical reasons, and has partnered with the Green Carpet Challenge and the Ethical Fashion Initiative – used these collections as platforms to push sustainable fashion. Perhaps one day they will.

For now though, as Karen Walker says, 'it's about elevating the low, while diffusing the high-end. It is the story of the our age.'[6]

Walker herself has worked with Uniqlo on a childrenswear line. 'It's valuable cross-pollination,' she told me, on the eve of a smaller project with Swedish sock brand Happy Socks. 'Do you know who *they* worked with before us?' she said. 'Snoop Dogg.'

Label conscious

Charles Frederick Worth is often credited with inventing the designer label. If there were others before him, they've been forgotten. In the 1860s he had the name of his business (House of Worth and Bobergh) stamped in gold on white Petersham ribbon and sewn inside the waistbands of his dresses. By the 1870s (having dropped Mr Bobergh) he was attaching woven 'Worth Paris' labels to the linings of all his models, and rival houses such as Doucet had followed suit. When fakes became an issue in the 1890s, the House of Worth (now run by Charles's sons Jean-Philippe and Gaston) began attaching numbered tapes to garments, identifying designs by collection and year.

Worth was the first designer in the modern sense – although Rose Bertin created trends for Marie Antoinette, she didn't market and distribute them like Worth did. He was the first to sell models to American department stores, and to seek out celebrities to dress. His house took orders by mail and later phone, and opened subsidiary branches (in London, and the chic resort towns of Dinard, Biarritz and Cannes).

Mr Worth liked to listen to Verdi when 'composing' his designs. He wafted about his gilded salons at 7 Rue de la Paix in fur-trimmed robes, and kept twin black spaniels, each with a green velvet chair to loll in. His best work, he insisted, was done lying on a sofa around 5 p.m. – there was inspiration to be found in the way the setting sun glanced through the windows of his salon, apparently.

And yet a person less likely to conquer French fashion you'd be hard pushed to find. Worth was born in a Lincolnshire market town in 1825, the son of a solicitor who liked a tipple. Early career details are sketchy, but it's likely his mother packed him off to London to escape. For a time the young Worth worked for silk merchants Lewis and Allenby – favourites of Queen Victoria.

Jean-Philippe Worth claimed his father's first job in Paris was as a shop assistant, but no one really knows why he moved there, or how he clawed his way up. Around 1850 he landed a sales role with the Paris equivalent of Lewis and Allenby. Gagelin-Opigez had royal connections too – their wares formed part of Empress Eugénie's trousseau. Worth designed his first gowns there, and had an office romance with a wily and well-connected girl named Marie Vernet. He married her, then struck out on his own with a cash injection from a like-minded Swede – before making his fortune in banking, Otto Bobergh had also been a lowly shop-boy. Marie brought her taste, sales experience and court connections to the new house.

Her husband's first stroke of genius was to combine dressmaking with the traditional supply of silks, embroideries, laces and *passementerie* under one roof – something no one seems to have thought of before. His second was to imagine the House of Worth as a comprehensive fashion brand targeting the glitterati.

Shopping at Worth put you in the right sort of company, from princess Pauline von Metternich and the Empress Eugénie, to Sarah Bernhardt and Nellie Melba. By the 1890s well-off women could buy a Worth dress made from Worth-designed silk, accessorised by Worth fripperies and even Worth eau de toilette – all bearing the Worth label.

Smells like chic

Personally, Worth hated perfume – fragranced clients upset him and he was always flinging windows open – but that didn't stop him selling cologne in his salon. It was a money-spinner, see? That said, it took his sons a while to launch the first official House of Worth perfume – Je Reviens, in 1932. You can still buy it.

Paul Poiret, society darling in the Belle Époque, was first to market the heck out of a fashion fragrance. He was the guy who liberated women from their corsets, and helped fuel the fever for Orientalism and the Ballets Russes. He too opened stores in chic resort towns, and courted glamorous clients (his Paris balls were legendary). Poiret's clothes were all about the senses – golden harem pants and fluid dresses, lampshade skirts and turbans. Why should they not smell as exotic as they looked? In 1911, the couturier set up Parfums de Rosine, which produced the earliest designer scents, including one called Chez Poiret. It took another decade for Chanel to bring out No. 5.

Chanel made perfume because she believed in it – she liked to say, 'a woman who doesn't use perfume has no future'. Her friend Claude Baillén describes her as leaving 'a wake of it' wherever she went.[7]

'They say I smell nice,' Chanel told Baillén. 'Of course I do, I know how to use scent! The French put a dab of it behind each ear, and one little bottle lasts them six months'. Madame went at the bottle hard; her atelier staff knew when she'd arrived by the smell of the air. No. 5 made Chanel rich, but it was authentic. I can't imagine Coco putting her name on a toaster.

Dior was the first couturier to license his name in the way that's so familiar today. 'I don't see why we should have our mannequins wear American-made stockings,' he complained after a show in July 1948.[8] 'Why don't we make Christian Dior stockings that someone would manufacture for us; that we could sell in our boutique and also some quality stores?' In 1949, Kayser-Roth delivered the first Christian Dior stockings to Saks, but it took one of Dior's employees to move licensing to the next level.

Pierre Cardin trained with a tailor in Vichy France, and worked in the ateliers of Paquin and Schiaparelli before arriving at Dior in 1946, aged twenty-four. Cardin started his own business four years later, but while he claimed 'I was successful immediately,' that's braggadocio – he made theatrical costumes before couture.

By the 1980s he was proudly telling journalists, 'My name is on everything' – and by then it was true. Having resigned from the Chambre Syndicale to focus on ready-to-wear in the '60s, he had proved himself a man for his age – forget art; Cardin was about commerce. He'd boldly wooed the Chinese and the Soviet markets way before any of his contemporaries. He'd practically invented the '70s dandy with his tight suits and frill-front shirts. Pierre Cardin was a household name; it made sense to cash in on that. 'If I dress the man,' he said, 'why shouldn't I dress everything around the man, [including] his surroundings?'[9] At one point Cardin had 840 licensing agreements to sell products in ninety-four countries, granting use of his signature on everything from boxer shorts, electric shavers and ties to bottled water, pans and cans of sardines – none of which he designed.

In 2011, when the eighty-eight-year-old Mr Cardin announced that he was ready to sell his company, he reckoned it was worth €1 billion. Critics have long accused 'The Licensing King' of trashing fashion, but most of his peers took his cue.

In America there were Bill Blass chocolates, backgammon boards, even a car. Geoffrey Beene passed away in 2004, but you can still buy shirts with his name on made by PVH, which owns Calvin Klein. Klein, of course, put his name to a lot more than jeans.

'In a label-conscious world, where the fashion designer's stamp has crept onto place mats and pillow cases, automobiles and edibles, as well as nearly every article of clothing imaginable, are we ready for the first designer cigarette?'[10] asked the *Los Angeles Times* when Yves Saint Laurent announced exactly that in 1985. His puffers were produced under license by the R.J. Reynolds Tobacco Company. Saint Laurent himself oversaw the packaging and commissioned Helmut Newton for the ad campaign, but while the designer had bouts of smoking 150 fags a day,[11] he favoured Peter Stuyvesant.[12]

You can buy Cartier ciggies, which I pretentiously smoked as a teen, thinking they'd bring me closer to chic. Yeah right. They were produced by the same lot that made Benson & Hedges (wouldn't have been caught dead). What's in a name? So much, and yet nothing at all.

In her memoir *The Woman I Wanted to Be*, Diane von Fursten-berg describes how, in the mid-'70s, her homewares line for Sears, 'quickly grew beyond sheets and towels into curtains, tableware, rugs – eventually even furniture,' to ring up sales of more than $100 million a year,[13] but by the early '80s she was struggling. Her payroll was 'enormous', and warehouses were full of excess wrap dress stock. Then along came Carl Rosen, fresh from his deal with Klein and keen to license DVF. 'Not only would he buy and dispose of my aging inventory, but he would run the business and pay me a royalty,' she writes.[14] She signed, and soon after offloaded her makeup business too (to British pharmaceuticals company Beecham).

'I had very little say in the design, quality, and most importantly distribution of the many licensed products,' von Furstenberg writes. 'Little by little, the simple dress I'd made had disappeared ... The dresses were given shoulder pads and lost their identity as I had lost control.'[15] While she turned it around later on, she admits her brand 'lost its character and much of its value' when it was licensed to the hilt.[16] So why were we were still buying it?

In 2011, Dutch researchers Rob Nelissen and Marijn Meijers published a study on how designer clothing with visible branding affects perceptions of the wearer. By showing volunteers snaps of a man first in a Lacoste shirt and then in one with no logo, they discovered that people judged Mr Label as wealthier and of higher status. People trusted him more, too. In another test the pair sent a woman in a Tommy Hilfiger sweater to do a survey in a shopping mall, then sent her back in a logo-free sweater – more than half those she approached agreed to answer her questions when she was designered-up, versus just 13 per cent when she wasn't. Further experiments demonstrated that designer labels endeared the wearer to potential employers and partners.

'This study confirms a wider phenomenon,' observed the *Economist*. 'A work of art's value, for example, can change radically, depending on who is believed to have created it, even though the artwork itself is unchanged. And people will willingly buy counterfeit goods, knowing they are knock-offs, if they bear the right label ... If everyone agrees something has high status, then it does. But that agreement often transfers the status from the *thing* to the *label*.'[17]

Remember 'logomania'? The trend for flashy status dressing was big in the noughties, when head-to-toe Burberry checks were the chav's choice, and it was cool to show off the waistband of your Calvin Klein shorts above your jeans. In 2013, the newspapers were reporting logomania's return. Only this time it really was maniacal.

That was the year Sofia Coppola's movie *The Bling Ring* hit cinemas, based on the true story of the teenage label hunters who burgled Paris Hilton's closet in LA. It was also the year that London teenager Aamna Aliani made headlines for her fraud-funded shopping spree. Aliani and two male friends scammed cash from a bank, then spent it at Louis Vuitton, Gucci and Prada. It was the logos that gave them away, when police caught them struggling to get their clearly branded swag into the car. And because this is the era of the 'share' and 'like', photos from Aliani's mobile phone were soon leaked to the press. They showed her seventeenth birthday cake – it was shaped like a Louis Vuitton handbag.

CHAPTER 7

Revolution Baby

Beautiful on the inside

I'm becoming obsessed with how things are made, and what from. Running around the park used to be a way to clear my brain, but this week it's more crowded in there than Westfield on Christmas Eve. As I jog I play a game of Spot the Synthetics, making a mental tally: my tank top, that girl's running shorts, that man's bum bag, that entire footy team's jerseys, that dog's … what? *Banana-yellow Sou'wester*? Are you kidding me?

It is beginning to drizzle and the football players pack up, but the schnauzer in his raincoat is damp-proof and trots happily after a swallow it has no hope of slaying. I picture the container arriving from Shanghai; inside, the Great Wall of Boxes made from cardboard bricks, and inside these, hundreds of miniature yellow mackintoshes packed flat. Did the garment workers think they were sewing for children in some rain-sodden land where fishing was popular, the Scottish highlands perhaps, as they stitched the little yellow hoods and the stunted sleeves destined for doggie paws?

The sky is threatening to crack but I stick it out. I need to blow the cobwebs away. I haven't been sleeping well since a man with a hiking habit invaded my dreams.

On the night in question, instead of watching the end of *Midsomer Murders*, I went out to a Fashion Revolution Day talk. We revolutionaries convened in a pub, the sort that makes you glad it's too dark to see what is making the floorboards sticky. An energetic Irish blonde named Avis was the host. A former Dublin recruitment consultant, she'd packed her bags and moved to Africa where she did things like run a surf camp and teach yoga and try to change the world, then Sydney, where she founded Think Act Change to encourage people to step up and commit to something.

Turns out being an activist is quite tiring, which might explain why most of the Think Act Change audience was half my age. There were no chairs and no food, and when I left three hours after I'd arrived, the event showed no signs of wrapping up. As I yawned and wondered who was killing the bell ringers in Midsomer Parva (Was it the toff from up at the big house? It's *always* the toff) I worked out that the last time I'd been to a political rally I was at university in Sheffield, in my purple suede mini-skirt phase. I really, really liked purple then. I drove a 1970s Beetle sprayed metallic violet. It rattled like a lawnmower and had no heating; on winter journeys the only way to stay alive was to wrap yourself in a blanket like an Armenian peasant woman and take a lot of drugs. It was a different life.

In this life, my friend Melinda was on stage in a Katharine Hamnett SAVE THE FUTURE slogan tee. She made a stirring speech about Rana Plaza. 'It's time to ask more questions about how our clothes were made,' she said. 'It's time to wake up.'

She'd briefed me on all this, so I knew at some point during the evening I would be asked to fess up about the label in my jumper, but I'd been so busy with murder (the bell ringers were being garrotted; it was positively medieval) I'd forgotten to change. My unacceptable knitwear was a double whammy of badness: cheap cashmere, made in China. I moved out of the shadows into the very dark shadows and hoped no one would notice me.

Avis acted as MC and in between the speeches she gave away prizes (a copy of an ethical fashion book, an organic T-shirt) and swore like Jo Brand. Or Russell Brand. Or the bastard child of Russell and Jo, if said child had been raised by Irish gangsta rappers.

'Okay, let's get fucking going, people! I want you all to turn to the nearest person you haven't met and ask them where they got their clothes. Let's look at some motherfucking labels!' After a suitable pause, she shouted, 'Anyone learn something they'd like to share?'

A lady in red stepped up. 'Truth is I had no idea,' she said. 'But when I found out I was coming tonight I checked my label. It's made in Australia.'

'Winning!' called Avis, and flung her a T-shirt.

The next girl to her feet (there were men in the audience, but none spoke up) proclaimed proudly that her jacket was vintage. It was embroidered with tiny bronze sequins, the telltale shine of polyester gleaming through.

'Winning!' shouted Avis again, this time adding the suffix: 'like a motherfucker!' Cue more whoops, but not from a sixty-something lady standing beside me, her striped cardi dutifully turned inside out. I watched her brow furrow, and as she shook her head I caught her eye and we volleyed a little shrug between us, as if to say, 'Kids! What can you do?' *Wash your mouth out with soap* ...

'Vintage is a great way to shop because it's already there!' said Avis, sparking a wave of WOOT! WOOTs! The prize for sequins-woman was a book, and as Avis lobbed it skyward it arced gracefully as if in slow motion, balletic somehow, and also blessed; it narrowly missed grazing heads. I ducked, thinking about the flaws in that argument: that something otherwise morally questionable might be excused if it's vintage, because *it's already there*; because if the damage has already been done to the Mongolian sands, to the mink or the Finnish raccoon or the chinchilla, to the labourer sewing thousands of tiny sequins for punishing shifts in poor light, then perhaps the greater crime is to waste the results. It's an argument popular with vintage fur fans; an argument I've made myself (truth be told I own big Russian coat that makes me feel like Marisa Berenson: it's 1970s/ it's vintage/it's not hurting any Arctic foxes today, is it?).

At which point I started to think about sneaking off home, because while we were all there for the right reasons, it seemed too easy to descend into mutual back-slapping. *Well done, made-in-Australia lady! Snaps to you, with your vintage jacket!* Not that anyone would say 'well done' to me if they knew about the white Russian.

Plucking hell

I was trying to consciously uncouple my boot from the floor when the place went quiet. I looked up to see a man arrive on stage in a collared shirt, and I felt a flicker of kinship (he'd probably sacrificed *Midsomer* too), so I stayed.

He began to explain how the American outdoor gear brand Patagonia has been working on supply chain transparency since the '90s, but he lost me when he started on about hiking. There were polar fleeces involved and boots with moisture-wicking. I think I saw a yak in the distance. Now, I am a creature of the great indoors. I can just about handle a sweatshirt if you allow me a heel, but hiking, forget it. I went into a kind of trance, involving a lurid fantasy about Kettle Chips, as a goose farm appeared on the overhead projector.

'Mmm paté,' I thought.

Then, coming to, 'WAH! Not paté!'

'So we were surprised to discover that some of the feathers we were buying for our down jackets might have come from geese raised for *foie gras* production,' said Patagonia man, before launching into an explanation of the widespread practice of live plucking.

As in, THEY PLUCK THE BIRDS WHILE THEY ARE STILL ALIVE.

Down comes from the fluffy bit of a duck's or goose's chest. Unlike a feather, a single bit of down, called a plumule, is puffy in lots of different directions, so it traps air. It is this insulating situation that keeps the bird, and your down jacket, toasty. Have you ever thought about how it's procured?

Patagonia can now trace all their down back to cruelty-free farms, with birds certified non-force fed and non-live plucked. Rival outdoor gear brand The North Face has followed suit, and Ikea, which sells cushions and quilts as well as furniture, agrees officially that 'live-plucking is not acceptable'. But plenty of other companies sidestep traceability because it's a painstaking, expensive process. Mostly, the down that comes from wholesalers is all jumbled up, and when that happens there's no way of knowing which plumules come from where.

Everyone thinks goose down is automatically better quality than duck. Not so. Quality (that is, insulating powers, plus how long it keeps doing its job) depends on the size and maturity of the bird; down from immature birds will be less fluffy, ergo, less warm and puffy. So goose down isn't necessarily a luxurious treat, and it isn't necessarily an ethical one either.

Live plucking is banned in the EU and the US, but it still happens. The biggest down producers are China, where live plucking is legal, Poland and Hungary, where the loophole that 'gathering' feathers during moulting season is allowed comes in useful. During live plucking, workers hold the birds upside-down and rip the feathers out by hand; they do this to save the bird from death, thereby saving money – you can live-pluck several times before you need to slaughter.

Plucking often tears the skin, and when deep bleeding gashes form workers sew them up there and then with a needle and thread, which is probably not what you had in mind when you said hurrah for artisanal skills. Needless to say, there are no anaesthetics.

In recent years the down jacket has become a big seller, with leading brands attracting Wall Street investors. When luxury ski-wear brand Moncler floated on the Italian stock exchange in 2013, it was the strongest European debut of the year. Twelve months later Bloomberg was trumpeting 'puffy profits' – down jackets were no-brainer hits, attractive to retailers and consumers for their timeless design and easy fits: one-size-fits-many means customer returns are low.[1]

I thought of the goose down quilt my husband had bought the previous winter, which we tenderly call 'Cloud Bed' and consider the last word in luxury, and I thought of Liane Rossler asking if it is possible to find something glamorous if there's even a hint that someone (or some duck) has suffered to make it. I thought of the big tough feathers that broke Marisa's machine. And I thought of the Whistler Puffy in the Paws Point Boutique.

Why does a dog need a bloody coat anyway?

In the park, it is raining properly now, fat round drops that turn the grass to mush and make my mascara run, but it's still twenty degrees. This is Sydney, not Siberia, and in Siberia, I decide, any coats for animals or otherwise would probably be made of skins going spare, upcycling the cast-off pelt from the reindeer stew. It's lunchtime, but I have lost my appetite.

Dog day afternoon

Back home I Google 'Do huskies wear coats?' and have quite a nice time looking at pictures of these noble, wolf-like creatures tumbling through the snow. I find plenty in harnesses, some of which are jolly colours, but canine fashion is not a thing in indigenous husky circles. Turns out they don't need man-made macks because their natural coats are so efficient, with an insulating layer underneath and a water-resistant one on top. Lucky them.

Temperatures can drop to minus forty degrees Celsius in winter up north, when humans exposing the tips of their noses risk losing them, although that looks like changing: in December 2013 the *Siberian Times* ran pictures of the normally snow-blanketed towns of Krasnoyarsk and Barnaul exposed, sparkling with unseasonable rain and sunshine. Temperatures soared to minus three, while locals in Tomsk posed in bikinis with their moon boots to prove the point.

The indigenous Yakut people of the region were traditionally big on reindeer suede, which they used to make leather leggings, and puff-sleeved greatcoats, trimmed in fox or lynx fur. The sleeves had a purpose beyond costume drama; they protected the Yakuts' shoulder joints from the weather. Those who couldn't afford reindeer used horse- or cow-hide, hair-side in for warmth. It wasn't just a purple Beetle thing; everyone needed hats, scarves and mittens. They wore forehead bands with ear- and nose-flaps, held in place by plaited string (the best were made from wolf's paw leather). They packed dry grass into their shoes, and added fur socks.

In 1885, when the Russian Prince Shirinsky-Shikhmatov surveyed the area, a sort of furry girdle worn outside the shirt was popular. The Yakut have long used squirrel, fox and even bear skins for warmth. Sometimes, they used dog. But they didn't do it lightly – their dogs were precious, vital for hunting and transportation. No one skinned a dog just to make a jacket look cute.

In Canada's extreme northwest, on the border with Alaska, the indigenous people of the Yukon have a similar history to the Yakut. Their mountains are also bitter in winter, when temperatures drop to minus thirty-six, although things perk up in summer further down around the lakes. Like the Yakut, the first nation Yukon peoples traditionally lived in small groups following seasonal activities: hunting, trading, trapping. Archaeologists believe that the Inuit people of the Yukon once hunted woolly mammoth, but in more recent history they got their insulated clothing needs from reindeer and seal.

There's an intriguing waterproof parka in London's Victoria and Albert Museum made from seal guts. 'Gut parkas' were also made from sea lion, walrus and whale intestines, and were prized by European sailors for their lightness, but the indigenous Alaskans believed they had super powers. As noted in the exhibit, 'They were powerful garments that protected the wearer against both the elements and misfortune, and they attracted animals to the hunter.' The Alaskans considered humans and animals to be equals. 'The hunter will only succeed if the animal chooses to give its life as a gift in return for moral and respectful behaviour on the part of the whole community.' Traditionally, when a hunter killed a seal he poured cold water into its mouth to stop its soul from getting thirsty.

The reindeer of the Yukon region is the delightfully named porcupine caribou, and its fur is made from hollow hairs that help it float when it swims and shift colour from grey in winter to brown in summer, without any help from Clairol. The caribou is hunted primarily for meat, but all parts of the animal can be used – its hair and skin to make parkas, pantaloons with built-in moccasins, mittens, vests, and other garments. The sinew makes ideal sewing thread; it swells when it gets wet, thus waterproofing the seams. If the beasts' hoofs aren't boiled down for a popular local dish of jellied broth, they are dried and slung onto hunters' belts to act as 'caribou bells', which clack together in a sneaky imitation of caribou footsteps, fooling those who haven't yet become soup.

The level of craftswomanship involved was off the scale. Before imported factory-made clobber became the norm in the 1970s, a seamstress would take a month to make the clothes for her family. A girl was given an *ulu* knife as a right of passage, and when she married, her bridal trousseau consisted of her *ulu* and a lamp. She used her *ulu* to butcher seals, flense (skin) them, slice food cuts and carve off sinew for thread. The blade of an *ulu* was traditionally attached to its ivory handle with special glue made from seal blood, clay and dog hair.[2]

Dog hair had another use too. Since sheep were rare in these regions, women spun it into yarn and knitted with it. Some still do.

Melody MacMillan is a thirty-two-year-old 'yarn artist' specialising in *chiengora*, the name she's coined for the recycled dog hair that is her raw material of choice. Melody is based in Revelstoke, a popular mountain resort five hours drive west of Calgary, but she learnt her peculiar craft in remote Whitehorse, at the southern tip of the Yukon.

'People don't blink an eye when you mention dog hair up there, but I think it's probably the only place left on the planet where they don't,' she tells me.[3]

I found MacMillan on the internet. I don't know what I was expecting (okay, I do: some terrifying hybrid of Toni and Candace, the feminist bookstore owners from *Portlandia*) but she is nothing like the oddball crafter of my imagination. She's a pretty young mum. Our conversations happen over the phone a few days before she gives birth to her second child. In photographs she's wearing faded jeans and sneakers, her curly brown hair loose around her shoulders. On the slopes, she wears a down jacket not dissimilar to the Whistler Puffy, with a patterned bobble hat that would be unremarkable but for the fact that it's knitted from dog.

'I've always been an animal person,' she says. 'Every part of the world we lived, my parents always let us have a pet dog.'

MacMillan was born in Canada but grew up in South East Asia. Her parents were missionaries and moved around a lot, from Thailand to the Philippines, and for a time MacMillan went to boarding school in Malaysia. She remembers, 'always doing crafts, I was good with my hands'.

Back in Canada, MacMillan married a man from the Yukon. 'We were working up there one summer and I happened to meet his life-long neighbour, Mary. She was a dog hair spinner. I thought that was awesome and I had her teach me.' Mary, says MacMillan, 'probably started out spinning other fibres then gravitated to dog, because the thing is, [the fibre] is free. But she would spin all sorts of cool things. Fibre artists like to experiment. I know she tried working with fire-weed, which is their provincial flower – it produces a white cotton-like fibre. You can spin anything,' says MacMillan. 'You could spin your dryer lint if you wanted to.'

You can do that?

'Oh yeah. I've met people who save their own hair and spin it. I've actually had people request that from me, but it's not my thing.' MacMillan is dogged about dog. 'Canine yarn resembles angora in that it's very soft and it develops a halo effect,' she says. It lacks elasticity – no stretch equals fuzzy, a property MacMillan finds both distinctive and attractive. She considers canine yarn 'a luxury fibre like mohair or cashmere' – although she concedes its super-toastyness can freak some people out. 'It is 80 per cent warmer than wool,' she says. 'My international customers often go for the cushions rather than the fashion garments,' although blending the chiengora with Merino wool during spinning turns down both the heat and the fuzz.

'But that's not what most people are worried about,' says MacMillan.

They want to know if it smells.

'No,' she says. 'Just no. Once I'm done it doesn't smell at all.'

If it's so great, how come the fashion industry doesn't jump on the dog yarn train? (Actually, please please don't let the fashion industry buy that ticket.)

'I was just in Hong Kong with one of my clients who is trying to manufacture dog hair herself,' says MacMillan.

That sounds ominous, I say, thinking about Little Glam and the booming Chinese fur industry.

'I understand what you're asking but that's not what she's about,' says MacMillan. 'She wants to be able to send out her small orders to someone else to produce. She essentially contracted me to teach her how to do it by hand, because even in China they haven't figured out a way to commercially manufacture [chiengora] in a sustainable way.'

'One of the reasons is the fibre is not standardised. Domestic dogs are not like sheep; each one is completely different. You have to adapt your technique every single time.'

I want to say, what if they farmed a particular breed – then the hair would be standardised, wouldn't it? But I don't, because Melody MacMillan is only interested in the salvaged hair of family pets. 'Another reason is you're working with such small quantities each time,' she continues. 'We're talking ounces, not kilos.'

You could say that for anything upcycled or custom-made. Probably the reason someone like Marc Jacobs doesn't design dog yarn sweaters is that it's too weird and sounds a bit creepy ... okay probably the reason is that it hasn't occurred to him, but actually, the way

MacMillan does dog is ethical, sustainable and really rather lovely.

She works strictly with collected not clipped hair, and from donations. 'I don't ever want to see dog hair turned into something with a price tag. It's about creating something from what would otherwise have been thrown away.'

It is fully traceable because only MacMillan handles it, from fluff to finished garment. You can send hair from Fido and receive a blanket made entirely from ... Fido. A typical bespoke order takes about four weeks to make.

Customers send MacMillan pet hair they've found down the back of their sofas, or harvested from dog brushes and velvet trousers. They bag up this bounty and post it, unwashed, to MacMillan, who then sorts and launders it, before spinning it on her old-fashioned wheel and knitting it into hats, mittens or – her latest special project – a full chiengora parka.

'It's *major*,' she says, sounding suddenly like Rachel Zoe. 'It should take me at least two years, when it's finished it's going to be like a fur coat but entirely recycled out of dog hair.'

The first yarn MacMillan spun came from her own border collie. 'At that time he had a very soft belly undercoat so the yarn was exceptional, super-high quality beautiful soft puppy yarn.'

Since then she has worked with plenty of huskies, but recommends blending their fur: 'They tend to hover around the one- to two-inch length' – three inches is the holy coat-length grail – 'Husky is fine, husky can work.'

Just don't send her cat. 'Cat is a nightmare, it's too short, too soft.'

Often she must be content with mongrels. 'Most of the time I am working with mixed breeds with mediocre hair, but every once in a while ...' I can sense that I am losing her; she is daydreaming. 'You know, you hold out for the samoyed or the malamute, don't you?'

CHAPTER 8

The Dog Fur Private Eye

Think mink!

It's sandal weather in Manhattan and I'm fretting: fat chance of finding fur in May. I'm in New York to meet with Pierre Grzybowski, who has agreed to take me on an undercover mission to look for incorrectly labelled fur garments in the designer stores on the Upper East Side.

More than fifty million animals are killed for their fur each year. Globally the trade is worth more than US$40 billion. The International Fur Trade Federation (IFTF) promotes fur, being a natural fibre, as both sustainable and ethical. 'Fur is more popular than ever,' they say.[1]

Fur is back in fashion in a way that would've seemed inconceivable twenty years ago. According to the IFTF, global fur sales shot up 70 per cent in ten years, and 318 of the 450 fashion shows for the Autumn '14 season used fur. Milan topped the scale, where more than 90 per cent of designers used it.[2]

In the *New York Times*, fashion critic Eric Wilson asked, 'Did the designers forget that wearing fur is fraught with controversy? Or did they simply stop caring?' He noted that in 2010, 'for the first time in two decades, more designers were using fur than were not'.[3] This was no coincidence, or even the result of a collective creative consciousness, however. 'Rather, fur became a trend because of a marketing campaign.'

According to Wilson, furriers 'aggressively' court young designers such as Prabal Gurung and Derek Lam, doling out free furs for sampling. Alexander Wang attended a week-long junket in Copenhagen held by Saga Furs, 'a marketing company that represents 3,000 fur breeders in Finland and Norway'. The following season, Autumn '11, mink was all over Wang's runway – on full jackets, collars, earmuffs and even the arms of sunglasses. Maybe, as Wilson posited, Wang and gang were simply too young to remember how discordant fur *used* to seem?

Peta power

Anti-fur campaigns go back to at least the 1960s. In the '70s Doris Day was speaking out in favour of fake fur. People for the Ethical Treatment of Animals (PETA) began agitating to change minds about the real stuff being chic in the '80s. In the US, the first Fur Free Friday protests happened in 1985, on the traditional sale shopping day after Thanksgiving. Over the next decade or so, fur's image changed radically. Deemed both cruel and uncool, no one hip wanted a bar of it. Wearing fur was tragic, lame, vile. I remember this myself from school – girls were scared to wear granny's vintage sable for fear of public scorn (or, worse, looking like granny); in '90s Britain, fur was simply a no-go for anyone who didn't have a facelift.

In 1994, five models including Tatjana Patitz and Naomi Campbell stripped for a PETA campaign with the tagline 'We'd rather go naked than wear fur'. As PETA's co-founder Ingrid Newkirk has noted, it's easy to forget how bold that was at the time.[4] Remember, this was before raunch culture, #freethenipple and Miley Cyrus's wrecking ball. And Patitz and Campbell were big deals: 'supermodels' and MTV celebs who'd appeared in George Michael's *Freedom* video clip. 1994 was also the year that PETA occupied Calvin Klein's 7th Avenue offices – shortly afterwards Klein announced his brand would go fur-free.

Newkirk is PETA: she's the public face of provocation, the sixty-something pointy-chinned blonde who cast herself as the force-fed human goose (tied with ropes, blood trickling down her chin) in a campaign against *foie gras* production. She's the one who published her will as a public letter, detailing her wishes for her remains. She wants to be barbecued, apparently, in order to make us think about sausages, and asks that her 'skin, or a portion thereof, be removed and made into leather products, such as purses, to remind the world that human skin and the skin of other animals is the same and that neither is "fabric" nor needed'.[5] There's more, but let's not go there. Suffice to say, Newkirk is good at goading.

Dan Mathews, PETA's senior vice president, is not bad at it either. Square-jawed and tall with round blue eyes – he modelled a bit while he was studying – he looks like a cross between a Ken doll and a TV vet. But don't judge a book by its cover, not even Mathews' *own* book (he sports a bunny costume on the front).

In *Committed: A Rabble-Rouser's Memoir*, Mathews details the tactics he has employed to turn the fashion industry off fur. There are successes: it was Mathews who convinced Klein to watch a tape of 'chinchillas being genitally electrocuted ... minks having their necks crudely snapped'. And failures too: his repeated yelling at Karl Lagerfeld ('designer of death!') has done zip.

Often, the more you tell some people not to do something, the more they will do it. The season after PETA daubed his Paris store windows with red 'Death for Sale' graffiti in 2008, Jean Paul Gaultier presented an entire collection based on fur, complete with hats formed from furry heads with their ears and noses still on, many a dangling fox foot, and a soundtrack of howling wolves.

It was Mathews' idea to target designers 'and use their fame against them'.[6] So PETA people threw pies (tofu, not dairy cream) into the fashionable faces of Anna Wintour, Oscar de la Renta and Michael Kors. They called Donna Karan a 'bunny butcher' and got shouty at Roberto Cavalli and Burberry shows. Mathews personally rushed Gianfranco Ferré's runway in 2004, disguised as a priest. His message? 'Though shalt not kill.' But by far the best photo op came in 2002 when Gisele Bündchen, in stockings and suspenders, was surprised by protestors on the Victoria's Secret runway. It didn't last: the lights were dimmed, the campaigners dragged off, and the segment re-staged. When an imperious-looking Bündchen returned for round two she was met with thunderous applause.

In fact, Victoria's Secret is on the Humane Society of the United States' fur-free retailers, designers and brands list, along with Calvin Klein; Bünchen was targeted thanks to her campaign for US-based mink specialists Blackglama. She later told *Vanity Fair* that she regretted taking the Blackglama job. 'It was a bad decision,' she said, 'because I don't wear fur and I understand their [PETA's] cause. I am the biggest animal-lover in the world.'[7] Blackglama moved on to the next face: Cindy Crawford. And the next, and the next … Elle Macpherson, Carolyn Murphy, Hilary Rhoda.

In 2008, it was Liz Hurley – maybe she did it because of that time at Billy Zane's thirty-fifth birthday party at the Sunset Room in LA, when an activist chucked red wine on her white fur jacket and called her a 'murdering bitch'? Maybe Liz's Blackglama moment was just a big fuck-you to that: 'Whatevs, I'm Liz *Fur*ley now!' Or maybe she did it to pay her drycleaning bill, or just because everyone else was doing it.

The star of Blackglama's 'What Becomes a Legend Most' campaign for 2007 was Naomi Campbell. Rather go naked? Pah. That was officially over, mink-pullover.

Foxy ladies

Today, fur is back as a symbol of moneyed glamour. Lady Gaga has been seen in an Hermès shadow fox. Sharon Stone was pictured in a Fendi fur cape so big it should be a sofa throw. Kate Moss loves a fur chubby, while Kate Upton posed for *Sports Illustrated* in the snow, clad in little more than a Canada Goose parka trimmed with coyote. Rihanna stepped out in a Balmain leather jacket trimmed in raccoon dog fur (magazines tend to leave out the 'dog' bit of that description, but the animal in question is indeed a canid, native to Japan and East Asia).

Kanye West has long loved an extravagant pelt. His wife Kim Kardashian-West told me, five months after their wedding in 2014, that since meeting Kanye her own style has evolved: 'I think having the influence of my husband, who is *sooo* into fashion has just showed me [the way].'[8] Soon they were snapped wearing his 'n' hers furs. By Christmas 2015, Kim had posted a pic of their two-year-old daughter, North, on Instagram rocking the trend. The caption? 'Swag.'

Meanwhile, Fendi's mink and fox fur pompoms, known as 'Bag Bugs' and designed to clip onto its handbags, are enjoying cult status. The Bag Bug is the luxury equivalent of the emperor's new clothes. What is essentially a key chain with a fur offcut glued to it sells for $700 plus. I guess you could call it waste management.

The Karlito is the ultimate Bag Bug, designed in Lagerfeld's image, complete with his signature high white collar, black leather tie and dark glasses. Silvia Venturini Fendi had the first one made up as a gift for the designer, who loved it so much he put it into production.[9] When Cara Delevingne carried one on Fendi's Autumn '14 runway, fans went doolally – hundreds joined the waitlist for the chance to spend $1,750 on a fur Karlito.

And it won't even keep you warm.

When I ask Grzybowski if he's noticed a significant increase in the numbers of fur garments sold in American fashion stores since the IFTF posted those extraordinary figures, he says, no, not really, at least 'not being bought by the general public in the US.'[10]

Who is buying it then, apart from Kimye?

When the IFTF talks about the fur boom, it refers primarily to developing markets. In 'traditional markets', it says, demand has 'remained stable' but 'demand is growing not only in China but also in Korea, Ukraine and South America.'

In China, Japan and South Korea fur sales tripled in the ten years leading up to 2012. That year, Asian sales accounted for the biggest chunk (35 per cent) of the global total. Fur in these markets speaks of cash and cachet – it means you've made it. That's one reason why Grzybowski thinks full-length coats may be used as bribes for local officials to get things like new roads and pipelines built.

The first Louis Vuitton store opened in Beijing in 1992. *Vogue* China arrived in 2005, but the first major international fashion show didn't happen in China until 2007, when Fendi (which is LVMH-owned) commandeered the Great Wall. The extravaganza, for 500 guests, is rumoured to have cost US$10 million.

Fendi is the only luxury fashion house to maintain its own fur atelier. Fur is in its DNA, having started out in 1925 as a small leather goods and *haute fourrure* workshop in Rome. Lagerfeld became Fendi's creative director in 1965, and he came up with the 'FF' logo and coined the term 'fun fur'. That described his vision for fur as 'just another material'.

In his words, 'slowly, the very classic bourgeois coat disappeared and then [Fendi] became *the* fur business in Italy, because they accepted to remove the lining, to do things with fur [that] nobody had done before.'[11] He's talking about the couture approach to making a coat – for example, from hundreds of strips alternated with grosgrain ribbon – as much as the use of fur to make things like jumpers and skirts.

Whatever your thoughts on the raw material, Fendi's supply chain at the cut-make-trim end is exemplary: 70 per cent of its product is made in-house, and artisans train for ten years before they become Fendi fur cutters. Fendi's CEO, Pietro Beccari, is a fan of 'slow luxury' and has likened the *métier* of working with fur on this level to the art of cutting precious stones: 'It is like diamonds. It goes from generation to generation; from family to family.'[12]

But diamonds, as we know, can be bloody too.

I was at Fendi's Spring '15 show in Milan, which I have to note was gorgeous, with an orchid motif played out in fluid silk prints and textured denims, fluttery organza and laser-cut layers. There's no point in me pretending I don't admire the non-Bug designs of a house like this: Lagerfeld is fashion's Renaissance Man, a non-stop creator and innovator who somehow manages to design ready-to-wear, pre- and couture collections for Chanel at the same time as designing for Fendi *and* his own lines, publishing books and launching collabs, taking pictures and directing film clips – all while making a star out of his cat.

Anyway, there I was on row D when I noticed that the best seats in our section were reserved for the Asians. Rows A and B were full of Chinese actresses, Hong Kong DJs and Japanese buyers. Row C was

South East Asian bloggers. It was the end of September, still warm, but most all of them were furred up to the hilt in popsicle-bright bombers, Bugs on their bags, mink pompoms on their shoe-boots.

China is the biggest fur importer. The jury's out as to how long it will remain the factory of the world – but everyone agrees it's future is the mall.

Animal farm

Less than 15 per cent of the fur 'harvested' each year is wild, and almost all of that comes from Canada, Russia and the US. Thanks to the Asian boom, Canadian trappers are seeing unprecedented demand for wild otter, lynx, fox (grey, Arctic, red), beaver, marten and mink for use in the fashion industry. In 2013, the *Toronto Star* reported a 10 per cent rise in the numbers of trapping licence applications in Ontario, and North American Fur Auctions (NAFA) noted prices had 'tripled and in some cases quadrupled in two decades'.

Canada was the nation that made the most fuss when the EU pushed for an international ban on leg-hold traps in the mid-'90s, and the resultant 1997 Agreement on International Humane Trapping Standards was full of compromises: jaw-type leg-hold traps with teeth were banned, but so-called humane leg traps, without teeth, were exempt. Trapped animals have been known to gnaw off their own limbs.

The agreement did regulate killing times – but by species: a trap used on an ermine, for example, must legally put the animal out of its misery (by death or loss of consciousness) within 45 seconds; a marten is given two minutes, other species can legally be left alive a full five. And as Gryzbowski points out, traps frequently catch the wrong animals, from small mammals, birds and deer to hunting dogs and even pets. I'm no expert – I have never accompanied a trapper on his rounds – but I wonder how easy it really is to police this sort of thing in remote areas?

At least the trapped animal lived a natural life before it became a coat collar. I'd take the trapped fur over the farmed I think – not that I'd have an easy time isolating it. The Origin Assured (OA) labelling system (established by the IFTF and the auction houses) does not detail where a particular fur has come from, only that it's from 'a country where national or local regulations or standards governing fur production are in force'. It's bamboozling, to say the least, trying to work out what the laws are in various countries – and, when I look, many of the links from the OA website lead to defunct or otherwise inoperable regional sites. The specifics of OA are as clear as mud.

The only way to make sure fur is wild, not farmed, is to choose species that do not exist on farms, and hope the furrier or retailer has labelled it correctly – and even then there are no assurances as to how it was trapped.

Eight-five per cent of the fur produced globally is factory farmed, a practice outlawed in the UK in since 2003, following The Fur Farming (Prohibition) Act of 2000. In Parliament, Elliott Morely, then British Minister for Agriculture, Fisheries and Food, said the decision to ban was a moral one, although it presumably helped that there were less than twenty fur farms in Britain. The industry, said Morely, was 'not consistent with the proper value and respect for animal life'.

Fur farming is also outlawed in Austria and Croatia, and effectively banned in Switzerland. Italian law was changed in 2008 to require pens and swimming water on mink farms (although obviously the animals are still caged).

Even the Netherlands – the world's third-biggest mink producer, at five million skins a year – looks set to phase out the industry. Fox and chinchilla farming were outlawed there in the '90s, and in 2013 mink was next. Fur, the Dutch senate concluded, was an 'unnecessary luxury product'. Wages, countered farmers, were hardly that. In May 2014 they successfully overturned the ban at the Dutch national court in the Hague – the government was not allowed to take away their livelihoods without compensation. At the end of 2015, the ban was back – producers have until 2024 to close their farms.

As the British Farm Animal Welfare Council notes, minks and foxes, unlike herd animals, are 'essentially wild' – inquisitive predators particularly ill suited to confinement in small cages. Foxes like to dig. A mink will typically patrol riverbank stretches of several kilometres, and is semi-aquatic. The poor buggers – outside of Italy, farms aren't big on animal swimming pools.

A typical mink cage in Europe is 70cm high, 40cm deep and 45cm across. Nesting boxes are standard in most countries but stacked cages are common, and the floors are usually open wire, so there's nothing to protect animals on lower levels from falling excrement. The animals are usually kept two to a cage, further restricting movement – and anyway, where are they going to move to?

Then there's the killing. The squeamish should look away now. Methods vary from gassing (most common in the EU) and lethal injection, to neck-breaking and the unconscionable anal and oral electrocution (which induces a heart attack while the animal is conscious). At the time of writing, animal electrocution is legal in forty-nine American states. One of the issues raised during the European ban debates was that there's typically no legislation around staff training or qualifications when it comes to ending an animal's life.

There are also currently no laws regulating how fur farm animals are treated or killed in China, which produces 25 per cent of the world's pelts.

In the US, the federal Animal Welfare Act does not cover fur farms, and laws on farming standards and practices vary from state to state. Californian law, for example, dictates minimum cage sizes, but if you are a fur farmer in the biggest state player, Wisconsin, then it's up to you how you interpret the legal requirement to provide 'sufficient food' and housing for the animals in your charge. Some states don't require licences. Everywhere, farmers can choose whether or not to join the Fur Commission USA Merit Award Certification Program. Presumably the bad ones don't bother.

Telling it like it isn't

'Fur is tanned in the same way leather is, but uses chemicals gentle enough to ensure the natural hairs are not stripped from the skin,' claims the IFTF, which is clearly absolute tosh. Ah, the gentle formaldehyde, chromium and sulphuric acid. The International Labour Organization warns that tannery workers face 'a risk of ingestion of toxic dusts. Injurious vapours may arise from degreasing solvents and fumigating chemicals.' The World Bank identifies leather production (including fur) as among three most polluting industries on the planet.

The global fur trade – like the trade in exotic skins – is a big, unwieldy, amorphous and poorly regulated beast. Many suppliers no doubt do their best to operate ethically, but the industry is also home to those China-based producers who flog two million dog and cat skins each year. A 2005 joint investigation by Care for the Wild and Swiss Animal Protection uncovered evidence of animals being skinned alive on Chinese fur farms, and concluded that inhumane cages, 'rough treatment' in general, and the practice of slaughtering animals in front of those left living were routine.

The industry ain't pretty, and it most certainly isn't the sunset-dipped utopia awash with gentle chemicals and kindly farmers depicted on the IFTF website. And while we're on the subject, PETA is no blameless angel either. In 2014, a van marked PETA dog-napped a pet chihuahua named Maya from a trailer park in Accomack County, Virginia. A few days later, according to Maya's owner, PETA representatives delivered a fruit basket to the family. Maya had been killed. Oops, sorry about that.

Newkirk has admitted to 'euthanising' healthy animals.[13] The PETA Kills Animals website lists official numbers of animals received, adopted out or killed by PETA-run shelters in Virginia, where it is headquartered. These stats come from public records made available by the state's Department of Agriculture and Consumer Services, and the number of animals killed between 1998 and 2013 varies from a low of 72 per cent to a high of 97 per cent. PETA makes no secret that it would prefer 'the institution of "pet keeping" … never existed'.[14]

I asked my cat, Pix, who we adopted from a Cat Protection Society shelter, about Newkirk's suggestion that, 'our selfish desire to possess animals and receive love from them causes immeasurable suffering'. She strongly disagreed.

'But Pix, Ingrid says you "are restricted to human homes, where you must obey commands",' I said.

'I think you'll find it's the other way round,' said Pix. 'This is my home. You obey me.'

For a supposedly civilised society, the way we exploit and mistreat our animal resources is often pretty hideous. But that's economics – and politics – for you. And we don't fare much better with our labour 'resources' either. Or our natural ones.

Gum shoe tactics

I'm late and I'm running and I can feel a blister forming on my heel. Shop windows flash past: summer pastels, shorts, a fantastic silver pleated skirt that makes me pause. I seriously consider ducking in to try it on, but Grzybowski has already been waiting for me for fifteen minutes, and he has made the trip especially from Washington by train. I'm a selfish bitch. A selfish fashion addict bitch with no juice left in my phone, so I keep running. I'm breaking into a sweat.

I wonder if Grzybowski will be able to read my mind and find the chapter on the vintage Russian coat. I'm not alone – Ingrid Newkirk had a fur coat when she was nineteen[15] – but I hate mine now; it is shaming, it makes me feel like Eva Braun with her lamp-shades. I don't know how to make it go away. I've thought about burying it in the backyard, maybe reciting a poem and playing it a Leonard Cohen song.

Grzybowski is a big lean guy with a shaved head and oblong Prada glasses above a white shirt, no tie. He has the look of Ben Affleck about him, trying to keep the rage buttoned down inside his cruelty-free suit.

Later he will tell me, 'You wouldn't believe how hard it is to find a vegan suit,' turning back the collar on his jacket to show me the felt lining underneath. 'This bit is the bitch: it's usually wool.'

I will palpate it between my fingers and tell him, 'That's synthetic, I'm pretty sure,' and he will cut me off.

'Don't mess up my expensive gear. I used to make $23,000 a year. You think I want to spend it on clothes? Jeez,' he will shake his head. 'I hate it, getting dressed up like this, but you know, you wander into these stores in a cheap suit, your glasses held together with tape, they don't take you seriously.'

Being taken seriously in this context means being ignored; passing for a regular customer, just browsing, when really he is a spy. That's presumably why he doesn't bring a magnifying glass, which is a bit disappointing. I don't ask him about that because I'm scared it will make him cross. Anyway, he can see what he needs to see through his Pradas.

Grzybowski's girlfriend made him replace his old broken glasses; he'd had them since his days as a nightclub bouncer. ('I'm a martial arts man.') Those specs had one missing arm, replaced by a plastic cocktail straw and gaffer tape. I think he must be joking when he tells me this, but he's not. 'I like to fix things. Why buy more stuff?'

But all this is yet to come. Right now I am meeting Grzybowski for the first time.

He is folded into a booth in the restaurant attached to his cheap hotel, sucking up the dregs of a Coke. He has one of those tough, dry handshakes that makes you think he could save you in an Hollywood storm at sea. If he chose to. He might not. Might just let the waves drag you overboard.

'I'm sorry I'm late,' I say, and he nods. 'I like your shoes,' I say, because my brain's not working after all that running.

He is wearing tapered black dress-shoes. He lifts his leg to show them. 'Plastic,' he says. 'Two-hundred-eighty dollar shoes. I told the guy, they'd better last.'

As I take a seat, I kick my leather bag under the table. Then I decide: no. I'm not going to lie. I'm an animal lover, but like most people I eat meat and dairy, and I wear leather (less than 2 per cent of Australians are vegan). I have six designer handbags, which sounds excessive, grotesque even, but is it really? None of them have Bag Bugs attached. There's the big workaday black one I'm carrying now; a casual tan for jeans; dark brown for when the tan looks too pale; a smaller black one for going out; a sparkly evening clutch; and an old friend that cost me an arm and a leg from Anya Hindmarch, in her pre-cereal-box days.

According to a 2011 poll of 2,000 women conducted by Kellogg's (the very same company that sponsored Hindmarch's Spring '14 show), the average British woman owns seven handbags. How many do you have? They say Victoria Beckham has more than a hundred Birkins. Most men are immune, but not all. George Clooney, who I'd taken for a briefcase bloke, has been spotted with a satchel. I pick Grzybowski for the canvas backpack type, but I'm wrong. Later he will show me his strong box.

We play a dumb game of 'What If?' and I lose.

'What if you could prove an animal had been reared and killed humanely? Would you wear leather then?'

'I couldn't prove it, that's the problem.'

'What if I were an organic farmer in New Zealand and you came to my house and I went down to the bottom of the garden and milked a jersey cow called Tabitha, if I stroked her nose and she snuffled into my palm and it was clear that she loved me, and that I loved her enough to give her a name? And what if I milked her by hand into a bucket and I personally churned that milk into butter and spread it on an amazing scone, freshly baked in your honour? Would you eat it then? Because you'd offend me as a hostess if you didn't, and what if you had no tent and I kicked you out and you had to sleep in the dirt road? In the rain. Huh? How about that?'

'I would ask, why is that cow lactating? Where is the baby?' I roll my eyes, and he says, 'There's always some bullshit scenario. Nine times out of ten, that calf has been sold for veal production.'

He could have just asked for margarine.

We're getting off topic. We are here to talk about the fashion industry. Grzybowski is the Research and Enforcement Manager of the Humane Society of the United States' Fur-Free Campaign, or as he puts it, 'One man charged with protecting 100 million animals.'

There is one other person working full time on the campaign, which is donation funded. 'He's the carrot; I'm the stick,' says

Grzybowski. The colleague sets up the meetings with designers, dis-
tributors, retailers, big fashion, and tries to talk them into abandoning
fur. Grzybowski 'couldn't hack' that. He does the grunt work on the
ground; he's the gumshoe, the cop pounding the pavement beat.

His investigations focus on breaches of the Truth in Fur Labeling
Act of 2010, which requires mandatory labelling on all fur items sold
in the US. The EU has similar legislation. In Australia, we have no such
system (although cat and dog fur have been banned since 2004), which
seems astounding to me. Perhaps it's because for much of the year much
of Australia is too hot for fur clothes; perhaps it's because no one gives
a shit. Australia is not a 'green' country – it's a mining country, a fracking country, a country that is failing to protect its precious barrier reefs.

Sales of full fur coats might be paltry in Australia, but we're as
susceptible to the next country to the supposedly glamorous allure
of a fur highlight: two of my friends bought Céline's mink-lined slides
when they came out. And anyone with an Akubra habit should know
traditional millinery felt is made from rabbit fur. Rabbits, inciden-
tally, are not included in the IFTF's statistics on pelts. You might say
rabbits are pests – to which I would say, check out Wally and Molly
on Instagram (seriously, please do @wally_and_molly). And by the
way, shearling is the pelt of a dead sheep, in case you were thinking
the animal trotted off back to the paddock after shearing. Ponyhair
accessories are mostly cow, but if a fabric isn't labelled (or even if it
is), how do you really know? Another friend once went quite white
when someone asked if her expensive zebra-patterned sandals were
made of *real zebra* – maybe they were.

Are you fur real?
Any fur or fur-trimmed garment sold in the US must carry a label
detailing the type of animal and country of origin (COO) where the

animal was killed. Grzybowski wishes there was no such thing as designer fur, but since there is, this is his battleground.

He is looking for law-breakers: garments that are not labelled, or are mislabelled with incorrect species or COO. Worst are those labelled as fake, or 'faux', fur which are, in fact, made of the real animal-derived deal.

'Yes, that happens. It's too common. 2014 is one of the worst I've experienced since I started focusing on mislabelling in 2006,' he tells me. 'We've found real sold as fake in stores from every price-point: from discounters to the most expensive luxury retailers you can think of.' The 'faux' fur pompoms on a Stuart Weitzman ballet flat sold by Neiman Marcus online were found to be real fur; that neat removable faux fur collar on a Philip Lim parka in Barneys? Coyote. Raccoon dog is often mislabelled as raccoon or rabbit (because dog is gross, right?). 'Our lawsuits [have] named Neiman Marcus, Saks Fifth Avenue and Lord & Taylor among others, so we're talking big names here,' says Grzybowski. 'Despite repeated attempts to get companies to fix the problem, and push various agencies to take more strict enforcement actions, it still goes on.'

I ask him why, and he describes greedy, lazy corporations, and customers who aren't much better. Producers may lie, he says, because they don't care. Some retailers may lie because 'they think it's cheaper to run the risk of getting caught and dealing with it, than proactively doing adequate quality control'. There is a vein in Grzybowski's temple that throbs when he talks about this stuff.

'It must be difficult,' I say, 'to have to keep on delivering the same message to people who don't want to hear it?'

He shrugs. There are those who give up when the fight seems like too much hard work, and there's Grzybowski. I suspect he thrives off the challenge. Single-minded bolshiness gets things done;

the world needs disrupters to make change. I also think he's got more in common with Gaultier than he might think, but I don't tell him that either.

Grzybowski studied environmental policy and planning at college. 'A lot of our case studies dealt with food operations and pollution issues. Learning about the various environmental problems associated with producing animals for food, I decided to become vegetarian,' he says. 'Later on, learning about the dairy and egg industries, I decided to go vegan. The more I looked, the more I realised the depths of what went on. It was like jumping down a rabbit hole, there's no end to the new horrors you uncover.' Fur production, he says, 'stuck with me as surely the most grievous of all the animal abuses that go on, and the most indefensible'.

He conducts his investigation both online and on the streets. He buys suspect furs, and has them analysed in a lab (powerful microscopes help determine species). Those that break the law are archived in locked rooms and used as evidence. Sometimes Grzybowski responds to tip-offs from the public, like one time when a Humane Society of the United States member in New York spotted an advert for dog fur items in a Russian language magazine.

◉

We slip into a boutique off the main drag. Inside, are the sorts of lurid, bedazzled clothes I haven't seen since *Dynasty*. There are no customers, but two sales assistants, dolled-up ladies of a certain age.

'Doing some shopping today, darlin'? It's a beautiful day for it,' says the one with hair like Sylvester Stallone's mother. She pronounces it *beeoodeefool*.

'Just beautiful,' says the other one, who could be Linda Evans, twenty years after she played Krystle Carrington. 'Oh my! Is that cape something! Try it on! You're welcome. It's a little hot out today but come winter that will be a real beauty.' The air-con is whirring but it's still clammy in here. I pick up the cape: purple, embroidered with ribbon work, with a lattice-pattern of fur pompoms, interspersed with glinty crystals. It is hideous.

'Those are real crystals,' says Mrs Stallone.

Grzybowski makes a harrumphing sound.

Linda and Mrs S are being sweet to me, and I feel guilty duping them. 'Do you wanna try? Oh that coat could look so great on you,' says Linda.

'That purple would be pretty with your hair,' says Mrs S. 'And it's on sale.' She shows me the price tag, which has been fixed to the cape's turquoise silk lining with a tiny golden safety pin. The figure, '$6,700', has been hand-written, then scored out carefully with the same black pen. Underneath, in red, it says '$4,800.'

'Can we see the other labels?' says Grzybowski, glowering at the cape, subtle as a brick. 'What fur is this one? Where does it come from?'

He sees that there is no label apart from the price tag, and his eyes glitter like the crystals (they're not labelled either; they might be paste). 'There is no label,' he says.

'You know what?' I say, smiling at Linda. 'This is a little out of my price range. Don't get me wrong, it's beautiful,' – I draw the word out trying to speak her language – 'but I'm looking for something a little cheaper.' I beckon Grzybowski over to a display of scarves. 'Like this, this is cute.'

Mrs S has turned her back, and sighs before collecting herself: the show must go on. She whips around with surprising sprightliness, and smiles. 'Yes, yes, that stole is just the ticket.'

'Oh, I agree,' I say, and witter on a while about crisp winters in the mountains and how you can never have enough mufflers. We'll be back, I say, when we've had a think, and if she could just give me their details.

Outside, it's even hotter.

'So,' I say, adrenalin fizzing. 'Gonna bust 'em?'

'Nah,' says Grzybowski. 'Small fry.'

My shoulders sink further than Linda's did when she worked out I wasn't in the market for the papal purple.

'You were good,' he says.

'I should win an Oscar,' I say. 'How do the hell do you do this when you're on your own?'

'I get by.'

'But no one is going to believe you are doing some harmless coat shopping for a friend.'

'Well they do.'

We begin to sulk, both of us, pretending we are not.

'What was the name of Sylvester Stallone's mom?' I say. *Mom ...* I'm still in character.

Grzybowski doesn't know.

We walk a couple of blocks in silence, and suddenly we are outside the Fendi flagship. Now, I am carrying my second-best handbag and wearing hurty $150 J. Crew sandals with a pair of creased linen pants. I do not look like your typical buyer of $20,000 coats. Still, I think of Julia Roberts in *Pretty Woman* and I stick out my chin and suggest we hit this joint up. We fiddle about downstairs amidst the Bag Bugs for a bit, then head to where the serious stuff lives.

The sales assistant here is lovely too. She has lipstick on her teeth, which takes the edge off her intimidating elegance.

'What can I help you with today?'

'We'd like to see the furs,' says Grzybowski, approaching a rose pink shaved mink that costs more than my car. 'Where do they come from?'

I jump in and start talking about my fashion dream and how I've come to collect the Peekaboo bag I've been saving up for – but while I'm here I wanted to *peek* at the new ready-to-wear collection. 'Just to see it! We never come near this sort of workmanship back home,' I say. 'I look at the pictures, but it's not the same. Oh, just to look.' The bumpkin, the wide-eyed out-of-towner and bad pun fan, smitten by the fashion spell.

The vendeuse frowns at Grzybowski, who is fingering a mink shrug like it's road kill. He drops it and starts to study the stone-effect of the walls.

'This rock,' he says, 'is great.'

'He's a rock person,' I say, 'my ... brother. We're going to lunch. *So mean* of me to drag him shopping.'

I'm an only child. I'm Meryl Streeping it, knocking it out of the park. She is eating out of my hand.

'Actually,' she says, smiling, 'there are some very special pieces we just received from Italy. We had a private view for our top customers, so they're just here. I would be delighted to show you. They really are exquisite.'

And they are all correctly labelled. Grzybowski heads downstairs; he's not here for the good of his fashion health.

We try one more time in the opulent fur salon at Bergdorf's, where the security guard stands so close behind me as I look at (but don't touch) a J. Mendel fox jacket that I can feel his warm breath on my neck. I think longingly of Linda and Mrs S, I think of putting my feet up, of a gin and tonic and a club sandwich, but it is not to be. Grzybowski has something to show me.

If you scaled down Grzybowski so that he was the size of a mink, and you scaled down his hotel room in direct proportion, said room would be about the same size as the average European cage. It is white, except for the hulking black form of the plastic strong box. It's the size of a large suitcase, the kind you have to check in, and closed with two padlocks. 'If you can break that,' says Grzybowski, 'you'd have to be one of the top locksmiths in the world.'

The blanket is the size of a hand towel. It is made from the full pelts of three domestic dogs 'and various bits', stitched together. The hot room fills with an unspeakable stink, of wet dog – worse, rotting wet dog. 'It wasn't tanned properly, I guess,' says Grzybowski. It takes all my will not to retch. His expression is inscrutable.

'Doesn't this upset you?' I say, as he begins to secure his evidence away again.

'I can't be emotional,' he says. 'I have to stay detached. If I don't I'd go crazy, but mainly I'd be unable to do my job.'

Double standards

Why is the idea of fur so much more emotive than leather? The supers didn't front an ad campaign proclaiming, 'We'd rather go naked than wear leather trousers'. No one threw red paint at Jim Morrison. Why not?

The convenient, but inaccurate, answer is that leather is a byproduct of the meat industry, and not to use it would be a shameful waste. I've lost count how many times I've heard vegos justifying their leather habit in terms of saving resources. (Plus it's really hard to find pretty vegan shoes if you can't afford Stella McCartney.) But to borrow Al Gore's phrase, the inconvenient truth is that virgin rainforest is being razed daily to make way for cattle farms, while tannery chemicals are poisoning rivers. Our cheap leather habit is an environmental nightmare, but one that's socially more acceptable than fur.

The most obvious reason is that cows are not cute. Although research suggests they have friends and get lonely when they are separated, in general, we don't relate: bovines? Cheese factories. Whatever. But show us a *wabbit* ...

We are genetically pre-programmed to find small vulnerable creatures adorable, which is why when PETA released its 2013 video of workers in China tearing the fur out of live angora bunnies, we went right off our Christmas jumpers. The breed is ultra fluffy and sweet-looking, so when pictures of them simply sitting there being – as the Japanese call cute – *kawaii* (as opposed to being gorily abused by the heartless factory bods) hit social media, they were shared more than pictures of Harry Styles. Major fashion companies, including H&M, Primark, ASOS and Ted Baker, reacted by immediately dropping angora.

Catarina Midby, H&M's sustainable fashion advisor, was taking me through the brand's Autumn '14 sample collection when we came across an angora knit. 'We've stopped doing angora,' she told me. 'So it won't be like this sample, it will be mohair when it's delivered. It's horrible actually. We have always said the angora should be from good husbandry, and when we couldn't guarantee that anymore, because the industry has changed, we decide not to use it. We've also pledged to take back everything made from angora that was bought from H&M. So you can bring back a garment that is years old for a store credit.'[16]

I asked her what they'd do with the unwanted contraband.

'I don't know,' she admitted. Point was they were taking action, because customers demanded it. Torturing the cute thing is not a good look.

Then there's the immorality of the impractical. It's easy to argue that we need leather shoes to walk to work in, leather moto jackets to ride our bikes in, leather bags to carry our crap in (and steak to keep our iron levels up). When we say these things, reasonable, middle-of-the-road, nice people nod and scratch their chins and think, 'Hmm, yes, me too.'

But it is difficult to make the case for *needing* a fur item, unless you are living as your Inuit ancestors did in the wilds of Alaska, or shivering like Kate Upton did in her bikini in the snow. People buy fur because they think it makes them look sexy and expensive, and that makes the reasonable, middle-of-the-road, nice people feel uncomfortable. This time, when they scratch their chins they are thinking, *Like a fish needs a bicycle! Who do you think you are, you arrogant knob?* Fur is about luxury, vanity and exploitation. It's a hard one to defend.

Road kill

Petite Mort is the fashion label run by Pamela Paquin using fur from some of the one-million-plus animals that become roadkill in the US each year. She calls it 'accidental fur'. It all started when Paquin, who worked as a sustainability consultant in Denmark before moving back home to upstate New England, skinned and 'scraped' a roadkill raccoon, with a little help from a local taxidermist.

In 2013, she began doing it commercially, sending the pelts to a tannery in Idaho and making the results into mufflers, shrugs and even leg warmers. Paquin's motto, as detailed on her website, is 'because good taste is never at the expense of another', and she reckons fans 'may now wear fur down Main Street, or through Whole Foods, up the steps of the Opera House or off the slopes to your après-ski festivities with shameless pride'.

When Paquin's story was told in *Modern Farmer* magazine,[17] it sparked outraged comments from readers: 'What about the millions of dogs and cats killed in animal shelters each year? Why not use their fur/skin to make garments also?' Could selling such pelts be a good source of income for cash-strapped animal shelters, and what other 'niche markets could be created (highlighting the sick, exploitive nature of capitalism)'? Was brand Fido next?

Pierre Grzybowski's good ethics, Pamela Paquin's, yours, mine; they might be very different things. Like the answers to the questions: Are human rights more important than animal rights? Is it better to wear a vintage fur than throw it in landfill? Would you rather a roadkill carcass be used or left to rot? Are some types of fur 'better' or 'worse' than others? Trapped versus farmed, for example, or rare Russian sable versus the common nutria, or water rat, which is destroying Louisiana's marshes? And who are you to play God and decide? Or is it all the same as eating meat or wearing leather, and is that okay? Is fake fur unethical if it resembles the real thing, and perpetuates the trend for looking like a fluffy animal? What if it rejoices in its fakery, like that by UK label Shrimps? And what about its carbon footprint? It's complicated.

I've remembered the name of Stallone's mother: Jackie. When I get back to my hotel, I do a little research to see if she is still alive, so might possibly be working in an uptown boutique. Jackie Stallone has just turned ninety-two. She does indeed still work, but out of Santa Monica, not New York, and as a rumpologist, which is a sort-of ass psychic. Rumpologists don't read tea-leaves or palms or the bumps on your head; they tell your fortune by reading your bum. Jackie works from photos, to survey 'the lines, crevices, dimples, and folds of the buttocks' in order to divine character and destiny. According to Sylvester Stallone, his mother 'has successfully predicted every major event in my life'. According to Jackie, the left butt cheek will tell you what happened in your past, the right, what the future holds. The world is a place of infinite possibility and confusion.

CHAPTER 9

Counter Culture:
How Retail Evolved

Are you being served?

'John wants to buy some furs. Can you come over?'

It was Yoko Ono calling and she wanted Jack Cohen, then in charge of the fur department at Bergdorf Goodman, to nip on over to the Dakota building on West 72nd with some stock for John Lennon to have a shufty at. Ten trunks of it. Never mind that it was near closing time. Bergdorf's prides itself on customer service and anyway, furs are expensive – who knows what whims of the rich and famous the retailer had to accommodate? Well actually, I do, because I've watched the movie *Scatter My Ashes at Bergdorf's*, so I have it on good authority that Elizabeth Taylor once demanded 200 pairs of white mink earmuffs be made within a week for her to take on holiday to Gstaad. Anyway, if a Beatle says bring the mink, you bring the mink. Lennon ended up buying eighty furs, so it was a good night's work for Cohen.

Bergdorf's occupies the former site of the Vanderbilt mansion on the Upper East Side. To construct the so-called 'grandest house in America', Cornelius Vanderbilt II (who'd inherited squillions from his grandpop, the original Cornelius, a railroad baron) razed three brownstones on the corner of 5th Avenue and 57th Street, then five more around the corner. His finished pad had 130 rooms and was based, architecturally, on the palaces of French kings. But in 1927, just thirty-five years after it was completed, Vanderbilt's daughter Alice sold the building to developers, who knocked it down to build a shopping complex. (Alice donated the gates to Central Park, where, at the entrance to the Conservatory Garden, they stand as a spooky reminder of the Gilded Age.)

Upscale jewellers Van Cleef & Arpels were early tenants, as was Edwin Goodman, who had taken over Herman Bergdorf's women's clothing business in 1901. Goodman commissioned the developers to build him an apartment on the ninth floor of the new building, and installed his now iconic store in the 58th Street corner. By 1948 he'd taken over the entire place.

When personal shopper Betty Halbreich, immortalised at the age of eighty-five in *Scatter My Ashes*, began working at the store in the 1970s, Edwin Goodman's son Andrew still paced his kingdom daily. 'Mr Goodman would walk through the store every evening and talk to everybody,' Halbreich tells me, 'while we all smoked. I often wonder how the clothes smelled when they were shipped out. At five o'clock we'd bring the wine out. How those clothes ever got [delivered], I don't know! It's a mystery. It was a different time.'[1]

Wine aside, Halbreich remembers the store as 'in many ways very staid, but very beautiful – all the crystal chandeliers, the done-up doormen, the elevator men'. The legacy of the *Mad Men* era continued, and department stores wooed customers with a glamour and formality that is hard to imagine now. 'On the couture floor, a woman took your name and said, "Be seated", then she'd call and the vendeuse would come out, always dressed in black,' recalls Halbreich.

Customers still come to Bergdorf's for the experience, and Halbreich is part of it. I ask her to describe her role, which runs from arbiter of taste to fashion agony-aunt. 'I just sell the clothes and mouth a lot of foolishness,' she says. 'What do clients want? My heart! First they take my blood, then they take my heart, then they take my brain! That's literally true. I put [a garment] on someone, she will turn away from the mirror, look at me and say, "Betty, what do you think?" And I will spin her around again to face the mirror, [then to see] the back and the side, and say, "How do *you* feel? *I* am not going to be there when you wear this garment." It's some sort of assurance they want from me. But it's their money ... so I try to be conservative – and brutally honest.'

Halbreich is the last person to counsel buying a dress to wear once. She tells her clients to hold on to their best pieces, to treat them like art that will appreciate in value. She believes in buying the right thing, and making it work hard in your wardrobe, although she's no minimalist herself. She has twelve closets at home. 'Do as I say, not as I do,' is Halbreich's answer to that.

'The other day some poor soul put her arm in one sleeve and I said, "Don't even bother! That is the worst dress I have ever seen in my whole life!" She looked askance at me, and she said, "Betty, shouldn't I put the rest of it on?" I said, "DON'T BOTHER. I hate it, *more than* hate it." I whisked it out of the room: Gone!'

Halbreich's loyal customers – Joan Rivers was one – trust her eye, and know from experience that she can solve their wardrobe crises, but that's not all they come for. They come for the show.

Both the department store and shopping as entertainment are relatively recent concepts. That's not to say that shopping, with its opportunities for socialising and gossip, was not enjoyable as well as practical in, say, medieval times, when most of it was done at transitory markets and fairs – but we're talking daily bread here, not Louboutins. Ye olde shoppe was sustainable before sustainability was invented.

European towns began to develop in the sixteenth century, and high streets developed around marketplaces. Permanent shops were built with dwellings out the back or above, and from then on the butcher, baker and candlestick maker joined the church as physical focal points of communities – a system that worked well into the Regency era and beyond.

When Jane Austen's Emma looked upon Highbury village while her friend Harriet bought ribbons at Mr Ford's – 'the principal woollen-draper, linen-draper, and haberdasher's shop united; the shop first in size and fashion in the place' – she saw a typical scene: 'The butcher with his tray, a tidy old woman travelling homewards with her full basket, two curs quarrelling over a dirty bone, and a string of dawdling children round the baker's little bow-window eyeing the gingerbread.'[2]

Ford's shop plays a key role in Austen's novel *Emma*, as thousands like it would have done in the towns and villages of Georgian England. Austen describes the scene when eligible bachelor from out of town, Frank Churchill, strolling with Emma, happens upon Ford's. He says: 'Ha! This must be the very shop that every body attends every day of their lives, as my father informs me ... If it may not be inconvenient to you, pray let us go in, that I may prove myself to belong to the place, to be a true citizen of Highbury. I must buy something at Ford's ... I dare say they sell gloves?'

Emma replies: 'Oh! Yes, gloves and every thing. I do admire your patriotism. You will be adored in Highbury. You were very popular before you came ... but lay out half a guinea at Ford's, and your popularity will stand upon your own virtues.'

To fit in, you shopped local.

It was Napoleon who most famously called England 'a nation of shopkeepers', and Margaret Thatcher (the grocer's daughter) who is most closely associated with the comment – 'He meant to be unflattering, but we took his description as a compliment', she said – but it was the philosopher Adam Smith who first coined the phrase in the sixteenth century. Smith, like Thatcher, believed in laissez faire economics – that the pursuit of self-interest leads to community prosperity, that competition regulates greed and that the free market will naturally work for the good of society – although what he would have made of the age of the global corporation we can only guess.

Today 'Mr Ford's of Highbury' sounds impossibly quaint. The shopkeeper behind his counter is a dying breed. Good luck asking for a quick word with Mr Marks or Mr Spencer in Leeds (where they started out in 1894), or indeed in any of the hundreds of M&S stores now as far afield as India and Russia.

In London, the artistic Arthur Lasenby Liberty is gone from his fashionable Regent Street emporium. Once called Eastern Bazaar, it stocked exotic finds for discerning Edwardians; the current mock Tudor building was purpose-built and opened in 1924. Liberty London is now run by a private equity group called BlueGem Capital.

Benjamin Harvey and his modest Knightsbridge linen shop are gone, along with his partner James Nichols. There *is* one man behind the Harvey Nichols stores today – Hong Kong tycoon Dickson Poon – but I doubt you'll find him pacing the ladieswear department.

Harrods is owned by a nation state: Qatar. Mohamed Al-Fayed sold out to Qatar Holdings, part of the Qatar Investment Authority, in 2010. The fellow who founded the store in 1849 was Charles Henry Harrod and the first commodity he sold was tea. Harrod was also an early champion of the escalator. Who knew?

In Australia the big two are publicly listed companies, but there was once a real-life David Jones. A Welsh immigrant, he started selling his wares from Sydney's George Street in 1838. In 2014 the South African retail group Woolworths Holdings, which also controls Country Road, Mimco and Witchery in Australia, took over David Jones.

Mr Jones's future competitor Sidney Myer arrived in Bendigo, Victoria, from Russia in 1899. In the 1980s Myer's descendants launched the local version of Target (under licence from the US), merged with the now-defunct Grace Bros department store chain, and then with Coles. From 2006 to 2009, Mr Myer's namesake stores were spun off, and a private equity group headquartered in Texas stepped in. Shareholders in 2016 include Goldman Sachs.

When Edwin Goodman died in 1953, his son took over at Bergdorf's. Andrew Goodman sold out to the California-based Broadway-Hale Stores in 1972. Broadway-Hale became Carter Hawley Hale and at one time owned Wanamaker's of Philadelphia (John Wanamaker hadn't been near *his* counter since 1922), Canada's Holt Renfrew (Mr Holt left the building in 1915) and Neiman Marcus.

Neiman Marcus was opened in Dallas in 1907 by brother and sister team Herbert Marcus and Carrie Marcus Neiman. Herbert's son Stanley Marcus took over in the '50s, and it was he who struck the deal with Broadway-Hale.

In 2013, the Neiman Marcus Group – by now comprising no namesake family members, but forty-one Neiman Marcus stores, Bergdorf Goodman and the online homewares offering Horchow (yes there is a Mr Horchow: Roger) – sold for a reported US$6 billion. Benefitting shareholders included TPG, the Texan fund that had backed Myer. What a tangled web we weave. The buyers were a Californian private equity firm and a Canadian pensions fund – faceless suits.

Yet shops and shopping remain at the heart of discussions around community. As places where people interact, as well as transact, it's impossible to separate them from social history, whether we're talking about mom-and-pop outfits, department stores, designer boutiques, big-box discounters or suburban malls. And whoever's name is above the door.

Shock of the new

Glazed store windows appeared in the early 1800s, around the same time as the first arcades, starting with the Galeries de Bois in Paris. In his novel *Illusions Perdues* (Lost Illusions), Honoré de Balzac describes it as a 'gypsy encampment' where sex was for sale as readily as books, a place where gentlemen met to gamble and 'reputations were made and unmade, as well as political and financial deals'.

In London's Pall Mall, the contemporary Royal Opera Arcade was far more salubrious. Designed by John Nash (architect of Buckingham Palace), when it opened in 1818 shoppers would have found it very elegant, being used to the filth of London's open streets – where dung from the city's 40,000 horses congealed with the soot and dust to form a tar-like substance so thick and vile that well-to-do ladies used to order shopkeepers serve them in their carriages so as not to ruin their shoes.

Europe's department store craze began with Au Bon Marché, which opened in 1869 on Rue de Sevres in Paris's 7th arrondissement. Émile Zola used the store as inspiration for his novel *Au Bonheur des Dames* (The Ladies' Paradise), and it's still a big deal today – with the 'Au' replaced by 'Le'.

America too had its fine stores. In New York, Samuel Lord and George Taylor had been selling fashion since the 1820s, and from their dignified Broadway location since the 1860s. The Bloomingdale brothers expanded in the 1870s, and Macy's drew the crowds in the early 1900s – as a kid, founder Rowland Hussey Macy had worked on a whaling ship, where he got a tattoo of a red star on his hand; that star forms part of the Macy's logo.

In Chicago, Marshall Field (who in pictures looks like Steve Martin in *The Pink Panther*) went from being a penniless farmer's son to a multi-millionaire by exploiting the new wholesale market. By 1900 he was personally raking in US$40 million a year, roughly $800 million in today's money, and his name was above the city's biggest department store.[3]

According to Lindy Woodhead, author of *Shopping, Seduction and Mr Selfridge*, in the 1880s Chicago's ladies couldn't work. Their servants looked after the kids and the kitchen. 'There were no beauty parlours, no restaurants – certainly none where women could eat – and only one theatre.' It was either shop or go to church.

'Feminists have long raged about the consumer cult,' she writes, 'but the early women's champion Elizabeth Cady Stanton was quite clear on the subject. While she deplored the excesses of wealthy women "who only lived for fashion", she also implored women to seek independence through masterminding the family budget: "Go out and buy!" she would shout from the platform at conventions ... urging women to seize the initiative in equipping their household and clothing themselves – whether or not they were paying the bills.'[4]

Harry Gordon Selfridge rose to general manager of the Marshall Field's State Street store in the late 1880s, and much of what he introduced there he took to London, along with his mighty ambition, and unleashed on the wonder that was to become Selfridges on Oxford Street. Window-shopping, the bargain basement, newspaper advertising, twice-yearly sales, displays to encourage browsing – Selfridge pioneered them all. But above all, he put the show into shopping.

He arrived in London in 1906, and built the five-storey Selfridges building from scratch, hiring architect Daniel Burnham (who'd also worked for Marshall Field). Given that most of Selfridge's competitors were plying their wares in dimly lit rabbit warrens, with ancient clerks and stock hidden away, this building – with its mirrors, flowers and bright lights; its dazzling displays and in-store fashion shows; the pretty young female staff who called their customers 'sir' and 'madam'; and the smart restaurant that welcomed ladies – must have seemed like something from a dream. Or perhaps 'theme park' is the better description.

In 1909, after the French aviator Louis Blériot flew across the English Channel, Selfridge displayed the aircraft in his store, attracting more than 150,000 visitors. For King George V's Silver Jubilee in 1935, Selfridge draped his building with giant Union Jacks, and had a huge statue of Britannica erected on the roof, complete with gold lions. Selfridge claimed his store was 'the third biggest tourist attraction in town,'[5] after Westminster Abbey and the Tower of London.

In *A Cultural History of Fashion in the 20th and 21st Centuries*, Bonnie English describes how the grand nineteenth-century department stores aped museums, by displaying their treasures in glass cases and inviting visitors to ogle them, rapidly decreasing 'the gap between art and business'.[6]

This coincided with the invention of modern advertising. The language used to sell fashionable goods became more about 'seduction and showmanship' than value and need. 'The image of the product was paramount as it was closely tied with the status of ownership,' writes English. 'This form of conspicuous consumption, once restricted to the upper classes, now enticed middle class individuals.'

Woodhead notes that by the mid-nineteenth century the public was poised and ready to shop. The newly affluent boasted vast houses waiting to be filled, and the ladies of these were keen to dress up 'in as much as forty yards of fabric ... at least three if not four petticoats, in layers varying from flannel through muslin to white, starched cotton. Add to this a lace fichu, bead-trimmed cape, fur or embroidered muff, hat, gloves, parasol, stockings, button boots and recticule,'[7] and you're talking big business. A reticule was a dainty drawstring bag, often made of mesh. So now you know.

Women's dress became less fussy in the following decades. Department stores faced competition from new chain and speciality stores, as well as discount retailers. The Wall Street Crash of 1929 led to belt tightening all-round. Mr Selfridge hit tough times – he fell in with those terrible gamblers the Dolly sisters. In 1941 he was pushed out of his beloved store. Retired against his will, he lived out his days in a modest rented flat. And by the time Selfridge shuffled off this mortal coil in 1947, people were deserting city centres in favour of the suburbs.

In America in particular, the grand old department stores would have to wait decades for smart society to move back to town. Don't go thinking shopping was dead though – far from it.

According to plan

The new townships with their general stores that fed Marshall Field's riches sprang up along America's railway lines, but it was the highways that fuelled the rise of the mall.

In 1956, President Dwight Eisenhower signed the Federal-Aid Highway Act and began a giant public road-building program, stretching 41,000 miles and crisscrossing the nation to link the states. Eisenhower's aims were military, but the results were social. The highways spurred massive migration out of the cities into the 'burbs.

The prototype for what we now think of as the classic American suburb – pre-planned modern housing estates with all mod cons and uniform lawns to mow – was built in 1947 by the developer Levitt &

Sons. Levittown was designed to house returning war vets and their families in Long Island, New York.

Abraham Levitt and his two sons William and Alfred took inspiration from Henry Ford's car factory assembly lines. They pioneered a step-by-step construction process, with different teams of low-paid workers allocated to different stages of the build, starting with the pouring of a concrete slab in lieu of the fiddly old laying of foundations. The final stage was bolting in the washing machine. By removing skilled craftspeople from the equation, and using pre-cut, easy-to-assemble materials, Levitt & Sons could throw up a house in just one day. It was fabulous pre-fab! Family homes to go.

They designed curved streets, directing noisy traffic around rather than through communities, and wrote detailed rules into buyers' contracts regarding maintenance. They went so far as to ban residents from hanging their washing out so no one had to look at their neighbour's knickers.[8]

The new suburbs were marketed on the new television channels, as oases of clean air, and even cleaner morals, where perfect housewives kissed their perfect husbands off to work each day, then tended to rosy-cheeked children behind white picket fences – mercifully miles away from the vice and grime of the cities.

Britain could keep its 'nation of shopkeepers'; America would become, as Franklin D. Roosevelt had hoped, 'a nation of homeowners', and in doing so would prove Herbert Hoover right: home-ownership in the suburbs would result in 'a more wholesome, healthful and happy atmosphere in which to bring up children'. Or so they thought.

'In this business, a very important point is to figure your costs right down to the bone,' smiles Mr Norman Denny, vice president for materials, in a 1947 commercial for Levitt & Sons developments. He's talking about the wonders of asbestos. To build 'better homes at lower cost' for 'the new scientific age', the voiceover explains, 'the cost of the production of almost everything can be reduced by standard-ising materials and by mass production'.

Such thinking was also applied to consumer goods. The subur-ban housewife had new 'needs', from laundry powder – to feed that thrilling invention: the washing machine – to paint, to keep up the appearances of that pristine picket fence. But where to buy it all? There were no historic high streets in Levittown, no traditional mar-ketplaces or village squares.

Stepford Wives R Us

In *Cheap*, Ellen Ruppel Shell tells the story of Victor Gruen, the Aus-trian aesthete who in the 1950s envisioned a glittering future for middle America based on 'shopping towns', where 'both retail and nonretail functions would coexist symbiotically'.[9]

It was an appealing idea. Gruen envisaged wide-open spaces, tin-kling fountains, covered piazzas to shelter folk from inclement weather – places that would encourage shoppers to linger and socialise like the market squares and fairgrounds of yore. Gruen designed the first suburban malls: the roofless Northland outside Detroit opened in 1954 with its shops facing in, not out – a radical concept at the time. The fully enclosed Southdale, in Minneapolis, opened two years later.

Southdale was air-conditioned. In the region's uncomfortably hot summers and nippy winters, you can imagine the wow factor. Shop-pers came, and stuck around, just as Gruen had hoped they would. Weekend visits had a holiday feel. Who needed the beach? And because these complexes were built in the middle of nowhere, Gruen designed car parks allowing a public, newly enamoured with motor transport, to drive in (pack the kids! show off the wheels!), park, enjoy a day out – and at the end of it all, fill up with carloads of new purchases.

What could mar this consumer Utopia beyond the limitation of human arms? Well, there was only so much you could carry. Happily, Sylvan Goldman, a supermarketeer from Oklahoma City, had introduced the shopping trolley back in 1937. According to Ruppel Shell, Goldman's innovation was initially mocked – men didn't think the trolleys looked very masculine, and women took them as an insult.[10] *Like we're not strong enough to carry a basket? Or we're only good for pushing prams?* Goldman, undeterred, hired gorgeous models to push his trolleys up and down his aisles. The trend soon caught on. I wish Goldman could've seen the Anya Hindmarch and Chanel shows. Perhaps he did, from a front row cloud in the afterlife.

Victor Gruen was a socialist, who truly believed his shopping towns were problem solvers and catalysts for positive social change. His 'rosy optimism gradually soured,' writes Ruppel Shell, 'as he watched his dream towns co-opted into symbols of surburban isolation and commercial manipulation.'[11] Disillusioned, Gruen left America in 1967 – but mall culture stuck around, along with the concept of 'the gruen transfer'. The phrase refers to the zombie-like state of the mall shopper who has forgotten what he came for, wandering confused and disorientated, suggestible and susceptible to cynical marketers.

There is an Australian TV show called *The Gruen Transfer*, which pitches advertising experts against one another. This, they say, is the thinking behind their name: 'Factors such as the lighting, sounds, temperature and the spatial arrangements of stores and displays interact, leading the customer to lose control of their critical decision making processes. Our eyes glaze over, our jaws slacken, we … become impulse buyers. So if you go into a mall to buy a mop and walk out with a toaster, a block of cheese and a badminton set, then the gruen transfer has probably played a role.'

Buy now, pay later

'The '60s was a real turning point,' says Barbara Hulanicki, founder of London fashion game-changer Biba. 'My parents' generation had come through the war and they were still terribly Victorian [in attitude]; the younger generation had to burst out. We started earning money. We went to London and got jobs and had a great time. The pleasure of freedom was incredible. But there was absolutely nothing to buy.'[12]

Hulanicki is sharing her memories of the British fashion scene in the early 1960s before she came along and shook it up, good and proper. Apart from Mary Quant's Bazaar on the King's Road, high street fashion was rubbish. There were no cool chain stores, and although developers would soon give American mall culture a go – Birmingham's Bull Ring opened in 1964, in '65 came London's Elephant and Castle and the Arndale Centres up north – these early opportunities for 'coatless shopping' indoors were uninspiring in the UK. Top-end designer fashion was a yawn – there were no luxury flagships, precious few high-end ateliers or multi-brand boutiques; those that were in business catered to prim and proper ladies. Department store offerings were mostly dowdy. Other than Quant, who'd opened in 1955, the big names in London fashion when Hulanicki was a teen were Norman Hartnell and Hardy Amies – old men who dressed the Queen.

Hulanicki was at art school in Brighton when she won a fashion design competition in the *Evening Standard* – the prize was to have her design made up by Hartnell, of all people. Inspired by Audrey Hepburn in *Sabrina*, she'd dreamed up a striped beach suit with tiny shorts and a shirt collar. Hulanicki wasn't impressed with Hartnell's take on it – he used stuffy silk, rather than the youthful cotton she'd imagined – but visiting his atelier gave her ideas. Two years later, in 1957, she moved to London and found work as a freelance illustrator for *Vogue*, *Tatler* and *Women's Wear Daily* (*WWD*). She was twenty-one.

'I had a fabulous job, going to Paris and so on,' she tells me. 'I was desperate to get clothes but you couldn't just run out and buy something; you had to make it, or order it from a dressmaker. You made do with one precious thing, *if* you managed to get one. It was really very, very stressful.'

In 1963 the recently married Hulanicki and her husband Stephen Fitz-Simon, known always as 'Fitz', started up a mail-order business to market Hulanicki's original designs. Biba's Postal Boutique had some success with a brown maxi dress, less with a child's denim smock. 'We only did one size! Can you imagine?' says Hulanicki. She had no idea how to grade a pattern.

A fashion editor she'd done some illustration work for at the *Daily Mirror* featured Hulanicki in a new talent story, with a model in a pink gingham shift dress and matching headscarf. The caption read, 'It can be yours for 25s including the kerchief' and listed Biba's PO box address.[13] Hulanicki waited in the car while Fitz went to check the mail. 'I'll never forget the sight of him coming round the corner, lugging this great big sack,' she says. Same thing happened the next day, and the next. The gingham dress sold 17,000 units.

The first Biba shop opened on Abingdon Road, Kensington, in 1964, at a time when Carnaby Street was filling up with mod boutiques, and the mini skirt was happening. Hulanicki's customers were mostly young working women just like her. She hired a pattern-maker and took inspiration from the clean-lined modernity of Paris designer André Courrèges (*way* out of the ordinary Brit's price range), Hepburn's gamine chic and the childlike girl-women who lived in her illustrator's brain – but spun the whole thing on the cheap. Biba's mantra was affordable, available, fast. As Hulanicki told her biographer

Martin Pel, Biba fans 'wanted it there and then. They didn't want to wait, as they didn't look to the future in any way'.[14] It was all now, now, NOW – at prices you could afford on a typist's wage.

Schoolgirl Lesley Hornby was an early customer – she would later become the model Twiggy, and a Biba 'face'. The 1973 images that appeared in British *Vogue* of Twiggy lounging in gold palazzo pants and matching turban amidst the leopard print excess of the store's final incarnation have become icons of the era.

Biba soon outgrew Abingdon Road and took over roomier premises on Kensington Church Street and, in 1969, even bigger ones in a former carpet showroom on Kensington High Street (today it's a Zara Home).

The latter ran to 800 square metres, and allowed for expansion into branded cosmetics, homewares and menswear. You could buy the whole Biba look there, from separate departments: Biba gowns, boots, jewellery, lipstick, even cushions and paint, and all of it affordable. Hulanicki and Fitz sold a majority share of Biba to the Dorothy Perkins fashion group and started selling Biba merch in thirty countries, including the US.[15] In 1970, they opened a Biba concession inside Bergdorf Goodman.

It was around that time that Hulanicki began to think about the ailing Derry & Toms department on Kensington High Street. Joseph Toms and his brother-in-law Charles Derry had established their drapery business there in the 1860s. In the 1930s, new owners (and former local rivals) John Barker & Co. built a seven-storey Art Deco flagship on the site, complete with 1.5 acres of whimsical gardens on the roof. For a while they were home to a flamboyance of flamingos and the London smart set, who came to sip tea and cocktails. But then the war came. The gardens survived but were forgotten and the flamingos were moved on. In the chastened '40s and '50s, the era of the ration book, the Art Deco splendour faded. When Hulanicki got to know Derry & Toms, she says, it was still in business – just; the average age of the customer was 'about a hundred!'

'The whole street was absolutely decaying. It was grey; nobody went there. It was just [old] people shuffling around.' In 1971 the building went up for sale. Hulanicki believes it was in danger of being destroyed. She was smitten, although how she thought she'd tackle seven storeys and keep Biba the way she liked it is a mystery. (Delegation was not Hulanicki's forte; she insisted on approving every item of stock, down to the last fuchsia pink plastic mop bucket, and personally designing every dress.) All she can say is, 'it was very rare to see Art Deco in London, and then there was the tree.'

Derry & Toms was on her route to work. One day, she was with her young son when he looked up and noticed a tree. Could it really be there, growing up the in the sky like that? Spying the green branches, tantalising and very clearly alive, on the roof up above, became something mother and son looked forward to. Already under the building's spell, Hulanicki had begun to seriously think about trying to buy it. When she finally saw the gardens up close, she was a goner.

With help from the Dorothy Perkins people, they secured the lease, and 1973, Hulanicki, Fitz and planet Biba moved in. They built a cosmetics hall that stocked only Biba; a food hall that sold Biba champagne; and a 'couture department' like a 1930s Hollywood boudoir with white carpet. They renovated the old beauty parlour and created a childrenswear department with mini-me versions of Biba's signature skinny-sleeved purple smock dresses and metallic trouser suits. On the fifth floor, they restored the old Rainbow Room restaurant, and served 1200 lunches a day before turning it over to the party crowd in the evenings. The New York Dolls played opening night. Zandra Rhodes remembers sneaking in without a ticket to see Liberace perform, and haranguing him to autograph a bread roll.[16]

But the dream was short-lived. That same year Dorothy Perkins, hitherto a family business, was acquired by property developers British Land. They didn't favour Hulanicki's creative business strategies (or understand her feather boas). By 1975, Big Biba was shuttered, and Hulanicki lost the rights to the Biba name. 'The suits had won,' she says.

Today the building is home to a big M&S. Dorothy Perkins was on-sold to the Burton Group, which now goes by the name Arcadia. Remember them? We're back with Sir Philip Green again, the grand old duke of Topshop.

Twiggy was right when she said that Biba totally 'transformed the way the ordinary girl in the street dressed ... Not only did the clothes look amazing, you could afford to buy something new every week.'[17] Without Biba, would there be Topshop (for which Hulanicki has since designed capsule collections)? I reckon not.

In Britain, Biba started high street fashion as we know it – but it failed to kill DIY. There was a resilient strain: people still made what they couldn't afford to buy.

In the late '70s, DIY morphed into punk. You wanted a dress? You tore a hole in a plastic bin liner and shoved your head through it. Trousers falling apart? You held them together with safety pins like Sid Vicious did. Punk was anti-shopping, because it was anti-everything – until the world went truly mad, and then you could buy designer punk at the mall.

They're selling hippie wigs in Woolworths, man

'By its very definition, fashion is change. Clothes become looser or tighter, skirts get longer or shorter, bosoms flatten or protrude, orange is in, purple is out. It is all very simple, quite predictably cyclical, and as each new fashion comes in, women renew their wardrobes, buy clothes, alter or throw out the old, and the fashion industry prospers.'[18] These are the words of James Brady, *WWD*'s man in Paris in the '70s, a gent who was sure that 'fashion changes because, in general, women like change. They like to see themselves differently every season.'[19] But when he wrote these things, in his 1974 memoir *Superchic*, the pace of change was at least manageable.

Brady describes the fuss made in America in January 1970 after the Paris couturiers (inspired by hippie street culture) had lowered skirt lengths, heralding the death of the beloved '60s mini. *WWD* reported on the trend, and all kinds of folk unexpectedly lost the plot: 7th Avenue manufacturers, retailers who had stockpiled minis, women fearful that their hard-won right to bare legs was being attacked, men angry at being denied an eyeful of thigh. The midi skirt was declared un-American, and Brady, for supporting it, a 'sexist toad'.

Brady's boss John Fairchild made the cover of *Time*, branded a 'fashion dictator'. There were bomb threats at the Fairchild Building in New York. Meanwhile, Brady hit the US talk-show circuit, debating the long and the short of the issue – on one show, the hostess finished the segment by asking Brady if she might borrow his cigarette lighter, then used it to burn a copy of *WWD* on camera.

On it went. Department stores stocking the new longer lengths were boycotted. Glossies cropped fashion shots to edit out controversial hems. Echoing the protests against Dior's New Look, mini-militants (calling themselves GAMS, Girls Against More Skirt, and FADD, Fight Against Dictating Designers) took to the streets with placards reading 'Up your midi' and 'You can take a maxi up but you can't take a mini down'. Turns out 'women in general' didn't like change half so much as Brady thought they did.

In the McFashion era, trend speed has reached a whole new level. With new collections available every few weeks, we have been trained up to see ourselves differently every month, even every day. Rare is the fashion creature with a strong, consistent personal style.

Say you're a Brigitte Bardot type: you suit a cropped black Capri pant and a striped Breton T-shirt, black ballet flats and a red lip. Okay, but you won't get a buzz from buying a striped tee *every* three weeks, will you? So, you ditch Brigitte next time you head to the shops, and embrace your inner Biba bird or beatnik or cowgirl or punk. Don't know your Nietzsche from your nanna? No matter. By the time you've found the book online, let alone read it, punk will be out, hippie back in.

Dressing to respect religious views is about the only thing that keeps our muddled personal style in check today. If you're not into that, there's no longer any expectation that you subscribe to the politics, playlist, friendship circle or worldview of your chosen fashion tribe. We've forgotten how to commit; we are fashion sluts – and the fashion system is our enabler, churning out new trends at speed, and when they run out, mining the old ones, over and over until none of it makes sense.

You could argue that Vivienne Westwood and Malcolm McLaren 'invented' punk fashion in 1974 when they changed the name of their store at 430 King's Road, London, from Too Fast To Live, Too Young To Die to SEX.

TFTLTYTD had sold biker jackets, vintage Levi's and slogan rocker tees. SEX was a totally new proposition, selling rubber bondage gear, aggressively studded jackets, shirts and pants bound by canvas strapping reminiscent of straight jackets for the mad. This time, the T-shirts were much more provocative, printed with naked cowboys or an image of the 'Cambridge Rapist' in the creepy mask he'd supposedly bought from the shop. SEX's customers – and staff – bought into the anarchic ideology behind the look, underpinned by the new attitude in music. As McLaren explained it later, 'the clothes needed the groups'.[20] So he gave them the Sex Pistols. Most of their fans, and the kids who worked in the store, couldn't afford the SEX clothes – so they stole them, and Westwood turned a blind eye.

Forward wind. Nothing on this earth could possibly be less punk than Gwyneth Paltrow posing on the red carpet in a pink silk Valentino gown. Except perhaps Kim Kardashian in floral Givenchy and matching gloves, with a tuxedoed Kanye West on her arm. And yet both these apparitions visited the 2013 Met Gala to celebrate the exhibition *Punk: From Chaos to Couture*. I wasn't there, but I did see the exhibition later on. The show began with an epic floor-to-ceiling projection of '70s concert-goers. The clothes on the mannequins had rather less energy; there was something a bit *Sesame Street* about the spiky neon wigs. Still, it was fun to see some of Westwood's early creations close up, and to marvel that they'd hadn't been stomped on or set fire to back in the day. There was Liz Hurley's Versace safety pin dress, and some beautiful distressed designer imaginings (a hole-ridden Chanel suit!) that might owe an intellectual debt to the punk ethos but were hardly the sort of thing actual punks went in for. And finally: exit through the gift shop. Not a very punk concept, the gift shop, I have to say. Not even when it's selling rolls of duct tape printed with a safety-pin design. It was only $8.95 a roll; I should have bought it to patch my jeans with.

Two years have passed. The Met Store no longer stocks the duct tape, and my jeans are now mere memories of themselves, tattered ribbons that threatened to blow away on a breeze. A proper punk would nick some more stable trousers. But I am not a proper punk. Never was. The last thing I stole was a grape from Coles, and I still feel guilty about that. So I type the word 'punk' into Net-A-Porter instead. Sixty-eight suggestions spring up. They include a pair of

Giuseppe Zanotti leather ankle boots with zips on ($1,360); a white slogan tee by New York denim brand R13 ($288); a gold-plated Saint Laurent cuff ($795); a plaid shirt made of cashmere ($2,770); and a studded Alexander McQueen 'Hobo' bag ($1642). I'm not feeling it. I type in 'hippie' instead. My timing is right on. Spring '15 ready-to-wear is a hippie fest across the board.

I'd attended the shows this season. Witnessed Frida Giannini's last-ever Gucci show in Milan, with its topstitched suede, hippie denim and Bill Gibb-worthy prints. I'd noted the tasselled ponchos at Etro, worthy of a Human Be-In in San Francisco's Golden Gate Park. In London, I'd seen Henry Holland present a flower power collection with a Hendrix soundtrack. Now, the clothes have been delivered and Net-A-Porter is selling Stella McCartney bell-bottoms, Saint Laurent patchwork and fringed suede, and Valentino folk dresses. Matches has dubbed the trend 'Santa Fe Trip' and 'promises beautiful bohemia – think Joan Baez and Joni Mitchell'. Next week Zara will be full of cheesecloth.

Danny the drug dealer in *Withnail and I* pops into my head. 'London is a country coming down off its trip,' he says, passing a joint to Richard E. Grant's failed actor character. 'We are ninety-one days from the end of this decade and there's gonna be a lot of refugees.' It's 1969, the counter culture is crumbling, the future gearing up to be a total commercial sell out. 'They're selling hippie wigs in Woolworths, man,' he says, between tokes. 'The greatest decade in the history of mankind is over.' Don't worry Danny, it'll be back soon. After a fashion.

Everything must go

The writer Lee Siegel was only half joking when he quipped in the *New York Times* that, 'When the founding fathers penned those immortal words, "life, liberty and the pursuit of happiness", they were thinking of Bloomingdale's.'[21]

Siegel's 2012 essay 'The Department Store's Magic, Dispelled by Online Shopping' drips with nostalgia for 'that bygone house of treasures where my friends and I first discovered the alchemy that lay in purchasable things.' He played hide-and-seek in Women's Fashion, pretended to be his father in Furniture. In Electronics, Bedding, Sporting Goods and Toys, 'it was as if you were passing through the seasons and the cycles of life'.

It's unlikely that any kid of Siegel's would feel similarly inspired by what Vittorio Radice (boss of Selfridges in the early 2000s, now CEO at Italy's Rinascente stores) dubs 'monsters, anchoring the city centres'.[22]

The department store is still with us, but it ails. As I write, Myer in Australia has just reported a 23 per cent drop in half-yearly profits. Its CEO of seven years, Bernie Brookes, has moved on and, speaking to shareholders and media, the new guy Richard Umbers admitted that 'cost growth has outpaced sales growth, and profits have declined'. Customers, said Umbers, 'have changed the way they shop and their expectations of retailers have changed significantly'.

As self-styled 'retail prophet' and author of *The Retail Revival*, Doug Stephens tells me, 'The days of stack it high, watch it fly, have gone. It's not an exaggeration to suggest that we may not have the likes of Macy's, Walmart or any of these large retailers in the future, at least not in the form that we know them today.'[23]

In the US, department store sales have declined to around 2.4 per cent of the retail market. Individual departments have been transformed, truncated or closed. Henri Bendel in New York, for example, once a clothing leader, now sells only accessories and beauty products.

Few of us head to a department store to buy furniture, white goods, luggage or toys anymore; such departments limp on, leaving fashion, cosmetics and jazzed-up food halls to carry the whole.

Many of the old regional American names surrendered in the 1990s and 2000s, and either closed or were taken over (mostly by Macy's). The likes of Filene's, Foley's, Wanamaker's, the super-chic Beverley Hills fashion venue I. Magnin and even the mighty Marshall Field's were all folded into Macy's, Inc. and disappeared. J.C. Penny announced thirty-three store closures in 2014. Sears Holdings (which includes Kmart) shut nearly 300 stores between 2010 and 2015.

Contracting markets increase pressure to discount. According to Ruppel Shell, in 1955 only 5.2 per cent of department store goods were sold on sale; by the mid-1990s, only 20 per cent were sold at full price.[24] Half-yearly clearances used to be major events; now 'slow moving' stock hits the bargain bin if it hasn't sold in five or six weeks. Today, store buyers must factor in discount prices to their selections, and shoppers expect deep discounts all year round. And so we buy more, but cheaper. No wonder we value our purchases less.

Mall rats

There are more than 1200 shops in the Dubai Mall, the retail jewel in the United Arab Emirates crown. It's about the size of fifty football pitches, features an ice rink and an aquarium, and in 2014 hosted more tourists than Times Square.

Over in Macau, China, developers KHL Group are behind a US$5 billion mall-cum-hotel complex designed to resemble a mini Paris. Plans include a half-size replica of the Eiffel Tower, and 320,000 square feet of retail space housed along a fake Champs-Élysées and Rue du Faubourg Saint-Honoré.

Not every new mega mall is a success story. There's barely a tenant in the New South China Mall in Dongguan, Guangdong province. Developer Alex Hu Guirong made his millions selling noodles, and his vision for the biggest mall in the world featured seven 'zones' inspired by Paris, Amsterdam, Venice, Rome, Egypt, California and the Caribbean. He built it, but they didn't come. In 2013, six years after it opened, almost all of its 1500 stores remained vacant.

Meanwhile America, where it all began, has downed tools. Between 1950 and 2005, about 1500 malls were built in the US. Since 2006? Not a one. Retail analyst Robert Lewis predicts that by 2024, half America's malls will have closed.[25] So-called 'ghost malls' are popular blog subjects. The boarded-up Canton Centre in Ohio looks like a set from a sci-fi movie, a post-apocalyptic vision with smashed windows, greenery sprouting from the walls. Forty minutes' drive away in Akron, the Rolling Acres Mall has been empty, and open to the elements, since the owners went bankrupt in 2008. Last winter it filled with snow. In Arkansas, Phoenix Village is an abandoned shell. Parkway Centre in Pittsburgh is closed and sealed, but for a while the escalators still worked.

In February 2015, the UK's Local Data Company predicted that 20 per cent of empty shops in Britain 'would never be re-occupied' and suggested they should be demolished or converted into housing.

Doug Stephens calls changing spending patterns since the 1980s 'calamitous' for traditional middle tier retail. 'If you look at the period from, say, 1950 to 1980, most people were shopping in the mid tier, at department stores, for quality clothing – because most people aspired to be middle class,' he explains. 'But post 1980 we've seen a polarisation of wealth: between 1980 and 2005, if you were in the lowest quintile of income earners your income went down substantially. If you were in the highest quintile, your income went up substantially. But if you were in the middle tier, you were no further ahead financially – even though the economy doubled in size. Productivity went up but the wages of the average worker didn't.'

So the poor got poorer and the rich got richer?

'Right. And as a result we've seen a massive bifurcation in the retail market.' These are some of the economic reasons, says Stephens, behind the rise of fast fashion. 'People in the middle and at the bottom wanted what they needed and wanted it cheap; they didn't care so much if it lasted, they cared that it was within their budget.' Meanwhile big spenders are still spending at the top. 'Luxury continues to spin fast and move forward,' he says. 'It's the middle that really suffers.'

We haven't stopped shopping; we're just doing it differently, away from the high street *and* the gruen transfer. According to McKinsey, 'shopping behaviours are changing almost as fast as technology'.

Online's convenience, speed and range are hard to beat. eMarketer figures suggest global online retail sales will eclipse $US3.5 trillion by 2019, with the Asia Pacific market growing by 25 per cent in 2015. Australian growth lags behind that, but the National Australia Bank's Online Retail Sales Index shows we still spent more than $17.6 billion online in 2015, up nearly 6 per cent year on year. Of course that's not all fashion (booze and groceries are popular online purchases, as are appliances and things like music and movies). Shoppers are increasingly researching online before making targeted trips to physical stores to pick up pre-selected products at the cheapest price possible. Or they try on clothes and shoes in traditional stores so they know what size to look for – at a bargain price – online. All of which puts pressure on retailers shouldering the fixed costs of bricks and mortar operations.

We may be looking at a future where all transactions happen online, where malls and stores don't carry stock at all – but act instead as showrooms, selling 'experiences' to generate brand loyalty; Harry Gordon Selfridge's 'show 'em a good time' theory of opening wallets, updated. Some people said internet shopping would never take off. Some people were stupid.

Stand and deliver

Once upon a time, in the mid-'90s, there was a junior fashion editor at *Tatler*. Slight and quietly pretty, Natalie Massenet was eclipsed by her scene-stealing boss, the late Isabella Blow, who wore surrealist hats to the office and smudged her red lipstick on purpose to distract from her crooked teeth.

Today, Massenet is the one doing the eclipsing. She is an MBE, chair of the British Fashion Council and worth a shedload. Widely recognised as a business visionary, her innovation online helped change the way we shop for fashion.

Massenet was born in LA in 1965. Her parents Bob and Barbara Rooney were cosmopolitan types – Bob was a journo who'd worked as a foreign correspondent before moving into PR, and Barb once modelled for Chanel. As a child, Natalie spent time in Europe. After uni she did a bit of modelling herself in Japan. At twenty-seven she landed an LA-based job at *WWD*. A little later she swapped the West Coast for London and *Tatler*'s fashion cupboard.

In 1997 she was partying at Notting Hill Carnival when she met the man who would become her (now ex) husband, the dashing French banker Arnaud Massenet. He helped her raise £810,000[26] to go into the online fashion business with her friend Megan Quinn (fresh from the success of her cleaning business, Partners in Grime). It was not a bad investment.

When Richemont bought the Net-A-Porter Group (now including sale shop the Outnet; men's offering Mr Porter came later) in 2010, it was valued at £350 million. In 2015 there were rumours of a merge with Amazon, but that March a deal was struck with Italian fashion etailer Yoox: the new Yoox Net-A-Porter Group was worth an estimated €1.3 billion. Massenet, who stayed on as executive chair until September 2015, had this to say: 'Today we open the doors to the world's biggest luxury fashion store. It is a store that never closes, a store without geographical borders ... the best way to predict the future of fashion is to create it.'[27]

Massenet fell down the virtual rabbit hole in 1998. She'd left *Tatler* to go freelance, but was still assisting Blow, and one day Blow asked her to research Arts & Crafts porcelain for a shoot concept. 'From the moment I logged on and found out about fashion [online], I got sucked in,' Massenet explained to the *Los Angeles Times*.[28] Thinking about Amazon.com, she realised there was no high-fashion equivalent, nothing to give women who loved fashion the flexibility and accessibility offered by the hugely successful online bookseller. So Massenet tried (and failed) to persuade a friend who imported pashminas to sell on the internet. Okay, she decided: aim higher. She had contacts. What if she could persuade the likes of Anya Hindmarch and Jimmy Choo's Tamara Mellon to supply her with stock? What if she set up a sort of Amazon for luxury fashion?

Quinn, who left Net-A-Porter four years in and is a regular on the speaker circuit, often notes how the duo's backgrounds, not just good timing, made success possible. Both Massenet and Quinn were consumers – they had an innate understanding of their customers because *they were them.*

Quinn recalls meetings with moneymen who said things like, 'What sort of person buys a £400 handbag?' while the two women tried to keep straight faces. But also, 'We had been creating vehicles for women, for years, to shop.'[29] She's referring to her own career history in advertising and custom publishing and Massenet's experience as a fashion editor.

As Quinn has said, 'We knew who [our customers] were: they were cash rich and time poor.' The Net-A-Porter idea – simple, clever – was to take away the physical barriers to fashion shopping, just like Amazon was doing with books. 'No matter where you were, your office, your bed, an airport, a coffee shop, you'd be able to click on this editorial piece and buy the item.' Also, and this is key, 'No matter who you were, how much you spent ... we would treat you the same.'

Selling luxury fashion is about selling dreams, harnessing the power of glamour, of chic, of image – and making the customer believe that in buying whatever it is (the skirt, the necklace, the £400 handbag) they are also buying into those things. Net-A-Porter's founders knew the secret to making their customers happy – and making sure they returned – lay in replicating the flagship store experience. It was no use crumpling an expensive dress into a postal satchel. A classy delivery service and impressive packaging was called for. Quinn admits they spent absurd amounts on sturdy black gift-boxes, clouds of tissue and Petersham ribbons, but she says it was justified: they had to equal 'the handsome doormen at Gucci, the champagne in the Prada changing rooms'. Their solution played on the cliché of the five-star hotel bellhop, with his teetering pile of boxed purchases. That's what you would think of when your Net-A-Porter parcel arrived in rural Somerset or the South Australian bush – Quinn and Massenet were banking on it.

In the early days they worked out of a Chelsea flat, using a bedroom as a stock room and stacking those precious boxes up in the bathtub.[30] Net-A-Porter is now famed for its spectacular offices but it was, to quote Quinn again, 'an enormous struggle' to convince brands their idea would work. 'The internet was associated, back in 2000, with discounting and the high street rather than high end. They [the luxury brands] had spent fortunes on building their brands and their [flagship] stores and they wanted to protect them.'

They ploughed on, explaining that their focus was on designers and celebrating the heritage and stories behind the brands. Eventually some took a punt, attracted by Net-A-Porter's editorial interface and its founders' fashion nous.

Massenet and Quinn saw change coming. It was not just technology, sales channels and customer expectation that were shape-shifting, but the fashion system itself. As early as 2008, Massenet was pointing out that: 'The fashion cycle is outdated ... In the last five years, the consumer is more educated than ever. She gets to see the runway shows at the same time as the buyers and the editors, yet we are still treating her as if she hasn't seen them ... making her wait six months to buy it in the stores. We're telling her it's all about pointy-toed shoes next season, when what's in the stores now is round-toed shoes. You can't tell the customer that it's about two different things. She'll skip the round toe and go straight to the pointy toe, because that's what's coming next.'[31]

Way faster, much bigger, and in a state of constant flux – this is the story of fashion today. I interviewed Dana Thomas in 2015, eight years after her book about the business of fashion, *Deluxe*, came out. She was promoting her new one, about McQueen and Galliano, and we talked about the crazy pace and size of the industry today. 'Louis Vuitton had two stores in 1977,' she told me, 'now they have hundreds. When Galliano left Dior he was overseeing thirty-two collections a year ... In *Deluxe* I was writing about companies that had grown from small family businesses into these big multi-national companies; now they are billion dollar companies.'[32]

You don't grow like that by being shy. Luxury houses are increasing their standalone presence online – and most ship internationally. They run their own Facebook, Instagram and Snapchat accounts, and encourage their brand ambassadors to share the love on social media. Only a handful of cooler-than-thou names such as Céline resist selling clothing online – Céline's creative director Phoebe Philo once told UK *Vogue* she thinks 'the chicest thing is when you don't exist on Google'. But for how long? When not selling online is essentially not selling.

Yoox execs can only dream of the days of scant competition. Matches Fashion started in the '80s as husband and wife team Tom and Ruth Chapman's friendly local Wimbledon boutique. In 2015, when the pair stepped down as joint CEOs, online sales accounted for 85 per cent of the company's £130 million annual revenue. (About thirty mill of that is down to me, I reckon.)

The previous year Neiman Marcus was sufficiently impressed by the Munich-based MyTheresa, and its estimated US$130 million a year revenue, to buy it – the site now ships to more than 120 countries. Stylebop is also based in Munich, claims three-million-plus users and grew 40–50 per cent annually in the ten years from 2004.

In the US, Shopbop is a slightly more accessibly priced offering based out of Wisconsin that sells contemporary lines and designer denim labels. It's been owned by Amazon since 2006.

The other big one now is Farfetch, founded by London-based Portuguese tech guy José Neves in 2008 as an aggregated online marketplace – a digital interface between the global shopper and some of the world's best small boutiques that lacked their own ecommerce platforms. Farfetch is starting to buy its own stores – in 2015 it acquired Joan Burstein's iconic Browns. But who owns Farfetch? Condé Nast has been an investor since 2013. 'What's happened is that print and retailing were completely different experiences for the reader and the consumers,' said Jonathan Newhouse, chairman and chief executive of Condé Nast International when the deal was announced. We are now in a 'new reality'.[33]

Around the same time as the Yoox–Net-A-Porter news broke, Farfetch was valued at US$1 billion. Oh, and Condé Nast is turning Style.com into an ecommerce platform. In Australia, *marie claire* was the first glossy masthead to introduce ecommerce with StyledBy *marie claire* (full disclosure – I work there).

'Media used to be about driving people into stores,' Doug Stephens tells me. 'You'd place ads in newspapers and magazines, or on radio and TV, with the express intention of getting people to go to your distribution hubs: physical stores. Today media *is becoming the store*. Pretty much every form of media now has the potential to become a direct portal to purchase,' he says. 'It begs the question: what is the purpose of a physical store today?'

Stephens has a few ideas. For starters, he agrees with Robert Lewis that America is 'over-stored', by perhaps as much as half. The future, says Stephens, belongs to two kinds of retailers. The first: big retailers that sell the product they manufacture, companies like Nike, Lululemon and Burberry. The second: what Stephens calls 'experiential merchants', which will sell a variety of products within a category, *indirectly*, by creating such a powerful in-store experience that brands pay those retailers just to represent their products *whether or not* customers walk out the door with said product all tied up in fancy ribbons.

'Let's imagine you're a merchant,' says Stephens.

Okay, let's. Bags I be Arthur Lasenby Liberty.

'You sell a particular fashion brand,' says Stephens. 'The ask on the part of the brand is that you buy stock in quantity, warehouse it, ship it to your various stores, price it, and put it on your shelves. You train your sales assistants on this merchandise, and you sell it, at least you try to – you take some of it back in the form of returns, mark some of it down. Meanwhile, and this is happening on an increasing basis, your suppliers are selling direct to the consumer. Does that sound like a good business plan to you?'

Well, when you put like that ...

'For the retailer it's almost insane to keep doing this,' says Stephens, who believes the 'entire economic model of revenue and profitability for retailers and the suppliers they do business with is collapsing under its own weight.' Soon, he says, it will simply cease to function.

He predicts 'great retailers are going to emerge with a different model'. One possibility is that stores will start acting as agents for brands in return for a fixed fee. 'They will say, "Okay, so I will carry your product and represent it better than anyone else in the market place can, and whether you sell direct to the customer, or I do, or a competitor does, I don't really care, because you are going to pay me the same amount every year anyway." In order for that to work, the retailer is going to have to be responsible for measuring customer experience' – not, he concedes, 'something that happens today in a real way'.

Stephens thinks those old flagships are going to have to get with the modern program; they're going to have to forget about selling a certain number of units from the shop floor; forget measuring productivity by comparing those sales, by square foot, to the sales from last quarter, or last year; and unlearn everything about retail they *think they know*. 'Stores are going to have to move into the business of selling experiences first.' It's no use being just 'a box filled with other boxes'.

But where does sustainability fit into all this? Stephens says it must join the queue along with all the other factors that may, or may not, influence the shopper considering what to buy. In Stephens' view, it's not the big retailers or brands that hold the power. It's us.

CHAPTER 10

Seventh Heaven?

Streets style

In his book *Outliers: The Story of Success*, Malcolm Gladwell argues that arriving in New York City 'in the 1890s with a background in dressmaking or sewing or *schwittwaren handlung* [piece goods] was a stroke of extraordinary good fortune'. Gladwell likens it to 'showing up in Silicon Valley in 1986 with ten thousand hours of computer programming already under your belt'.[1] The timing was key: Singer sewing machines were being mass-produced, and Americans were ready to move away from home-sewn clothes.

While most of America's Irish and Italian immigrants were unskilled farm workers, Jewish immigrants from Eastern Europe in the nineteenth and early twentieth centuries tended to have backgrounds in making and selling stuff. Many had run small businesses in their old countries. They'd been shopkeepers, watchmakers, jewellery makers. 'Overwhelmingly, though,' writes Gladwell, 'their experience lay in the clothing trade'. They had the ambition to make a success of their new life, and the skills to make that happen; so they hustled, they scraped pennies together to buy materials; they sewed garments and sold them on the streets. They roped in family members to help sew at home, and soon some of them were able to formally become employers, and to rent workrooms.

Gladwell recounts the story of a Polish immigrant, Louis Borgenicht, who had been a draper's salesclerk before leaving Europe in 1889. Borgenicht had experience with handling both cloth and cash, he had the gift of the gab, and when he met his wife, a dressmaker, they'd opened their own small store, so he also had experience as an entrepreneur.

After a few false starts in Manhattan, the Borgenichts began making simple children's aprons, which Louis sold door to door. He talked a wholesaler into supplying him with fabric so that he didn't have to pay retail. With reduced costs and increased energy, Borgenicht worked his butt off and his business grew. He knocked on doors, and made sales to shops, so now *he* was the wholesaler. He expanded his product range and opened his own factory making children's clothes. One of his clients was Bloomingdales.

Writes Gladwell of Borgenicht's early years, 'When Borgenicht came home at night to his children, he may have been tired and poor and overwhelmed, but he was alive. He was his own boss. He was responsible for his own decisions and direction. His work was complex: it engaged his mind and his imagination. And in his work, there was a relationship between effort and reward.'[2] Gladwell believes this adds up to meaningful work, and compares it to the considerably less rosy lot of the unskilled immigrant Mexican worker who crossed the border into the US in the 1920s, and 'simply exchanged the life of a feudal peasant in Mexico for the life of a feudal peasant in California'.

Meaningful work is work that engages the mind and the imagination (even while it's hard – no one is saying those early garment workers had it easy). Work that allows for the possibility of advancement, for, as Gladwell writes, 'autonomy, complexity and a connection between effort and reward' – this is the labour that leads to success.

The children of people like the Borgenichts grew up to be New York's next generation of doctors and lawyers and the garment industry's future movers and shakers.

Ralph Lifschitz was born in 1939 in the Bronx. His father Frank, a first-generation immigrant from Belarus, was an artistic soul who dreamed of painting pictures but, with a young family to support, painted houses instead. As a kid Ralph shared a bedroom with his brothers, played basketball at weekends and attended Yeshiva like the good Jewish boy he was, but there was something unusual about him, at least unusual for the Bronx: he was fascinated by establishment American style.

He started calling himself Ralph Lauren (it was no fun being called Lifschitz in school, he said, since 'it has the word "shit" in it!'). To go with his new name, he created a new persona, dressing in button-down shirts and preppy sweaters. He stood out. While the other style-minded kids were buying rebel denim and classic '50s biker jackets, Ralph Lauren was dressing up like a wannabe WASP. When he couldn't afford the clothes he liked, he designed his own shirts and tweed Bermuda shorts. The next step, for an ambitious, well-brought up kid like Lauren, was to sell those clothes.

But Frank Lifschitz was keen for his son to get a proper job, so Lauren did time on the Brooks Brothers counter, then working as a New York salesman for a Boston-based neckwear company. He was twenty-six years old when he designed and sold his first range of men's ties. They were classy, cut wide in the European-style, and before too long, Neiman Marcus and Louis Borgenicht's old faithful Bloomingdales had placed orders.

Lauren opened his first Ralph Lauren store in 1971. His hit product, the thing that kept the customers coming, wasn't the ties though, it was the American dream: aspiration.

Oprah Winfrey once asked Lauren about his signature 'Polo' shirt,[3] so-called after the three-button, collared T-shirt worn by professional polo players on the field. 'I'd deliver my ties to stores wearing a bomber jacket and jeans,' recalled Lauren. 'One by one, the ties started selling and people started talking about them. That's when I began making other products. My symbol was always a polo player because I liked sports, and polo has a stylishness to it.'

'But you never played polo,' said Winfrey.

'No,' said Lauren, 'but I sort of wished I had. My clothes are all about a mood and style I like – such as tweed jackets. It's all about creating a dream I'd want for myself.'

'Ralph Lauren sells much more than fashion: He sells the life you'd like to lead,' is how Winfrey summed it up.

Me and my Calvin's

There must have been something in the water in the Bronx. Ralph Lauren and Calvin Klein weren't best buddies in the 1950s – Klein was three years younger – but they saw each other around the traps. They lived close by, they were both the sons of Jewish immigrants, both driven to succeed. Later they would be rivals.

Klein's father Leo had arrived in the US from Hungary at the age of five. He ran a grocery store in Harlem, worked long hours and often came home late – Klein probably got his work ethic from him. But it's his grandmother Molly whom Klein credits with his early interest in fashion. She was a seamstress and, as a boy, he used to hang around her alterations shop. Klein's mum encouraged him; she was clothesy too. The family must have been proud when Klein, having taught himself to sketch and sew, was accepted into the prestigious Fashion Institute of Technology in Manhattan. He graduated in 1963.

Course completed, the young Klein – wiry, handsome, charismatic – took a series of entry-level 7th Avenue jobs, sketching ideas and cutting samples for some of the hundreds of clothing manufacturers that operated in the area.

Problem was Klein was newly married with a baby on the way (Marci Klein was born in 1967), and he didn't appear to be getting anywhere fast. So when his childhood friend Barry Schwartz, another Jewish grocer's son, invited him to go halves in the supermarket business he was taking over from *his* father, Klein very nearly agreed. It was a close call, but fashion won out.

Instead of groceries, Klein persuaded Schwartz to invest $10,000 in a 'cloak and suit firm'.[4] They called it Calvin Klein Ltd. Tailoring was their focus, and it was a narrow one at first (the jeans, fragrances, undies and licensing deals would come later). Klein himself put in $2000, which he'd saved up from his 7th Avenue earnings. It was 1968 and it was all happening.

According to fashion industry folklore, fate smiled on their venture when Donald O'Brien, a manager from the Bonwit Teller department store, visited their building, stepped out of the lift on the wrong floor and stumbled across a rack of Klein's samples. O'Brien liked what he saw – 'Tomorrow you will have been discovered,'[5] he said – and arranged a meeting with the store's president, Mildred Custin. Klein, so the story goes, rolled that rack uptown himself; he must have been nervous. Custin was a tiny, silver-haired woman with a childlike soft voice,[6] but she had she a fierce rep – if she rated you, you made it; if she dismissed you, you may as well go wait tables. It was worth whatever sweating Klein did to get his clothes-on-wheels to 5th Avenue that day.

He left Custin's office with a $50,000 order.

Within five years, Calvin Klein had won his first of three COTY American Fashion Critics' Awards – the judges praised his 'classic' but 'nonconformist' vision. Reportedly, the company's wholesale volume tipped US $1 million a year in the early '70s. By 1981, it was said that Klein was personally worth $8.5 million.

Brooke Shields helped him earn a chunk of it. It was 1980 when the fifteen-year-old actress starred in the famous Calvin Klein Jeans TV commercial. Shields was hot property. Her castaway movie *Blue Lagoon* had come out that July, and Klein, hiring big gun Richard Avedon to shoot the commercial, must have suspected he had a hit on his hands – but no one could have predicted just how big it would be. On the 19th of November 1980, the CBS network banned the ad for being too sexy and provocative. The image of Shields purring, 'Do you want to know what comes between me and my Calvins? Nothing,' is still talked about. It sure shifted a lot of denim.

Of course Klein and Schwartz didn't sew those jeans themselves; the days of all hands on deck, of both their mums helping out by stitching-in labels, were long gone. Those jeans were made *and sold*, under licence, by a third party, name of Puritan Fashion Corp. It was Puritan that paid for the Brooke Shields billboard in Times Square. According to *Vanity Fair*, at one point Puritan was dispatching 500,000 pairs of Calvin Klein jeans a week. They cost $19.75 to make, and sold for $40. Even after paying royalties of $1 per pair, nothing got in the way of Puritan and their Calvins profits in the early '80s jeans boom. By 1983, they were selling 'about $500 million worth of jeans a year'.[7]

Established in the early 1900s by yet another Russian immigrant, Arthur Rosen, by the middle of last century Puritan was employing hundreds of busy hands: cutting, making and sewing clothes in New

York City. In 1977 when the Calvin Klein deal was signed, Arthur's son Carl Rosen was chairman. He'd already tried to persuade Pierre Cardin to work with Puritan on a jeans collection. Carl Rosen just knew that jeans were going to be the next big thing. He was a man of vision, tapped in to where the market was headed. It was men like Rosen who kept the wheels of the garment industry turning, and they needed to keep men like David Dubinsky, long-time president of the International Ladies' Garment Workers' Union (ILGWU), on side in order to do it.

The stakes were high. American fashion was at the start of a new phase, one that would soon be measured in billions rather than millions of dollars, driven as much by licences for branded lifestyle goods as designs for clothes.

It's a wrap

Meanwhile, two female designers were doing their bit to shake things up in the Garment District. Diane von Furstenberg, whose mother was a Belgian Holocaust survivor, arrived in New York from Europe in the early '70s with riveting cheekbones, an Austro-German prince for a husband and an inspired idea for a fashion business. She opened her 7th Avenue showroom in 1972 and filled it with the printed silk jersey frocks she'd had made in Italy. Those V-necked dresses wrapped around the bust like ballet cardigans, and featured crossover skirts, with a simple belt that tied at the waist holding the whole thing together. Von Furstenberg thought they were flattering and easy to wear – and American women agreed. By 1976 she'd sold five million of them and made the cover of *Newsweek*, as 'the most marketable female in fashion since Coco Chanel'. The canny Carl Rosen signed a licensing deal with von Furstenberg too.

Small wonder Donna Karan wanted a piece of the action. She had been working on 7th Avenue since 1974 (for Anne Klein, no relation to Calvin). Donna was born Donna Ivy Faske in Queens in 1948, and later lived in the affluent Jewish neighbourhood of Five Towns, Long Island, but her parents nicknamed her 'the 7th Avenue baby' because she grew up on the job; her father was a tailor, her mother a fit model.

As a child Karan was always drawing, and at fourteen she begged to be allowed to work in a dress shop; by eighteen she'd enrolled at Parsons. She set up her namesake label in 1985, and her stretchy black clothes helped define the era. Her first collection launched what she called her Seven Easy Pieces, designed to liberate women from the '80s power suit. Karan wore them herself: draped black minis, loose jackets and the ubiquitous black 'body' leotard, with its quick release crotch poppers underneath. Karan had energy and chic, and said things like 'I believe in comfort' and 'everything comes out of what works for me' – she was fabulous.

According to fashion-editor-turned-retailer Josh Patner, who worked for Karan in the '80s, 'she would breeze into her showroom in the 550 building at 4 p.m., and greet the staff with "Good morning, how's life in the big city?" and then work until 1 a.m. on the collection, often fitting and draping looks on herself'.[8]

John McDonnell, a photographer for the *Washington Post*, recalled how it was in the '70s and '80s documenting Karan's collections, as well as those by Lauren, Klein and Perry Ellis: 'Covering all of the shows meant running all over the Garment District to cram into small designer showrooms to see one show, and then rush off to the next and the next, all day long.'[9] McDonnell occasionally snapped the starrier show attendees – Bianca Jagger and Andy Warhol were regulars – but he was really there to shoot the clothes. It was all about the clothes.

The wider world was falling in love with American sportswear, and 7th Avenue was where it lived. The scene was buzzy, it was cool, and – looking back on it now – it is tempting to feel nostalgic for its simplicity. Fashion was still a local industry. Most collections were manufactured around the corner from where they were designed. Union boss David Dubinsky's daughter Jean Appleton remembered 'pushing [her] way through the hundreds of master cutters and pattern-makers who crowded the sidewalk along 38th Street at lunchtime, dodging the hand trucks carrying stylish garments that later appeared on the backs of women from east coast to west.'[10] Little had changed since the '50s when more than a third of all the clothing worn in the US was made there.'

Now just 3 per cent of the clothing worn in America is made in *America*, never mind in Manhattan. The remaining 97 per cent – including the vast majority of so-called American sportswear – is manufactured overseas.

In 1994, the ILGWU merged with the Amalgamated Clothing Textile and Workers Union, and was renamed UNITE. Today it also reps the hospitality industry.

When Carl Rosen died in 1983, his son Andrew, just twenty-six at the time, was running Puritan. Sale of the company to Calvin Klein was completed by 1984, and Andrew Rosen stayed on for a few more years, then disappeared from view. In 1997, he was back with the contemporary brand Theory, which he co-founded with Elie Tahari. Since then he has invested in, and mentored, the indie labels Rag & Bone and Alice + Olivia. In 2011, Andrew Rosen was part of a group that invested in homegrown luxury brand Proenza Schouler.

Andrew Rosen's passion is 'Made in America'. In 2012, he said, 30 per cent of Theory garments, and 65 per cent of Rag & Bone's were made in NYC.[11] In 2013, Rosen launched the Fashion Manufacturing Initiative with the Council of Fashion Designers of America and the New York City Economic Development Corporation. Some are saying fashion can breathe life into 7th Avenue yet.

Mob rule

It wasn't Rosen or Dubinsky or Klein or Lauren who was named the Garment District's 'Man of the Year' for 1981. No. Feted that year at a fashion industry dinner at the Plaza was a *mafioso* from New York's most powerful crime family. Thomas 'Tommy' Gambino is the son of notorious protection racketeer and 'Boss of Bosses' Carlo Gambino, one of the inspirations for *The Godfather*.

The small-time street gangs of the 1920s had paved the way for New York's answer to the Cosa Nostra. Prohibition offered plenty of opportunities for organised crime, but when it ended, in 1933, the gangs were forced to pursue alternative avenues for revenue-raising. The unions provided an obvious one – there was a market for thugs to 'persuade' workers not to break strikes. On the other side, some manufacturers were keen to 'talk' workers back into the factories, if you know what I mean.

In 1988, ex-mobster turned FBI informant Vincent Cafaro told a senate enquiry that the 'real power' of the mafia lay with union control, and that 'some of the most important industries in New York City' – including the waterfront, shipping and construction industries, and the garment centre – 'were all subject to mob influence and control'.

Until 1993, when he was finally convicted of racketeering, Tommy (with his brother Joe) ran the Consolidated Carriers Corporation trucking company. It had a 'virtual monopoly on garment deliveries throughout the city,' so whenever patterns, fabric, cutwork or finished garments had to be moved – which was all the time – the Gambinos' boys did the driving.

According to Ralph Blumenthal in the *New York Times*,[12] 'virtually every sewing shop [in Manhattan] was allocated, or "married", to one of several large truckers linked to a cartel dominated by the Gambino family or their rivals, the Luccheses. The truckers sold or traded shops among themselves, with no say on the part of the often-reluctant brides. If a manufacturer wanted to move goods in his own trucks or hire a "gypsy", or independent hauler, he had to pay his regular trucker anyway.'

As Blumenthal puts it: 'The cartel's dominance was so entrenched that violence was all but unnecessary. A glance, a whispered name – "Gambino" – and would-be renegades tended to fall quickly into line.'

A former production manager for a small designer brand in Manhattan testified at the trial. 'If you want trucks, you just have to play their game,' he said. 'And you can't do anything about it.'

Looked at one garment at a time, the mob tax was trifling – 'perhaps only 40 cents' a piece – but it all added up. Thomas Gambino was said to be personally worth $75 million by 1992. Between 1986 and '89, the family trucking businesses grossed nearly $50 million shuttling garments back and forth across the city.[13]

The police went to extreme lengths to catch Gambino – and this is where the story starts to sound more like 21 Jump Street than real life – coughing up $10,000 to buy a small garment business and packing it with undercover cops. They must have been convincing performers, because their cover wasn't blown as they blatantly side-stepped Consolidated Carriers and hired independent drivers to deliver their 'garments' – I'm not sure if these were real garments or real deliveries or where they were sent, but the ruse worked. Consolidated sent their heavies to protest – too much. It was a sting!

Gambino got out of jail in 2000, aged seventy-one, and retired to Florida. The Garment District no longer suffers from a mob-run trucking monopoly – but then again there aren't enough clothes made there to justify one. The garment industry Man of the Year Award is no more. The CFDA Fashion Awards do a rather better job of recognising excellence in the field – Andrew Rosen scooped one in 2012.

Cheap and nasty

Between 1828 and 1858, New York's clothing industry grew faster than any other in the city. By 1910, it employed around 46 per cent of NYC's industrial labour force, many of them unregulated 'homeworkers', who made garments where they slept and ate in tenement dwellings downtown.

In 1911, the New York State Factory Investigating Committee called for an end to home-work, citing concerns over rat-infestations and the threat of smallpox, which, it turned out, could be carried on garments. Who knew? Fashion wasn't just killing those who made it in fetid conditions, but those who consumed it too – and not just in NYC. Disease spread by clothing was a problem throughout the industrialised world.

In London, back in 1850, the Christian socialist novelist Charles Kingsley (author of *The Water-Babies*) had reported on the phenomenon in his revelationary tract *Cheap Clothes and Nasty*: 'These wretched creatures [garment workers], when they have pawned their own clothes and bedding, will use as substitutes the very garments they are making, So Lord—'s coat has been seen covering a group of children blotched with small pox. The Rev. D— finds himself suddenly unpresentable from a cutaneous disease ... little dreaming that the shivering dirty being who made his coat has been sitting with his arms in the sleeves for warmth while he stitched at the tails. The charming Miss C is swept off by typhus or scarlatina, and her parents talk about "God's heavy judgment and visitation" – had they tracked the girl's new riding habit back to the stifling undrained hovel where it served as a blanket to the fever-stricken slop worker, they would have seen *why* God had visited them, seen that his judgments are true judgments,' he wrote.[14]

Kingsley visited the wretched garrets of London's East End, typically two small rooms in which 'about six men' lived and worked, often with their wives and children, receiving cloth and stitching orders via middlemen.

One such worker described his lot to the writer: 'I was near losing my life there, the foul air of so many people working all day in the place, and sleeping there at night, was quite suffocating. Almost all the men were consumptive, and I myself attended the dispensary for disease of the lungs. The room in which we all slept was not more than six feet square. We were all sick and weak.' They existed, just, on rations of tea and bread doled out by the original horrible bosses.

Cheap Clothes and Nasty details the two types of tailor operating in Victorian England: the traditional sort, who employed skilled men and paid them a reasonable wage, and what Kingsley, appropriating contemporary tailors' slang, calls the 'sweaters', echoing the term so familiar today: sweatshop.

This 'dishonourable trade', writes Kingsley, exploited men 'altogether unanimous in their descriptions of the misery and slavery which they endured'.

Unscrupulous recruiters 'kidnapped' potential workers from the streets: 'Young tailors, fresh from the country, are decoyed by the sweatees' wives into their miserable dens, under extravagant promises of employment, to find themselves deceived, imprisoned, and starved, often unable to make their escape for months perhaps years; and then only fleeing from one dungeon to another as abominable!'

Anyone who knew of the conditions and bought clothes made under them should be ashamed of themselves as 'past contempt', wrote Kingsley.

In 1906, an exhibition sponsored by the *Daily News* was held in London in order 'to acquaint the public with the evils of Sweating'. Inspired by a similar venture in Germany, it filled Queen's Hall in Langham Place (later bombed in the Blitz) with photographs, written statements and forty-five workers demonstrating their trades, in real time. They included the obvious (tailors, makers of shirts, coats, button-holes, lace and women's underclothing) and the now-obscure (umbrella coverers, hook-and-eye carders, bristle pickers, shawl fringers and pompom makers).

Over 30,000 visitors attended, including many of the well-to-do. Checking out the trades was a social scene hit that season. We can only guess how many fashionable ladies read Mary Neal's words in the exhibition 'handbook' and felt pangs of guilt over their frocks and furbelows.

Neal, the daughter of a Birmingham button manufacturer, was a social worker, unionist and suffragette assigned to observe dressmakers for the exhibition. She speculated that the very idea of the expensive, glamorous goods they handled might send them over the edge: 'I think,' she writes, 'that the display and luxury with which young girls just at the age when they love finery and pleasure are brought into contact, is very bad for them. The contrast between their lives of drudgery and the lives of the girls for whom they make pretty frocks, for parties of all sorts, for open-air pleasures and indoor revels, cannot fail to give them false ideas of what real beauty is. And I know that in some of them, often of the finest spirit, it implants a bitterness which no after experience can obliterate.'

Many of the most shabbily treated were women. Also writing in the handbook, Margaret Irwin, another suffragette, notes the plight of those females who sewed women's and children's underclothes, identified as one of the most terribly paid home-work trades. 'The worker's "day" frequently includes several hours after midnight. One woman said she "sat as long as she could go at it." Another frequently did not go to bed until two [a.m.], while she rose again at five. Sometimes she sat up all night. Another said she was "kept sitting every night until she was dizzy and could hardly see." Her average day was from six in the morning until ten at night. Her husband, who was partially invalided, did the housework.'

At risk of sounding like one of Monty Python's Four Yorkshiremen, the female buttonhole makers had it worse. 'The worker is obliged to sit stooping, one knee over the other, so as to have the garment in the best position for rapid working; this posture often causes very serious internal trouble from which the worker has to suffer all her life.' The worker was required to finish her task within an hour of the buttonless coat being delivered, wrestling with its cumbersome heavy wool. And because it was impossible to tell when that might be, she had to make herself available at all times just in case. In busy periods, the worker is 'so driven that she has not a reasonable time to have her meals.'

In quiet times, there was often no work at all.

As well as boosting support for the fledgling women's rights movement, the exhibition spurred the establishment of the National Anti-Sweating League in the UK, inspired by the organisation of the same name in Australia, where the government had already legislated to tackle living wage issues in 1890s. Britain got its first minimum wage bill in 1909 – a watershed moment in the history of labour rights, even though the first law covered only four trades: tailoring, lace-making, paper-box making and chain-making.

The US would have to wait until Roosevelt's New Deal before they got their turn (The Fair Labor Standards Act, 1938), but the Anti-Sweater effect did not go unnoticed in America. The ILGWU was formed in 1900 by seven local unions in New York. One of the things it did in the early days was push for a law against home-working – but it wasn't happy with conditions in the new factories either.

In fact, there were lofty ideas behind the Manhattan loft boom. Light, space, ventilation, a formal separation between home and work – all this added up to better conditions, surely? That was true, as far as it went. But the new buildings brought new dangers, as factory foremen took to following workers around to stop slacking, and locking exits to stop stealing or early leaving.

Doesn't this sound familiar?

The story of the Triangle Shirtwaist Factory disaster, which happened in New York on the 25th March 1911, echoes that of Rana Plaza a century later.

Terrible waist

The shirtwaist was a type of ladies' blouse made popular in Harry Gordon Selfridge's time. Made from cotton or linen, usually cream and trimmed with lace, it was worn with a long skirt, and its simplicity (compared to the fussy, heavy dresses that preceded it) felt like a fashion revolution – freeing up ladies to dash about, perhaps even accessorised by the suffragette's purple sash.

As Lindy Woodhead notes in *Mr Selfridge*, women loved the new blouses, and 'ever-increasing demand put added pressure on production space and staff costs, leading to a marked increase in "sweated labour"'[15] in both the UK and the US.

Skilled tailors and seamstresses, either in independent ateliers or the department stores' on-site workrooms, mostly still made complicated outfits. But shirtwaists, along with that oh-so-badly-paid-for-underwear Margaret Irwin writes of, were run up in their thousands by homeworkers, outworkers (who banded together to rent cramped workrooms) or the new factory workers in their lofts.

In the early 1900s, many of New York's shirtwaists were made in factories like the Triangle, which was run by Max Blanck and Isaac Harris from the Asch Building on the corner of Greene Street and Washington Place.

In 1911, the Triangle employed about 600 people, mostly teenage girls, who were cheap labour. The fact that most, being new immigrants, couldn't speak English and were unlikely to join unions was a bonus. Blanck and Harris had been in trouble with the unions before.

They were dodgy characters. They paid their child workers fifteen dollars a week, to work twelve hours a day, seven days a week. During the ILGWU strike in 1909, they hired thugs to beat the workers up. That winter, Triangle fired 150 union sympathisers.

Blanck and Harris knew all about dangers of factory fires, too. The Triangle had copped it twice, and another of their enterprises, the Diamond Waist Company, had also burnt after hours. Some said the bosses lit the blazes on purpose for the insurance money. All this experience with flames, however, didn't stop them from locking the Triangle's doors from the outside during the working day. It was to prevent theft, they said.

There were four elevators in the Asch Building, but only one was in working order. When fire tore through the eighth and ninth floors, management, based on the floors above, was able to escape via the roof. The young workers were left to queue in single file, along a skinny corridor, to access the elevator. Twelve people could squash inside, and the elevator made four trips before it was too late. Of the two stairwells that led to the street, one ended with a door that opened inwards; the other was bolted. It was a death trap, and 146 people died as a result.

The fire brigade rushed in, but their ladders were too short. Girls began to jump from the windows. Fifty-eight people died hitting the sidewalk. Some of their bodies landed on the hoses before the firemen had chance to use them. The sheer number of corpses overwhelmed the ambulance men, and surrounding merchants helped out with barrows, setting up makeshift morgues in shops.

'This is not the first time girls have been burned alive in the city,' said spirited unionist speaker Rose Schneiderman at a memorial event held in the unlikely environs of the Metropolitan Opera House. (Schneiderman worked in a cap-making factory before she took up politics, but the Met audience was mostly posh lady feminists.) 'Every week I must learn of the untimely death of one of my sister workers. Every year thousands of us are maimed. The life of men and women is so cheap and property is so sacred. There are so many of us for one job it matters little if 146 of us are burned to death.'

Thousands came to gawp at the bodies, many of which were so badly burned they couldn't be identified.

Factory fires are no longer an issue in Manhattan, but they still happen elsewhere. To quote the sociologist Robert Ross, 'It's as if the 1911 conditions had been lifted up by an evil hand and dropped into Bangladesh.'[16]

The race offshore

Although he didn't plan it, Thomas Gambino's exit was well timed. The American apparel manufacturing sector buckled in the late '90s as China began to boom. The same thing happened in Europe and Australia: for big companies the cost reductions of producing offshore were irresistible.

According to Werner International Management Consultants, in 2014, for example, wages in the formal economy for the average US-based textile worker involved in spinning, weaving and dyeing and finishing were US$17.71 per hour. In the UK the dollar equivalent was $24 an hour. In Australia (the second highest-paying country), it climbed to US$38.67. The top slot went to Switzerland, paying more than fifty bucks an hour. But guess how much Mexican workers got? A shade over three dollars. In China, the average textile worker was earning $2.65 per hour – in Bangladesh they got 62 cents. Read that again. *Sixty-two cents.*

Imagine you are a fat cat clothing manufacturer facing pressures from consumers to lower prices, and from shareholders to increase your bottom line – where would you choose to make your clothes? And now ask yourself how much you'd really care about the Bangladesh Fire and Building Safety Accord.

The seeds of a truly globalised market were sown with the invention of the shipping container in 1956. Before that, goods like silk, shipped from distant lands, were seen as exotic luxuries. Moving them around the globe was a logistical headache, time-consuming and costly – which is why my grandparents in the UK were thrilled when they found an orange in their Christmas stockings as kids. The Maharaja of Kapurthala may have ordered Louis Vuitton trunks from Paris to keep his swords and turbans tidy, but ordinary people shopped local – and that included fashion as well as fruit.

It's hard to get excited about shipping containers, but those corrugated storage cubes were change-makers. As their use became standard after the '70s, ships were built with the sole purpose of carrying them. Ports were modified, longshoremen laid off, new trucks built and drivers laid on, new retailers and markets invented – because why not fill the stores with cheap goods from overseas if they could be bought for a song and delivered in a jiffy, with greatly reduced freight and handling costs, and little chance of theft?

Meanwhile, cargo ships got bigger, faster, and more reliable. The next logical step? Entrepreneurs in those once-far-flung countries, where labour is cheap, produce more low-value stuff to supply demand in countries where workers have wages to spare. Shipping containers are the reason we have $2 shops, and there are entire towns in China producing Christmas decorations all year round. So ubiquitous is this tinsel-covered tat nowadays, I too would get excited about an orange in my stocking.

No matter how many shipping containers were at its disposal, for years the fashion industry missed out on the new global market for super-cheap because of a sticky bit of red tape called the Multi Fibre Arrangement.

The MFA was designed to protect domestic markets in Europe and North America, and was introduced in 1974, when the Brits and Americans were freaking out over cheap imports from Hong Kong. What this did was protect local manufacturers by way of a complicated system of import quotas and tariffs. Dismantling it was one of China's conditions for joining the World Trade Organization in 1995. The phase-out of the MFA was complete by 2005; many were surprised it had lasted so long – protectionism is not popular in the modern globalised economy.

Big American apparel companies with no intention of making stuff in expensive local factories had been playing a game of 'chasing the cheapest needle',[17] which meant different parts of the same garment were being made in as many as six different countries to keep costs down.

Killing the quotas meant supply chain simplification – it also meant entire garments would be made in China in increasing numbers, because China, at that time, provided by far the best combination of cheap and abundant labour, sophisticated new factories and government incentives. It was a perfect storm for clunky, pricey, old-style manufacturing.

CHAPTER 11

Grand Social

Unions squared

Rosario Dawson is telling me a story about a birthday present. It's not something you can tie up with ribbons. 'After my grandmother died, I brought my mom to Sierra Leone for her fiftieth. She planned on a week, but she stayed for three months because it was the only thing that helped her get over it; she was inconsolable. My grandmother was a very powerful woman.'[1]

'More powerful than you?' I say, because that's hard to imagine. Dawson, who has a shaved undercut and is wearing a blue scarf of African *bogolan* mudcloth, is a force to be reckoned with. She looks sideways at me, like 'come *on*,' and keeps talking.

'So my mom is in Sierra Leone, and the civil war is over but the aftermath is very palpable, so she is walking in communities, talking to the people she meets, and they are like, "Oh! You lost *your* mother, I am sorry." And they really empathise, and they say, "I lost my dad, my uncle, my cousin, my brother, all my sons." And they say, "We're all brothers and sisters here. We grew up together as orphans in the bush so that's family, and you are welcome, like family too."'

Dawson describes a sign that greets arrivals at Sierra Leone's Lungi International Airport, 'The land of smiles!', and we talk about how plenty of visitors from places like New York, trained to be cynical, must think, 'You have nothing, and you're smiling? Like that's not a tourism sound bite.' Not that tourism is booming in Sierra Leone – Dawson's mother made her trip before the 2014 Ebola outbreak that killed at least 4,000 people in a year and saw lockdowns, quarantines and curfews across the country.

'But you know what?' says Dawson about those smiles. 'It's totally true. You talk to people and they have the most horrific stories, but this indomitable spirit. When you have community, when you care about and support each other, anything is possible.'

Dawson calls herself an 'actrivist', because she is part movie star – she debuted in the cult 1995 film *Kids* – and part activist. She's done thrillers with Bruce Willis and Ryan Reynolds, comedy with Chris Rock and played Channing Tatum's love interest. She sings and dances in *Rent*, and kicks ass in *Sin City* and Quentin Tarantino's *Death Proof*. Occasionally she turns up on a red carpet, but, she says, there has to be a good reason, like supporting her beloved Lower Eastside Girls Club in New York. In her twenties, Dawson refused to dress up for auditions, and drove her agent nuts attending castings in baggy old sweats – she wanted to be chosen for her talent, not her looks. But mostly she wanted to change the world.

In 2004 she co-founded Voto Latino to encourage civic engagement amongst America's Latin population (her own heritage is mixed Puerto Rican, Afro-Cuban, Native Indian and Irish). She's vocal about climate change and injustice in general. She works with V-Day and the One Billion Rising campaign to end violence against women.

It was Eve Ensler, a feminist playwright and friend of Dawson's, who started V-Day. Ensler wrote *The Vagina Monologues* and in 1998, buoyed by its success, she had an idea: what if the profits from ticket sales wherever the play was staged on this particular day went to support victims of sexual violence in local communities? The concept took on a life of its own, with protests, 'teach-ins' and workshops, and has since raised more than $100 million to fund education, safe houses and shelters all over the world.

'But the statistics haven't changed. One in three women will be raped, killed or beaten in their lifetime,' says Dawson. 'Are you okay with that?'

Obviously I'm not. But I am glad that now ethical fashion has Dawson on its side too. People listen to her – in fact, they are listening to us now, leaning in and nodding (and probably going away and thinking, *let's do something about those violence figures*; at least I hope they are).

We are having this conversation in the eighteenth century Palazzo Morando on Milan's Via Sant'Andrea, during fashion week. Last night, Italian *Vogue* held a cocktail party here for Who Is On Next? – their annual celebration of young fashion design talent.

Dawson and her childhood-friend-turned-business-partner Abrima Erwiah made the cut with their startup brand Studio One Eighty Nine. It's a social enterprise, rather than a conventional fashion label, really. They work with organisations like Shine On Sierra Leone and the UN's Ethical Fashion Initiative to make collections in Africa, providing regular work for people who might otherwise have none, and keeping traditional artisanal techniques alive. Erwiah and Dawson design the products alongside the people who craft them.

So far, they've made both men's and women's apparel, and accessories, such as backpacks in West African batik cloth. Their glass bead necklaces were wine bottles in a former life; and their 'Bottletop' bags were made by women in Brazil out of upcycled aluminum ring-pulls. Their Fashion Rising collection features batik cottons hand-painted and sewn in Ghana (where Erwiah is now partly based), *bogolan* from Mali and hand-dyed Somalian indigo cloth. It's early days, and the collection is small. They sell through their own website but don't wholesale yet – which is not to say it won't evolve that way.

One of the things I have come to realise about ethical fashion is that the product needs to speak for itself, without the backstory; that designers have to build consumer desire to sell in sufficient numbers to create change.

Dawson and Erwiah are determined to make that happen. 'Opportunity does an incredible thing,' says Dawson. 'You see the possibility for change. You can get yourself out of places that the statistics say you shouldn't expect to get out of. If I help you and you help me – we can grow.'

Dawson grew up on the Lower East Side. Her mother Isabel Celeste worked at a shelter for battered women and volunteered at Housing Works, helping families and homeless people living with HIV and AIDS. Money was always tight.

'My parents moved into a squat when I was a little girl. At first we didn't have electricity, but they created a home around us,' says Dawson. With their neighbours, they tidied the place up and built a stoop to keep the drug dealers at bay. That's where Dawson was sitting when she was spotted by *Kids* director Larry Clark and writer Harmony Korine.

'New York at that time was about HIV and homeless rights, the crack epidemic, child pregnancy. My mum was a teenager when she got pregnant with me,' says Dawson. 'It was expected that I would do the same – the negative cycles always seemed to be perpetuated, because people couldn't see an alternative.' *Kids* provided one, but if that opportunity hadn't come out of the blue, I'll bet Isabel Celeste would've worked out another.

The fighter instinct is a Dawson family trait. Isabel Celeste's mom was Isabel, a labour rights activist in the 1970s. And Isabel's mom – Dawson's great-grandmother – was Celestina, a seamstress who worked in New York's Garment District, and was a vocal member of the ILGWU.

Dawson was four when Celestina died of cancer, so her physical memory of her is hazy. But the legacy is clear. It was Celestina who sparked the long line of activism that powers the women in Dawson's family. 'Celestina was the person my grandmother fought for. Isabel would go to marches, protests, labour meetings and translate what was said into Spanish so the workers could understand,' says Dawson. 'She would take my mom with her. And my mom did the same thing with me when I was growing up. Mom worked at a women's shelter, she worked with housing, she was involved with one of the first recycling centres in New York. I was raised in activism. That's been always my first experience.'

Erwiah is 'a New Yorker West African by way of Ivory Coast and Ghana' who went to NYU and then studied in Florence. Back in New York, she worked for the Italian brand Bottega Veneta. Her first role was in marketing, not design, but she says being in that luxury environment made her 'think carefully about the meaning of craftsmanship, artisanship and heritage'.[2]

Bottega Veneta (owned by Kering) is one of the most discreet luxury brands. At its helm is German designer Tomas Maier, a man so less-is-more he edited the superfluous 'h' out of his first name. He is ex-Hermès, and once told the *New Yorker*, 'the It Bag is a totally marketed bullshit crap'.[3] Maier sends the same bag designs down the runway season after season.

One of the first things he did when became creative director of Bottega in 2001 was remove the logos from the brand's designs. He also pushed the company to open a leather-making college, Scuola della Pelletteria, to help save traditional craftsmanship in Veneto. Maier's line is, 'Everything we create is intended to last a lifetime ... We don't believe in cutting corners for a quick profit. We want to have the least harmful environmental impact because this is our heritage to protect—both people and place.'[4]

'Tomas taught me to really think about what has to happen to craft something,' says Erwiah. 'It takes a lot of time for someone to learn the skills to make a garment or an accessory on this level, to build the work from scratch, and if we, the consumers, take the time to respect that, the end result has more value.'

Erwiah loved her time at Bottega Veneta, but by 2011 she was ready to move on – she just wasn't sure where. Then Dawson took her travelling, through Kenya and Rwanda to Bukavu in the Democratic Republic of Congo. There, near Lake Kivu, stands a place called the City of Joy. The name comes from what it hopes to achieve, not what brings its citizens to its doors. Ask Eve Ensler about that.

'I have just returned from hell,' is how she described her first visit to Bukavu's Panzi Hosptial, which treats survivors of sexual violence. 'How do I convey these stories of atrocities without your shutting down, quickly turning the page or feeling too disturbed? How do I tell you of girls as young as nine raped by gangs of soldiers, of women whose insides were blown apart by rifle blasts and whose bodies now leak uncontrollable streams of urine and feces?'[5]

With the help of a one-off donation from UNICEF, Ensler hooked V-Day up with the Panzi Foundation to establish the City of Joy. A 'centre for revolutionary change', it takes in ninety women at a time, who each stay for several months. They are survivors not victims, say organisers, and they learn practical skills for advancement (for example, literacy) as part of the therapy process. A thousand women leaders are expected to graduate from the program by 2017.

'Some of these women have been used as tactical weapons,' says Dawson. 'It doesn't get any worse. After they've gone through the physical healing process, many of them end up with fistula and incontinence as a result of the rapes. City of Joy was set up by them, for them, to heal them emotionally. While they are there something remarkable happens to these women, they remember their strength.'

I tell her about the photo I saw in a newspaper. In it, Dawson watches a laughing Ensler fend off hugs at the project's official opening party. With their colourful headwraps, the Congolese women wear black slogan tees that read 'Stop the rape of our most precious resource', and they are smiling and jumping up and down, and Dawson is smiling too but with her mouth clamped shut trying to keep back her tears. Erwiah was at the party too but she's not in the picture.

'It was such a *feeling* to be there, I can't describe,' says Dawson. 'The obvious word is joy but it's more than that. I'm talking to a mother and she tells me her mother *and her daughter* were raped, so *three generations*, but they are not broken, they are beaming at you because they are in this space, and they created it – and with it, hope.'

Anyone experiencing this would want to help, raise awareness and funds, but Erwiah, with her fashion background, found herself looking at it from a different angle. 'What I saw was all these women making crafts and fashion objects as a form of microenterprise – they take the money they get from selling them and invest it into sustainable farming to feed their kids,' she says. 'It's one of the ways to break the cycle of violence and build community, but also independence. We were like, what can we do to be a part of this?'

It's the oldest trick in the book – people make stuff; they sell it; that creates jobs; now maybe their kids will have a better start than they did. It's back to Malcolm Gladwell's theories on success. But also, if you want to take it personally, it's back to Dawson's great-grandmother Celestina. And it's textbook example of what Simone Cipriani, founder of the Ethical Fashion Initiative, calls 'not charity, just work'.

Speak of the devil.

'Hello hello!' says Cipriani popping up from behind the *bogolan*, and folding me into a bear hug. 'I see you have found the beautiful Studio One Eighty Nine! How you like?'

'I like very much,' I say.

Missionary position

'I am not a fashionable man,' says Cipriani.[6] 'Ha ha HA!' He has a laugh that makes me think of firesides and Brian Blessed in a Shakespeare play. Cipriani's eyes crinkle behind his glasses and his mighty beard shakes.

'But I appreciate fashion. I think fashion is a formidable force. I am Italian, and in my culture, fashion is everywhere. When I was young I saw fashion and beauty all around me, and these ideas were always linked to humanity,' he says.

'Whether it is a piece of art or a luxury item, it was made by human hands, and celebrating these hands – the artist's or artisan's skill – was an accepted part of the story. To understand how something is made is to add to its beauty.'

If Cipriani sounds like Maier here, it's because he kind of is, albeit without the clichéd German reserve. Cipriani is the archetypal exuberant Italian, much given to back slapping and throwing his arms in the air; think Roberto Benigni in *Life is Beautiful*, but less bonkers. Cipriani's charisma isn't haphazard – it's targeted with military precision. Karen Walker admits to being 'immediately spellbound' by him. He is a very persuasive man, a useful trait in his line of work – that is, directing the International Trade Centre's Ethical Fashion Initiative (EFI).

The EFI links artisanal microproducers in Africa (Kenya, Ghana, Burkina Faso, Mali), as well as places such as Haiti, Cambodia and Palestine, with big fashion – mostly, so far, in Europe, but also in Australia, Japan and South America. They find partners anywhere established designers are open to the prospect: in London with Stella McCartney, in Tokyo with Hirofumi Kurino of United Arrows, in Rio with Osklen's Oskar Metsavaht, in Melbourne with Mimco. Think of Cipriani as a fashion matchmaker.

His obsession with artisanship has its roots in the heritage of Italian craft, and in his own cultural background. Cipriani was born in Pistoia, Tuscany, about thirty kilometres from Florence, which is home to some of the biggest names in Italian fashion: Guccio Gucci, Emilio Pucci and Salvatore Ferragamo. Between Pistoia and Florence lies Prato, where Italy's textiles industry is concentrated. The first woollen mills were established in the region in the medieval age, and tanneries have lined the local Arno River around Santa Croce for centuries. Traditionally, these tanneries used natural tannins derived from tree barks to process skins over several weeks, and 'Made in Tuscany' still signals added fashion magic – it speaks of history, authenticity, legend and chic. You grow up with all this, it rubs off.

Cipriani studied international development at university then went to work for a local shoe manufacturer, but his focus was always expansive. As a kid he dreamed of being a mountaineer. He loves travel – lucky, as he now spends eight months of the year on the road with the EFI. He earned his stripes managing an Italian NGO, which helped leather producers with training in developing markets, and consulting for agencies within the European Union and the UN. At one point he worked for a leather producer sourcing factories in India, Vietnam and Indonesia.

He saw plenty of examples of how not to do it. Today 90 per cent of the world's leather, including most used by luxury brands, is chromium tanned. Tuscan producers have been recycling their chromium salts since 1984, some even recycle waste fats and skin shavings for use in fertiliser and soap production, but elsewhere the industry is not so advanced. Tanneries in Kanpur, India, produce fifty million litres of toxic waste water every day; most of it ends up in the Ganges, where children wade and livestock drink. But what Cipriani kept coming back to was the notion that steady, fair work could change communities for the better. An empowered population might even tackle pollution.

'Responsible fashion means being responsible towards people ... but it also means being responsible towards the environment,' he says. 'How can we improve production processes to minimise the destruction of natural habitats? This is a big question.'

Cipriani is driven by what he calls 'a virtuous circle', where employment provides the possibility of lifting people out of poverty by their own means, 'which creates self confidence'.

I once watched him deliver a rousing speech on this subject at the Melbourne Fashion Festival. 'As people work together towards this,' he said, 'they improve their attitudes towards solidarity and cooperation, so they widen their social networks, which means they have to organise themselves better, which means they develop better business skills. *Better skills, more work, better communities.*' With each point his voice rose. 'Work empowers people to lead the flourishing life,' he said, bringing the tempo down again, the expert conductor. 'That's about more than just improved nourishment or sanitation; it allows people to use their emotions, their thinking capacities, their senses, to be fully part of society.'

Cipriani observed this first hand in Africa in mid-2000s, when the United Nations Industrial Development Organization (UNIDO) tapped him to help build up Ethiopia's leather industry. With his wife and their three daughters, he moved to Addis Ababa, the birthplace of Haile Selassie's African Union, then home to around three million people, an increasing number of them displaced farmers. The civil war that had raged since the '70s, and helped cause the terrible famine of the '80s, had been over since 1991, but its legacy remained. If your average Westerner thought about Ethiopia at all when Cipriani arrived, it was in relation to Bob Geldof and Live Aid, not for designer handbags sold in American department stores. But that's exactly what Cipriani had in mind with Ethiopia's first luxury leather brand, Taytu.

Ethiopia was rich in sheep and goats (producing about five million hides a year), but its farmers and tanneries were poor. A farmer selling a Bati goatskin, much prized for its fine suppleness, might get $2 a pop for his troubles. The exporting tannery could earn $40 per hide, but the luxury brand manufacturing a coat from this skin in Europe would rake in hundreds. Taytu aimed to flip that around. Set up as a cooperative of local tanneries, it would design and manufacture products locally.

The collections scored coverage in *Time* magazine and shelf space in Barneys and Hollywood retailer Fred Segal, but Taytu didn't really fly. Cipriani says they failed to think about long-term markets properly – they were too busy focusing on the product. They also had an image problem; affluent shoppers in LA and Manhattan knew their Gucci from their Pucci – Taytu, not so much.

Next time, Cipriani decided, he would do things differently. He lay awake at nights, trying to figure out how to drive his virtuous circle. It was no use making bags, however beautiful, if capricious fashion fans didn't buy them consistently. 'You can't have sustainable fashion without a sustainable market,' he says.

His UNIDO work took him more frequently to Kenya, and whenever he got a weekend off in Nairobi, he'd hang out with his friend

Gino Filippini – a fellow Italian and a missionary with the Servizio Volontario Internazionale, who'd made his home in the Korogocho slum. There, an estimated 150,000 residents were crammed into one square kilometre, paying rent on tin- or plastic-roofed shacks.

More than two-and-a-half million people live in Nairobi's slums, which include Korogocho and the vast Kibera, but also smaller, satellite settlements – and new neighbourhoods pop up every day. One in six people on earth live this way, and their numbers continue to swell.

The Economist describes Kibera as 'a thriving economic machine' run on power stolen from the city grid.[7] Because the government treats its residents as squatters, and fails to take out the trash or fix the roads or run schools or hospitals there, they must get on and do it for themselves. The report likens Kibera to 'an African version of a Chinese boomtown, an advertisement for solid human ambition'. It says that 'to equate slums with idleness and misery, is to misunderstand them'. Anyway, New York's Upper East Side was once a shantytown.

Brass tacks

Steven Adawo Kine is one of Kibera's entrepreneurs. Fondly known as Steve Brass, he is a welder who melts down old padlocks and scrap metal to make jewellery. When Cipriani met him, Kine was using a bicycle pump to pressurise his gas tank, and operating his small furnace by hand – it took him forty minutes to reach the 950-degree boiling point for brass. When asked about safety issues, Kine said, 'Well I know I can't do any mistakes, I would not only burn myself but a good part of the slum!'[8]

Cipriani offered Kine a regular market for his upcycled brass creations – making buttons and buckles for Vivienne Westwood bags. A buck for a buckle.

Westwood came to Kibera to meet Kine (she sat on his stool, a story he likes to tell), and she brought video cameras, her husband Andreas Kronthaler, the fashion photographer Juergen Teller and Cipriani's team. Well, Cipriani's team brought them all really, but it doesn't matter – what matters is that a famous London designer came to Kibera, and told everyone about Kine's skill, and the success of Cipriani's EFI program. It was by no means a sure thing.

Cipriani's UN bosses in Geneva initially funded his project for twelve months, 'to see if I can make it work,' he says. 'Possibly, they thought I can't! Ha ha!'[9] But make it work he did, by setting up production hubs in places where skilled workers lived. These hubs are run as social enterprises, with the EFI managing logistics. What began as an experiment has become a stable industry. Word spreads.

Cipriani likens the people who care about ethical fashion to accumulating snow – one day, he says, these 'little avalanches' will become one big avalanche and come crashing down to sweep away the old order.

I'm sure he must have his head-in-his-hands days when it comes to working in Africa, over the wretchedness of things like Ebola and Boko Haram, but he's not admitting it. 'Hope!' he says. 'Hope changes the world. What keeps me going? The real change I see in communities.' The EFI has created steady jobs for at least 7000 people in Africa. 'In order to prove your case, you must measure results,' Cipriani tells me. 'We can see very clearly how the lives of people can be affected by these programs: we see the most common diseases decrease, we see housing conditions improve, the numbers of children in school.'

Are Steve Brass's buttons enough? Vivienne Westwood has been accused of tokenism, and called out for her non-EFI supply chain, but we have to start somewhere. Cipriani's aim is to steadily increase business through the EFI hubs, and he believes the fashion world is in the early stages of 'moving beyond mass production'. He wants to foster business relationships not just with African artisans but with African designers, too.

Since 2013 the EFI has partnered with Rome's AltaRoma fashion week to present emerging designers. That has seen Ghanaian designers wow on the runway, and the likes of Senegalese designer Sophie Zinga get her work in front of fashion editors.

I met Zinga in Milan and she showed me her beautiful dresses, made from ombre lace layered with hand-embroidery. Zinga is making her collections in Senegal to sell in Senegal. 'I have a store in Dakar,' she told me. 'Retail is picking up there.' Dakar has had its own fashion week since 2002. This is not only about the so-called developed world's appetite for the artisanal.

By 2015 Westwood had been working with the EFI for ten seasons, producing hand-beaded clutches with Maasai artisans, using recycled canvas from Kibera, and placing orders with a fabric hub in Burkina Faso. In 2014, when she re-designed the cabin crew uniforms for Virgin Atlantic, she included EFI-made handbags to match the red recycled polyester suits. It's Stella McCartney's 'something is better than nothing' philosophy taken to its logical conclusion – and it makes sense to me. One step leads to another.

'The smallest thing can have an impact,' McCartney told *Business of Fashion*. 'We are all living on this land with limited resources, and we all have to be conscious about how we consume and how we manufacture and how we source.'[10]

Why should Westwood get grief for giving it a go, when countless other brands don't even try? I would rather Cipriani and his team changed the way some things were made by some people, than nothing by no one.

Ask him about that and he says simply, 'We *can* do more, and you can help. Consumers are the most important driving factor in all of this. DON'T FEEL POWERLESS.' I'm reminded of the way he concluded that seminar speech: 'Every time you allow one person to live a flourishing life, humankind takes a step towards a better world. A world without poverty, hunger, violence without conflict, without war. It is extremely beautiful to work together towards this, to strive together for something bigger than us. I know so many people who do this! Why don't you join us? Now!'

The first bit was an invitation. 'Now' was an order.

Rebel rebel

When Cipriani was looking for markets for Taytu, he focused on the US and Europe. He looked out, because his price points were high and there wasn't an obvious market within. But make those price points more friendly and there is. When Bethlehem Tilahun Alemu decided to start an accessories business in Addis Ababa, she reckoned it was about time Ethiopians had access to a global brand made at home.

She looked around her and what she saw was Nike, Adidas, Puma. Where were the African shoe brands? 'Imagine if your favourite "developing nation" had a Nike of its own,' she says. 'A globally present and highly successful brand owned and operated by the actors from that developing nation; *that* changes the entire paradigm and holds the seeds of a new type of prosperity.'[11]

Alemu is fed up with what she sees as patronising foreigners swooping in to help 'poor' Africa. 'We've been inundated with multitude "projects" all purporting to "help" us, but which have ultimately served to enrich [either] those proffering the "help" or the project while, ultimately, enfeebling us,' she tells me via email from Addis Ababa.

'Let's get this out of the way,' she says. 'Contracting out production in a low cost/low wage country is not a new idea. It's been around forever. Covering it in a Fair Trade gloss is simply [adding] cosmetics

[to] the overall equation. What's far more life-changing and nation-changing for the long term, is people from those so-called "low cost", "low wage" nations creating and building, and controlling, competitive global brands, producing world class products that leverage their talents and resources and bring direct prosperity to their community members. That model is A TOTAL REVOLUTION.'

In fact, Alemu's shoe company soleRebels is Fair Trade Certified, but its founder worries about the semantics. She takes issue with Fair Trade's 'standard promise'. 'By assisting in product development, purchasing and importing these artisans' products, this organisation has created mutually beneficial, long-term partnerships with low income, refugee and fair trade artisan groups in *pick your poor country and insert name here ...*'

This kind of thinking, she says, paints artisans into a 'low income' corner, and presumes they will stay there, so that Fair Trade companies 'can keep feeling good about themselves'.

You can feel the frustration bouncing off her words. What Alemu wants is for the principles of Fair Trade to be the principles of sustainable business – actually, of business full stop.

'Think of it like this,' she says, 'do artisan-based companies like Prada, Louis Vuitton, Armani, Tod's, Gucci, Fendi, Hermès et al. try to make you feel shamed into buying their products? Like, "Buy this Hermès bag and help an artisan"? No, of course not ... They get you to buy their goods because they pour a tonne of creative energy and resources into ensuring they [are] top-notch. Then they pour tonnes more creative energy and resources into ensuring that you, the consumer, understands, appreciates and embraces that value. That's exactly what we do.'

Alemu grew up in the rundown Zenabwork neighbourhood of Addis Ababa, the eldest child of a cook and an electrician. 'My parents encouraged me to get a higher education,' she says. At sixteen, her first job was in a clothes shop. She got herself to university, where she majored in accountancy. When she wasn't in class she was earning her living, mostly in retail, sometimes for international footwear brands – the usual sports shoe suspects – and she watched as local money flowed into decidedly non-local coffers. All this made her want to focus on her own community. 'I knew that there were so many talented people here who could do great things if only given a chance,' she says. 'They were my neighbours, my family members.'

As a kid, she'd watched her mother spin cotton with an *inzert*, a traditional wooden drop spindle; she'd done it herself. 'We also grew up watching *shemmanies* [weavers] hand loom the threads that we'd spun into magical, gorgeous fabrics to make *netalla* and *gabbis* [traditional scarves and blankets].' Similar fabric was used to make traditional shoes, called *selate* and *barabasso* – slip-ons with rubber soles cut from old car tyres.

Alemu knew she wanted to start a business manufacturing a product. Shoes, she says, were the obvious choice. Everybody needs them. *Selate* are affordable, and they use local materials (Ethiopia has been growing cotton for centuries), plus with their fabric uppers they lend themselves to attractive, easily adaptable designs. They're also vegan, handmade and have a low carbon footprint. Tick, tick, tick for trendy potential customers in Europe and the US, as well as local fans.

The name soleRebels, Alemu says, sprang like 'a piece of magical serendipitous poetry' – because her business plan was a rebellious one (make for the domestic market first, go global, stay locally owned), and because the rebels who overthrew the communist dictatorship in 1991 marched into Addis Ababa in *selate* shoes. Similar shoes were worn by Haile Selassie's Army of the Ethiopian Empire to fight Mussolini's troops in the 1930s.

In 2004, Alemu set up a workshop in her grandmother's Zenabwork backyard. It was 'pretty basic'– just Alemu and five paid workers, cutting up the old tyres, spinning and looming the cotton, and sewing the uppers to the soles.

They started making flip-flops and leather sandals, and Alemu's brothers joined the company: Kirubel, an IT grad, took over marketing while Brook, with a degree in economics, streamlined production. Within four years they were distributing on Amazon. They cut deals with Urban Outfitters and Whole Foods in the US. Less than a decade after they made their very first *selate*, there were standalone soleRebels stores in Athens, Vienna, Barcelona, Taiwan and Singapore. They've opened in Silicon Valley, with 'fifty to sixty' more stores planned. 'We're on track to generate US$250 million of revenue by 2018,' Alemu tells me. She's aiming for billions.

All the shoes are still produced in Zenabwork, in a bigger, better factory next to the original workshop. SoleRebels employs more than 130 workers there, and pays them between four and five times the legal minimum wage. The success of the factory feeds success for its suppliers, says Alemu, explaining how they partner with only small-scale organic cotton farmers, something that's actually not as hard as it sounds. 'Owing to the privations endured here most small-scale cotton farmers never used anything more complex than animal dung as fertiliser,' she says.

Hand-making stuff using local materials makes the most economic sense, but the knock-on effect of a low or zero carbon footprint is more healthy for the community anyway. While she bristles at labels – 'what we offer, I believe, goes far beyond "green"' – Alemu says she couldn't imagine founding an unsustainable, eco-ignorant or unethical brand. 'Ethiopians have been recycling for years without ever calling it recycling. When you have limited resources everything is valued and valuable.' Theirs is not a throwaway society (at least it hasn't been traditionally, although Ethiopia is Africa's fastest-growing economy so perhaps it soon will be – with prosperity comes consumerism, and with consumerism, waste). For now though, says Alemu, the old ways persist and either there's an obvious second life for something, 'or there isn't and so people invent one'. Alemu calls this 'equal parts ingenuity and resourcefulness'. Cutting up bald truck tyres to use as shoe soles saves them from landfill, where they are notorious space-stealers and methane gas trappers. Or it prevents them from being burned, which releases toxic gases into the air.

Alemu wants to reiterate that she grew up, studied and established soleRebels in the same town. 'This is a small but very critical point. You see, there is a distorted but powerful conventional wisdom, here and across Africa, that says if you want to succeed then get out and go, especially West,' she says. Alemu keeps making *Forbes* power lists ('World's 100 Most Powerful Women', 'Africa's Most Successful Women', '20 Youngest Power Women in Africa') by *working from home*. Accolades: whatever. What gives Alemu a thrill is the idea that her success proves a point: 'as a powerful counter to generations of media that have attempted to show Ethiopians as helpless, passive recipients of aid. My story runs counter to that narrative, and has in fact flipped the discourse on African development from one of poverty alleviation orchestrated by external actors, to one about prosperity *creation* driven by local Africans.'

CHAPTER 12

The Ethical Runway

Truth, desire and reconciliation

What makes a human rights lawyer think he can take on the Paris runway?

Paul van Zyl is a forty-something South African with a boyish grin. He is a careful, measured speaker, and in some ways there is little difference between the way he used to talk to the media about the indefensibility of Dick Cheney's stance on waterboarding, and the way he talks these days about beautiful clothes.

The subject matter couldn't be more different – but if you've ever questioned whether fashion can be a serious concern, van Zyl is the man to convince you it can.

'The trajectory of my life has always been about a sense of fairness, justice and dignity,' he tells me.[1] 'Apartheid in South Africa was precisely the opposite of those things. Working [as executive secretary] for the Truth and Reconciliation Commission, and after that for various NGOs, I became convinced that while part of what makes a successful country is justice and rights and laws, part of it is making sure that the people who are at the bottom of the pyramid are able to lead dignified lives.

189

Which generally means access to work and opportunity. Without that it's not just difficult for them, it's a risk to the country as a whole because you get an angry, marginalised, disaffected people.'

The giant global textiles, clothing and footwear industry, he says, is an obvious employer. Not that he knew much about fashion before he co-founded Maiyet; the first Paris show he ever attended was his own.

In 2011, 'fashion' was just a word he and Daniel Lubetzky wrote on a list while they were trying to figure out how to work together. Lubetzky is the social entrepreneur behind Kind snackbars. 'Daniel grew Kind from nothing to a company worth hundreds millions of dollars,' says van Zyl. 'I wanted him to do it again, and I wanted to be part of it. After looking at a number of different options, we thought we should do something in the fashion space. I looked at him and said, "You're a food guy." He looked at me and said, "You're a human rights lawyer." That wasn't a recipe for success, so we went out and found a third co-founder in Kristy.'

Kristy Caylor's previous job was running an indie fashion label called Band of Outsiders, but she had also worked on Gap (Product) RED. Bono co-founded RED in the mid 2000s to support the Global Fund to Fight AIDs, Tuberculosis and Malaria, and (Product) RED is the logo they license to megabrands (like Gap, Nike, Coca-Cola and Apple) to use on stuff designed specifically to raise money for the Fund. There is plenty of (Product) RED apparel, but it's mostly T-shirts and hoodies – not serious fashion.

Maiyet is a totally different proposition: a high-end fashion brand which aims to compete with the storied French luxury houses; to hold its own on the designer fashion floors of the world's chicest department stores.

Van Zyl has known from the start that worthy aims aren't enough. He calls it 'the yoghurt principle'. It's desire, stupid. 'We have to build a brand that is truly covetable, that people want to buy regardless of the underlying social mission. If you're going to develop the quintessential ethical yoghurt brand, with an organic family farm in upstate Vermont, it still has to taste good.'

The obvious way is to start small, tinker, get it right while the scale is manageable, but van Zyl and Lubetzky don't think like that. They raised $10 million in startup investment from people like Richard Branson and Abigail Disney (Walt was her great uncle), and aimed for sales of $100 million within five years. Their vision was brave, brilliant, grand, possibly arrogant and probably nuts – they had no idea what they were letting themselves in for in Fashion Land.

'Luxury was our aim from the outset,' says van Zyl. 'It's a $300 billion industry and part of the hypothesis of Maiyet is that there's a really amazing opportunity to redirect some of that buying power to places that would benefit from it.' Places like Kenya, India, Colombia and Peru, where van Zyl says they have found 'the next generation of global artisans'.

Maiyet doesn't use the phrase 'garment workers', and they don't have 'suppliers'; they have 'partners'. All follow the Fair Trade philosophy (although they're not usually accredited). So how are things like fair wages monitored? 'First, it's about being smart about who you select as partners, up front,' says van Zyl. 'We look for people who have fair or minimum wage certificates already, or they might be part of a co-op movement, or they are deeply committed to these kinds of processes as individuals. Second, we do very deep audits, both at the start and then on an annual basis to make sure certain standards are met.'

How did they find these partners?

'We just get on planes and look.' With their not-for-profit partner Nest (which works with artisans to train, develop and build sustainable businesses), they visited twenty-five countries in six months.

Van Zyl was 'looking for companies that we could grow to have a positive social impact', and Caylor for 'beautiful work she could integrate into her collections'.

In Indonesia they found batik artists, in Peru fantastic knits. In India, so impressed were they by the skill of Varanasi's traditional silk weavers (most of whom still work on pit looms in family homes where, says van Zyl, interloping 'goats are often a problem'), that they commissioned an ambitious new workshop building in partnership with Nest. Designed by architect David Adjaye, it will include childcare facilities and civic spaces, and when it opens in 2016 will exist for the common good, not just Maiyet's – everyone signs non-exclusivity agreements. 'We don't put people into golden handcuffs and say: you can only source to us. We genuinely want them to grow, and that means they are free to transact with anybody. In a decade's time my litmus test will be: did they thrive and grow and are they sourcing to a large enough group [of brands, designers, fabric wholesalers] to keep on doing that.'

Take, for example, one of Maiyet's first partners in Kenya, Anton Onyango Otiende and his wife Benta. They make 'beautiful hand-carved wood and bone, and hand-poured metals, hand-cast' in Nairobi. 'They were doing this on the side of their house with their kids running around,' says van Zyl, 'literally with a bicycle pump fanning the flames of the furnace, and sand and molasses moulds.' Otiende is now a regular Maiyet supplier. 'He was making something we valued. So [with Nest] we found some land, built a workshop, provided tools and safety equipment, and in an amazingly wonderful passing-it-on story, what Anton is now doing in his spare time is taking on orphan kids from the surrounding areas and teaching them. We have miles to go with Anton, we're just getting warmed up. We want to do deeper stuff, get him gold plating facilities. He has sixteen staff now; he trains them and he pays them decent wages.'

I ask about Anton's background, if he lost a job in a factory some-where, but van Zyl says, 'No, I don't think so. He was a self-taught entrepreneur, surviving from hand to mouth, and thinking, "Here's an opportunity, I am going to teach myself." There are hundreds and thousands of Antons in the world, they have talent and ability, but what those Antons lack is connections – they have no idea how to get their product into Barneys.'

Maiyet's business plan detailed selling to stores like Barneys and Net-A-Porter, and showing in Paris. 'Within two years we were on the official schedule showing at 8 p.m. on the Saturday night. The other 8 p.m. brands [included] Saint Laurent, McQueen, [and] Givenchy we like that company,' says van Zyl. 'My team comes from Chanel, Louis Vuitton, Saint Laurent, Alessandro Dell'Acqua.'

◉

Eighteen months after launch, the buzz about Maiyet was all good. There was a New York flagship store in Crosby Street, Soho, and chic campaigns featuring model Daria Werbowy. Suzy Menkes had praised their 'modern clothes and accessories with a human touch,'[2] and *Business of Fashion* proclaimed Maiyet had 'done what other brands have tried and failed to do: fuse a luxury sensibility with eth-ical credentials'.[3] But then fickle fashion, as it so often does, moved on to the next thing.

On Style.com, Maya Singer described Caylor's silhouettes for Spring '15 as 'a bit of a muddle'; 'nothing popped,' she said.[4] Menkes was still impressed – reporting on Maiyet's Autumn '15 collection for *Vogue*, she concluded that they had 'strived – and succeeded – to avoid making this a do-good brand for so-called "pity purchasing". Their clothes and accessories are luxury products, all first rate in design and make'[5] – but what happened to the 8 p.m. buzz?

That same season, Style.com's then executive editor Nicole Phelps (she's now director of Vogue Runway) suggested the brand was 'at a crucial juncture'.[6] 'With eight Paris shows behind it,' she wrote, '. . . it's no longer the new kid on the block. The curiosity factor has started to wear off – an issue made clear by the empty seats at the label's Hôtel Salomon de Rothschild venue. It didn't help that the show was wedged into a difficult time slot between two big Paris tickets, but the point is that Maiyet will only succeed now if creative director Kristy Caylor can give it a distinctive voice.'

By Resort '16 Caylor was out of the design room (she remains the company's president), and Declan Kearney, formerly at Alexander Wang, was in. Explaining the decision, van Zyl proved he'd been paying attention: 'It's a response to the growth and a way to expand our reach ... We are *at a crucial juncture*,' he said.[7]

For his part, Kearney promised 'a shift in the way the brand looks ... I'm very inspired by New York, and what women wear on the subway'.[8]

Singer approved. 'For the women who have championed Maiyet on principle, today was a banner day,' she wrote on seeing Kearney's first collection.[9] Kearney 'has made it possible to endorse this ethical brand in practice, i.e., by *wearing* it'. Singer thought the clothes 'came off as pleasingly familiar, but there was a sense of handmade-ness that allowed them to feel novel'. Kearney had 'revisited various nuts-and-bolts pieces from a stylish downtown girl's wardrobe and added a liberal application of warmth. Some of that was due to the craft elements – not just traditional ethnic techniques, but couture ones, too, like faggoting and fil coupé – and some of that was due to the tactility of the collection as a whole.' There was much to like, including great tailoring and maxi dresses with built-in bras.

'Women with more ample breasts will rejoice,' concluded Singer. 'So will all the women who have been aching to support the Maiyet mission and now have some genuinely cool clothes to choose from ... Do good, look good. Here's to that.'

◉

Maiyet is an interesting case study because most ethical fashion launches don't aim at the runway, and most existing runway brands don't have sustainability in their DNA. And here's Maiyet saying, we are in business to make a difference, *and we want to compete with Saint Laurent, McQueen and Givenchy* and all the rest of them. I love it, don't you? It might be risky, but any new label is a risk these days. We've passed peak label. We already have more than enough, so why not try to do things differently? To succeed takes more than money and ideas though – you need good timing, and a thick skin. That said, pots of money can't hurt.

Ethical luxury is a hard sell. Over a four-year period, Bono and his wife Ali Hewson reportedly sunk US$20 million of their own money into their brand Edun ('nude' spelled backwards), before LVMH bought a 49 per cent share of it in 2009. Even then profits weren't a given. For 2011/12, Edun Apparel (which is registered in Ireland, but has its head office in New York) reported losses of roughly $8.5 million.

Edun's business plan was to create luxury ready-to-wear entirely manufactured in sub-Saharan Africa. In the US, the brand – pitched as 'the expression of a new Africa, steeped in dynamism, creativity and a spirit of enterprise' – launched splashily into Saks, only to lose the account later on.

There were teething problems with the made-in-Africa collections. According to the *Wall Street Journal*, late deliveries and unreliable fits affected sales, and retailers complained.[10] By 2010, Edun was making most of its main line in China and Peru.

'The whole point of the mission is that we do sell clothes, and then the company grows and therefore we work more in Africa,' said Hewson in 2014. By now, they were '85 per cent there'[11] with the amount they were making in Africa, she said, plus they had a brilliant new creative director in Danielle Sherman (who'd co-founded The Row with the Olsen twins). Sherman's confident, modern collections won back buyers and secured a new fanbase, while sidestepping the obvious – the 'craft' angle was kept to a minimum; Sherman was more likely to splice her wool crepe with black leather or PVC than hand-beaded panels. Edun's New York fashion week shows scored strong reviews, and Net-A-Porter snapped up the brand's sleek jumpsuits and monochrome separates. As the UK *Telegraph* noted after the brand's Spring '16 show, 'The fact that [such pieces] were made in Madagascar by a team of local women is incidental.'[12]

'The aesthetic is the most important thing,' confirmed Hewson. 'Or else it's not fashion and it's not going to be a business.'

Stella McCartney probably has the biggest designer business associated with the ethical fashion cause. She has close to forty of her own stores, and wholesale accounts with about 600 more. Her Paris shows are hugely influential, her customers are glamorous (friends Kate Moss and Gwyneth Paltrow represent) and her name is synonymous with cool British fashion. But McCartney has refused to compromise her ethics while growing her brand. She turned her vegan bags and shoes into cult hits against the odds – parent company Kering makes most of its profits from leather goods. McCartney went inside-out for Fashion Revolution Day, helped launch the Clevercare initiative (which educates consumers about more environmentally friendly clothes-washing) with H&M, and works with Livia Firth's Green Carpet Challenge. But, ultimately, does she define her brand as 'sustainable fashion' or 'ethical fashion'? Not quite.

Officially, she uses the phrase, 'committed to being responsible, honest and modern' to describe her approach. 'I design clothes that are meant to last. I believe in creating pieces that aren't going to get burnt, that aren't going to landfills, that aren't going to damage the environment,' she has said. But the only label McCartney is plastering on her brand is her own.

The language that we use

Ethical fashion has an image problem, something Kristy Caylor has noted: 'It's the public perception that something ethical is sacrificing on design. It's granola or fair trade; it looks very hippie – all those assumptions.'[13]

I think we should change its name. Sustainable fashion is no better. Both words are clunky, inelegant and invoke ideas of hemp. I don't hate 'eco' but 'eco-chic' is unbearable, and what does 'green' mean nowadays?

'Don't ever, *ever* put the words "fashion" and "sustainability" too close together,' counsels Fashion Revolution's Orsola de Castro. 'There has to be something in between, otherwise it makes no sense.'[14]

In Rome, Stella Jean, one of my favourite designers, works with the EFI, but like the Hermès scarf-printer Kamel Hamadou, she describes her process as 'story-telling'. 'My aim is to make a reportage that starts with Italy where I live and comes back to Haiti,' she says. Her father is a jewellery designer from Turin; her mother is Haitian. Sustainability, she says, 'is not a commercial act, it's part of my culture'.

Londoner Duro Olowu, an exquisite tailor of Nigerian descent and another friend of the EFI, is often spoken of as a sustainable designer because he favours the hand-made, and uses traditional African fabrics as well as couture-worthy ones, but Olowu is having none of your categories, conceding only that he does things 'differently' and is 'inspired by the world'.[15]

Suno is a New York-based label known for its cool prints, founded by former filmmaker Max Osterweis and designed by Erin Beatty. They work with artisans in Kenya, Peru and India, and won a CFDA emerging talent award in 2013. Osterweis had often holidayed in Kenya, and told *Time* magazine that it was after Nairobi's post-election riots in 2007–08 that he decided, 'I wanted to create long-term employment and also set an example to show that investment in Africa need not be about building more safari lodges … I wanted to do a collection women could wear to an art opening, to dinner. I didn't want to do an "ethnic collection," whatever that means.'[16] They describe their offer, which is sold in department stores across the world, as 'a high-end collection with a conscience'.

Sydney-based Kit Willow walked away from her Willow brand in 2013, and now runs 'design-led ethical and sustainable' brand KITX. 'It was born,' she says, 'out of a spirit of kindness, integrity and transparency – the X represents the future.' She talks about designing 'with people and the planet in mind' as well as her customers. 'Some of them will be really proud of the fact that our clothes haven't had a negative impact,' she says. 'Others may not even know, and it doesn't matter, you know? Because it's KITX's responsibility to make those smart choices for them – whether they are aware of it or not.'[17]

'Slow fashion is a good one,'[18] Carry Somers, another Fash-Revette, told me during London fashion week, when we tried to come up with more palatable phrases. 'I can see a bit of a shift towards "slow" on the runways, with some collections becoming a bit more classic: more of an evolution than an about-turn each season. These are the kinds of pieces you can invest in.' She showed me her shoes: Céline. 'They were seriously expensive, but I know I will wear them for the next decade,' she said. 'They have nails in the bottom of the sole. When did you last see that?' Those shoes were a poke in the eye for disposable fashion.

Should we, then, be talking more in terms of quality and longevity? It is certainly true that many designers who care about the beauty of craft, and about creating garments that will live beyond next season, are reluctant to call themselves 'sustainable fashionistas' (and not just because 'fashionistas' is more cringe-worthy than 'eco-chic', if that's possible). In fact, most are more than reticent; they are locked out, because the criteria for the 'ethical/sustainable fashion' tag are rightly strict. Can you be a little bit sustainable? Ethical by degrees?

Lydia Pearson, who with Pamela Easton runs the beautiful, carefully made Australian brand Easton Pearson says, 'There is so much talk about ethical fashion now but I'm not sure we're able to use that label. It's so difficult to sign a Fair Trade agreement, for example, and to promise that absolutely everything you do comes from a sustainable source. We know the weavers of the fabric before we even start on the embellishment, but we don't know who spun the sewing thread. We can only say that we try as hard as we can.'[19]

Melbourne-based designer Roopa Pemmaraju says simply, 'Social entrepreneurship is a happy side product of the way we are set up.'[20] Her womenswear collections are sewn in her native Bangalore, India, in a workroom run to upskill disempowered women, and she develops her silk prints with indigenous communities in Australia.

De Castro sums it up: 'The reality is that sustainable fashion really is *fashion*. It's everything else that isn't sustainable that should be called [out] as such. Choose whichever name you like the least, such as "unethical fashion" or "unsustainable fashion" to describe the way that [rest of] the industry operates.'[21]

◎

For some designers even the word 'fashion' is problematic. Wayne and Gerardine Hemingway started the awesome UK brand Red or Dead in the '80s because they wanted to change the world. 'We were not going to be normal fashion company,' says Wayne Hemingway.[22] 'The name came from the Cold War. "Better red than dead" was what very provocative young people were saying, because we'd prefer to be communist and side with the Russians, than side with the aggressive Americans.'

Okay, but Red or Dead were British Fashion Council darlings, they showed at London fashion week, and they opened twenty-three shops. They were indisputably part of the fashion system. And yet Hemingway is right when he says, 'We were so un-commercial. We were so bloody brave, not in the way that Alexander McQueen was kind of calculated brave; this was coming from the heart – we wanted it to be affordable, we wanted it to be political.'

In 1993, they visited the high-security Full Sutton Prison in Yorkshire to see a fashion show put on by inmates, who'd designed and sewn clothes as part of a Home Office–sanctioned program. 'It's better than locking someone up and throwing away the key,' says Hemingway, of what came to be known as Keyhole Clothing. 'You give them a chance to learn something.'

Read or Dead's Autumn '94 collection was inspired by prison life, and included workwear made from sustainable hemp, and sewn in the prison. The tabloids pounced: 'Jailhouse Shock!', 'Crime Does Pay!' It didn't help that Peter Sutcliffe, aka the Yorkshire Ripper, was serving a life sentence in Full Sutton. 'Sutcliffe didn't make our things, but the truth didn't matter,' says Hemingway. 'We ended up on the front pages with made-up stories. They said the inmates were smoking the hemp fabric, which isn't even possible. The press were trying interview our kids at a show we were doing. I nearly hit someone.

I remember them saying, "What do you think about your parents supporting murderers?"'

Spring '96 got Red or Dead into trouble again. This time the headlines branded them a 'Bloody Disgrace!', called them, 'The Sick Face of British Fashion', thanks to a show inspired by desperate housewives that featured knives and fake blood. 'At that stage we had those laminated *Elle* cards in the shop, we probably had some *Vogue* ones too, you know, [displaying] shoots that had used our clothes? We took them all down! We were like, okay, we're not doing any of that now. We'll put up "The Sick Face of British Fashion" [clippings], and just campaign from now on. We did that right until the end.'

The weird thing was, the less they tried to make commercial collections, the more fashion they sold. There was no getting away from it – they were a successful commercial streetwear brand. At what point do you say, enough? You can't fight the system if you're part of it. The most ethical fashion brand of all, the one with guaranteed zero carbon footprint, the one that doesn't exploit a single person or thing, is the brand that does not exist.

In 1996, the Hemingways sold a chunk of Red or Dead to the Pentland Group, which today owns Speedo, Boxfresh and part of Hunter wellies. Two years later, they signed away the rest. 'Gerardine didn't really want to sell, but she's happy now that we did,' says Hemingway. 'I was desperate to get out. I didn't ever feel part of the industry, and I also didn't want to be. I would never in an interview allow myself to be called a fashion designer. I'd say, "I'm a designer". I always tried to keep us out of it, but [Red or Dead] was still a fashion brand.'

These days Wayne, Gerardine and two of their grownup children run Hemingway Design, a British company 'with its feet firmly planted in societal needs'. They organise car boot sales and a fete called the Festival of Thrift. They revamp tired old housing estates in places like King's Lynn, and are creative directors on Margate's Dreamland theme park regeneration project. Very occasionally they design clothes – in 2015, they did the new uniforms for Transport for London workers – but they don't do fashion. Wayne Hemingway can say that and mean it these days.

CHAPTER 13

Silent Spring/Summer

Choose life

In 1989, Katharine Hamnett decided she'd had enough of fashion too. 'I hit the wall,' she says.[1] 'We were on such a roll. It was so just so easy. Success was pouring in. We were selling to something like 700 shops, but I battled from that point. I'd always thought that the key to being successful was being a decent human being.'

Turns out it isn't. I could have told her that.

On a cold spring day we are sitting in a café by Regent's Canal in London. Actually, we are sitting outside it, so that Hamnett can smoke as she drinks her espresso coffee and talks about organic cotton, saving Britain's bees and people power. And what a fine mess the fashion industry is in.

Hamnett has been one of the coolest names in London fashion since the '80s. Back then the Blitz kids loved her, along with Body-Map and Vivienne Westwood. This was before fashion became global big business and got so serious, back when models used to dance down runways (I wish they still danced). The Hamnett look was bright and bold, part club scene, part power-dresser, with skinny leggings and oversized everything else – giant protest tees and para-chute silk parkas, baggy trench coats, big makeup, hair. Later, Hamnett's coloured denim was a cult thing. In the '90s and noughties she did skinny black jersey, more denim, and even the odd bit of targeted rhinestone bedazzlement – Naomi Campbell walked her runway barely dressed, with a sparkling 'Use A Condom' slogan on her knickers – Hamnett was subversive, underground, cool.

Not that she was small scale. The BFC crowned Hamnett Designer of the Year in 1984. There was Katharine Hamnett menswear, eyewear, swimwear; she had a London flagship on Sloane Street; sold collections in forty countries and hired photographers like Terry Richardson and Juergen Teller, before they were famous, to shoot her campaigns.

The daughter of a diplomat, Hamnett went to boarding school in England, because the family moved around a lot. She has fond memories of Paris; at one point they lived in Romania. Observing the international brat scene – she remembers 'the Saudi ambassador's daughter' at school getting about in Courrèges[2] – as well as her mother's chic style informed Hamnett's early love of clothes. 'Fashion is in my blood. I come from a long line of fancy dressers, all of whom dress much better than me, I have to say.' Today she's in her 'uniform' of black jumper, black mini skirt, black tights and boots. The jumper is Uniqlo; 'I shop there like everybody else.' Her hair is scraped back in a ballerina bun and she's brought her lovely scruffy dog along; he keeps trying to sit on the table and she keeps pushing him down. 'I'm in love with textiles,' she continues. 'Always have been; when I was a child we used to go on holiday to the south of France and I'd insist on bringing little bits of silk velvet with me.'[3]

At eighteen Hamnett arrived at Saint Martins to study fashion. She graduated in 1969, and went straight into business with her friend Anne Buck. Their label Tuttabankem sold to Browns and Saks, but by 1974 it was over. Hamnett freelanced for five years, including a stint with an Italian sportswear company, then hit the bank up for a £500 loan and went out alone. Securing a backer in Peter Bertelsen helped – he ran Ralph Lauren's wholesale business in Europe, and was behind Valentino and Armani opening London stores. Hamnett was playing with the grownups.

As with Westwood, her designs were widely copied, but rather than turn a blind eye Hamnett decided to tap into the power of that. She made her first slogan T-shirts to promote a friend's Buddhism-themed art exhibition in the early '80s. If people knocked the shirts off, she thought, fantastic; they'd be spreading a meaningful message.

'I've always been quite interested in Buddhism as a philosophy,' she tells me. 'I mean, I'm a heathen, but I took divinity at school because I thought it was interesting. And I thought Buddhism came over best because they talk about the "gatefold path" and "right livelihood" – the goal of not hurting any living thing.' Hamnett's own philosophy of 'not being a shit of a person', and expecting what goes around to come around, echoes this. 'The Buddhists refine that thinking of course, but the basic idea of right livelihood, it's a good one, isn't it?'

Indeed it is.

Alas 'right livelihood' is not the most pithy of statements, so Hamnett settled on 'Choose Life' for those T-shirts, and printed the letters in black block capitals as big as they could be.

She was right on both counts: the T-shirts were undeniable statement-makers and, boy, were they copied.

In Wham!'s 'Wake Me Up Before You Go-Go' video, the 'Choose Life' tees George Michael and Andrew Ridgeley wore were Hamnett originals – by this point, in 1984, the slogan was being read as a call to arms against drug abuse and youth suicide. Not Hamnett's intention, but she didn't mind. She did when anti-abortionists appropriated the slogan though: 'Yes, well, that pisses me off, obviously.'

Shortly after 'Go-Go', ex-*NME* journalist Paul Morley copied Hamnett's T-shirt concept to promote an act signed to his fledgling record label ZTT. The band was Frankie Goes to Hollywood, and Morley's shirts, in similar lettering to Hamnett's, read, 'Frankie Say Relax' (these, in turn, have also been much copied – the more obvious fakes add an 's' on the end of 'say', in case you're searching on eBay). Morley doesn't even try to pretend they were his idea. He told the *Guardian*, 'What persuaded me was reading [about] Katharine Hamnett saying she *wanted* the T-shirts ripped off, which reminded me of [publisher] Mark P saying he wanted [punk fanzine] *Sniffin' Glue* to be ripped off. And I mean, I did a fanzine, so when I read that I thought, great, fanzine T-shirts!'[4]

But Hamnett wasn't selling records; she was selling politics. She produced T-shirts – sometimes in silk; one reason why they were so big is that there was no stretch in the fabric – with such battle cries as 'Worldwide Nuclear Ban Now' and 'Protest and Survive'.

Recession and a simmering resentment between rich and poor gripped early '80s Britain. There were two-and-a-half million unemployed in April 1981 when riots erupted in Brixton. By July, the unrest had spread to hard-up neighbourhoods of Birmingham, Leeds and Liverpool. The following January, unemployment passed the three million mark. The pissed-off people of Britain protested – they wanted to smash things up.

Prime Minister Margaret Thatcher, the Iron Lady, was doing the same, but from a different angle – slashing government spending, smashing unions and dismantling public services. Twelve months after Brixton, when it looked like its power at home was in real danger of collapse, the Thatcher government announced military action to defend the Falkland Islands from Argentine invasion.

Meanwhile, the Cold War raged on, along with the fear of nuclear Armageddon. Perhaps the end of days really was only the touch of a button away. Perhaps it still is. The bombs haven't disappeared just because the Iron Curtain has; we've just stopped obsessing over them.

'You have to deter a potential aggressor, to stop him from being tempted to use his armaments to attack,' said Thatcher during a TV interview in January 1983. 'Weakness would tempt him. Strength stops him.' As part of its NATO commitments, Britain was on track to deploy 572 cruise and two Pershing missiles before the end of the year. The ban the bomb movement swelled. In October an estimated one million people turned out in Europe to march for the Campaign for Nuclear Disarmament, with a 200,000-strong crowd bringing central London to a standstill.

Hamnett's next ad campaign, shot by *Vogue* favourite Peter Lindbergh, featured a gang of scowling, disaffected-looking guys and girls, and two big-eyed children in enormous white tees, their slogans urging 'Stop Acid Rain' and 'Education Not Missiles'. It was all very Zeitgeisty, but life, as is its habit, went on.

In March 1984, the BFC brought London's designer showings together in Olympia and the city finally had its fashion week. The government sensed the economic benefits of a more professionally organised event, and duly dispatched Norman Lamont (he of the crazy eyebrows, then Minister for Industry) to attend various catwalk shows. Princess Diana turned up to peruse the exhibition stands, spending fifteen minutes with one of her favourite designers, Jasper Conran.[5] Someone had the bright idea to hold a fashion week reception at 10 Downing Street, and on Saturday March 17th, 200 guests mingled with the PM at home. Mrs T wore a black velvet suit with one of her signature pussy-bow blouses, her lacquered hair like a general's helmet; Zandra Rhodes was in chiffon; and Di's wedding dress designers David and Elizabeth Emanuel turned up in their gladrags.[6]

Hamnett recalls discussing with Conran whether they should boycott the party. She remembers he said something like, 'Why should we go and have a glass of warm white wine with that murderess?'[7] It was Thatcher who ordered the sinking of Argentine ship the *Belgrano*, no getting away from that. But as for the wine, surely they could have the red? In the end it was too good an opportunity to miss. Hamnett conceived of the perfect outfit – but had just hours to get it together. 'I went quickly to a photographic studios and had the lettering done on linen, which I had to stitch on to the T-shirt, so it wasn't far off a proper sandwich-board outfit,' she recalled in an interview with the *Independent*.'[8] It wasn't a regular T-shirt, but a long white linen T-shirt-dress bearing the slogan: '58% don't want Pershing'. To arrive at the shindig, she hid it under a coat. Her leggings and white Converse sneakers poked out. When the PM came to shake her hand, Hamnett dropped the wrap.

After that, as Hamnett tells it, Vivienne Westwood was about the only person who dared talk to her: 'Everybody else avoided me like the plague.'[9]

Job done, lesser women would have legged it. Or been kicked out (but perhaps it was decided that line of action would make for saucier news headlines). Hamnett stayed until the bitter end, when she chased Thatcher round the room and asked her about acid rain. The prime minister was not amused: 'We don't know what causes acid rain, and I am a scientist,' she said. 'Goodnight!'

Now the slogan tee was everywhere; in the streets, the clubs, even the Albert Hall – which, in November 1985, was commandeered by Fashion Aid. Think Band Aid with designers. The event raised money for famine victims in Ethiopia, and concluded with a mock royal wedding expertly costumed by the Emanuels. Freddie Mercury made a charming prince kissing his 'bride' (actress Jane Seymour) while pageboys in blue velvet and flower girls, in puffy dresses just like the ones at Charles and Di's wedding, looked on. Bob Geldof harangued the crowd to 'Give me your fucking money, give it to me now!' prompting Nicholas Coleridge to lament in the *Spectator* 'hectoring and ranting are new to the catwalk'.[10]

The Hamnett T-shirt worn by Yasmin Le Bon to dance down the Fashion Aid runway read 'Stay Alive In 85'. Le Bon was smiling (this was a fundraiser, no need to bring the mood down), but the subtext was that people everywhere were *not* saying alive; they were dying – of AIDs, of drugs, of poverty, of unjust wars and famine. Four years later, Hamnett would add toxic pesticides and the greedy, heartless fashion industry to that list.

◉

'In '89 we commissioned some research on the impact of clothing and textiles production, socially and environmentally,' Hamnett tells me.[11] 'That was the brick wall for me, the epiphany.' What she discovered, via the Pesticide Action Network (PAN) UK, was that, globally, cotton accounts for nearly half the fibre used to make clothing and other textiles. And worldwide, that cotton production accounts for 25 per cent of insecticide (targeted insect killers) use, and 10 per cent of herbicide (weed killers) use. Pesticides, by the way, is an umbrella term that includes insecticides, herbicides and chemicals to kill bacteria, fungus and other pests.

Many different species of insects and mites can attack cotton crops, but the biggest threat is the bollworm, which feasts on the plant and causes rot. Organophosphates are the most commonly applied chemicals in the battle against the bollworm.

Pre-1940, most pesticides were plant-derived, bar a few grim ones made from heavy metals such as arsenic, but the Second World War saw the development of new synthetic carbon-containing (organic) compounds on an industrial scale. The organochlorine DDT was one, heralded as broad-spectrum (killed all sorts), persistent (meaning it didn't break down in the environment rapidly, hence no frequent re-sprays) and practically insoluble in water (so rain didn't wash it away) – all of which to modern ears sound like reasons to be very afraid, but back then seemed like pluses. The Swiss scientist Paul Müller developed DDT as an insecticide – he received a Nobel Prize for his efforts in 1948.

It was DDT that controlled the Naples typhus outbreak of 1943, and was sprayed aerially over the South Pacific to prevent malaria a few years later. It was used on troops to kill lice. In the '50s, the British government extended its aerial spraying program to dump gallons of another synthetic organic compound, Herbicide Orange, over the Malay Peninsula. Take that, forests and crops in communist strongholds! The Americans decided this was a top idea – and also that the Brits had set a legal precedent – and followed suit in the '60s, when an estimated twenty million gallons of the stuff was dumped on Vietnam. The biggest producers of what came to be known as Agent Orange? Two names you might have heard of – Dow and Monsanto.

Back home, farmers in the US fell for the chemical companies' marketing spiel, and signed up to rid their fields of their own enemies – insects. If for some reason you weren't keen on spraying DDT on your crops from the '50s to the '70s, you could try dieldrin – another organochlorine; this one acted like a nerve gas. Dieldrin poisoned mozzies too but unfortunately it didn't stop at those pesky bollworms.

In her explosive 1962 book *Silent Spring*, biologist Rachel Carson blew the whistle on organochlorines as Persistent Organic Pollutants (POPs) that not only stick around in the environment, but proliferate.

Carson sets the scene by describing an Eden-like location 'in the heart of America, where all life seemed to live in harmony with its surroundings. The town lay in the midst of the checkerboard of prosperous farms, with fields of grain and hillsides of orchards.' She describes a rural idyll once renowned 'for the abundance and variety of its bird life', and crossed by streams 'which flowed clear and cold out of the hills' and teemed with fish – before 'a strange blight crept over the area and everything began to change'. The birds stopping singing, the livestock died, the farmers and their families sickened. 'Everywhere was the shadow of death.'[12]

Carson reveals 'the true complexity of the chemical world of the hydrocarbons', explaining how systemic pesticides have 'the ability to permeate all the tissues of a plant or animal and make them toxic',[13] and how they might bioaccumulate through the food chain by building up in fatty tissue, muscle and bone. When the bird eats the insect, it eats the chemical deposits within it too, which then magnify inside the bird until something bigger eats it, and so on.

Carson tells how twenty-five farm labourers in California's San Joaquin Valley were 'seized with sudden illness' after handling cotton seeds coated in insecticides,[14] and how fish in Alabama's Flint Creek, flooded by runoff, appeared dazed then died en masse. 'Evidence of the deadly presence of the chemicals was obtained by placing test goldfish in cages in the river; they were dead within a day,' she writes.[15] She talks of the poisoning of earthworms as well as soils. Of hydrocarbons causing birds to lay eggs with thinner shells, more likely to crack and fail. Of American's bald eagles, those predators at the top of the bioaccumulation tree, failing to reproduce and disappearing from the skies. And she raises the spectre of a cancer link.

Carson asks, 'Who has decided – who has the *right* to decide – for the countless legions of people who were not consulted that the supreme value is a world without insects, even though it be also a sterile world, ungraced by the curving wing of a bird in flight?'[16]

The chemical giants scrambled to discredit Carson. *Monsanto Magazine* (yes, that was a thing) parodied her work.[17] The National Agricultural Chemicals Association reportedly spent $250,000 (a lot of money then) on a smear campaign. Carson was dismissed as 'probably a communist'[18] by the former US Secretary of Agriculture Ezra Taft Benson, who wondered why a childless 'spinster' should worry about future generations. Nice. People still argue today that Carson's role in pushing governments to ban DDT killed more people, via malaria, than it saved.[19] For the record, Carson argued for careful use, reduced use, and a rethink of indiscriminate crop dusting – anyone who has actually read her book will know it's ludicrous to blame her for malaria outbreaks.

By April 1964, less than two years after the first serialised pages of *Silent Spring* appeared in the *New Yorker*, Carson was dead from breast cancer, but not before President Kennedy had ordered an investigation into the charges detailed in *Silent Spring*. Use of DDT on crops was banned in the US in 1972. The US Environmental Protection Agency now recognises that dieldrin and aldrin 'pose a substantial risk of cancer' and that they 'do not break down easily in our environment and [do] become more concentrated as [they] move up the food chain.' The links between these substances and sickness (cancer, birth defects, immune system and reproductive disorders) are now widely acknowledged. Organochlorines do us no good, they hang about, and get into all sorts of places they shouldn't. Heptachlor, for instance, has been found in human breast milk.

In the mid-'90s the UN Environment Programme moved to impose worldwide restrictions on their use. The Stockholm Convention on POPs finally came into force in 2004, detailing the banning, phasing out and cleaning up of twelve key POPs including dieldrin, aldrin, DDT (with limited exceptions to control malaria) and heptachlor.

Companies like Monstano, Dow and Bayer responded by pushing new-wave organophosphates. These degrade on exposure to sunlight and air, but that doesn't mean they aren't dangerous. They are generally more soluble (so, more likely to contaminate groundwater) and have greater acute toxicity than organochlorines. They are also nerve agents. Yet here they are, the next big thing.

According to the World Health Organization (WHO), at least 20,000 agricultural workers die each year from pesticide poisoning. 'Millions are hospitalised and we don't know how many more are affected,' says Hamnett. 'This stuff just goes on killing.' In South India's cotton region, the Mahatma Gandhi Memorial Hospital in the market city of Warangal, Telangana state, admitted more than 8,000 people with pesticide poisoning between 1997 and 2002.

Most of the people out there in the fields applying these chemicals are poor farmers or itinerant labourers. Too often they cannot read the warning labels on the containers. Training is insufficient or non-existent, and many resist wearing protective gear in the heat, even when it is provided. When poisoning occurs, poor nutrition and generalised ill health make recovery less likely.

A 2010 report by the International Cotton Advisory Committee flagged that while the Indian government has restricted DDT use, other 'highly hazardous' pesticides are gamely sprayed over cotton crops every day. They singled out monocrotophos, a nasty organophosphate 'with suspected genotoxicity'. While it is banned or severely restricted in China, the US, the EU and Australia, in places like Telangana and neighbouring Maharashtra state, farmers ladle it out of cartons with their bare hands. They have been known to rinse empty containers in the river for reuse. In 2013, in the northern state of Bihar, twenty-three primary-school children died from acciden-tally poisoned lunches. The oil used to cook their rice and lentils had allegedly been stored in a recycled monocrotophos container.

Why do we, as consumers of cotton, tolerate this situation? Hamnett figured it was because we did not know. 'Looking back I was terrifically naive because I thought, I will tell people and they will say, "Oh this is awful, let's change it." Only they didn't.'

Hamnett's initial idea was to work with PAN UK to raise money for farmer education. She designed a special jeans collection, with a view to donating 10 per cent of sales to help support an organic cot-ton farming cooperative in Senegal. It proved more trouble than it was worth. Her denim was produced under licence in Italy, and get-ting the money out of her partners was ridiculously hard. 'By the second season I was desperate,' she says.[20] 'I've got the Pesticide Action Network on the phone begging me to get this money to the farmers, and I've got this guy who's not answering my fucking calls or faxes because they weren't intending to do this, ever, so what are you going to do? I had to go in there with a Channel 4 TV crew, hid-den in a huge limo, and upbraid the guy outside his office to get the cheque. That was the end of that relationship.'

Maybe it was about changing the way she designed – she decided to source organic cottons for her next ready-to-wear. 'But I'd go round huge trade fairs to people I'd bought thousands of meters [of regular cotton] from in the past, and say, "Have you got any organic cotton?" And they'd say, "Why?" I was the only one asking for it.' When she did break through, her Italian manufacturers 'substituted all the beautiful sustainable fabrics I'd found. They told me the day the collection was going out to sell, and I said, "WHAT?" And the guy said, "If you carry on with this ethical environmental stuff you can take your collection and fuck off." And this is one of the top factories in Italy.'

'Really?' I say. 'Why would they do that?' It sounds crazy to me, when the sourcing slog had already been done, and also because it was Hamnett they were dealing with, hardly someone likely to back down without a fight.

'Because it wasn't convenient, because it was more expensive, because they were stupid,' she says. 'Oh I don't know. They thought the issue was going to go away, I suppose.'

I ask how she felt coming up against such resistance, and she says, 'I wanted to cry. The Italian situation was just infuriating'. So she took her business elsewhere, and she continued to tell anyone who would listen about the benefits of organic cotton. 'For the farming communities, it literally flips their lives from starvation and poisoning, destitution, losing their children at the breast, to the possibility of a decent, healthy existence – it's better for the soil, the country, everybody that's involved with processing *and* you get a better price for it.' Hamnett journeyed to Mali with PAN to make a film about cotton farmers. She cancelled her licences, and renamed her business Katharine E Hamnett – the 'e' stands for ethical.

In 2007, Lynn Barber wrote in the *Observer* that fashion had finally caught up with Hamnett after 'all those wilderness years when she was out of sight, she was working on the problem of how to make fashion more ethical, more environmentally sound, how to produce clothes that didn't use petrochemicals or pesticides, that relied entirely on organic and recyclable materials.'[21] But had it really caught up?

That was the year Hamnett pulled out of Choose Love, her organic cotton Fair Trade range for Tesco, saying, 'I was initially really excited about the tie up because I thought we could increase demand for ethical products. But I've come to the conclusion that [Tesco] simply wants to appear ethical, rather than make a full commitment to the range.'[22]

On the first anniversary of Rana Plaza, Hamnett joined War On Want protestors in London calling out Gap's failure to sign the Bangladesh Accord. The T-shirt she wore to demonstrate outside Gap's Oxford Street store read 'Pay Living Wage Now'.

In 2014, Hamnett was busy petitioning her local Hackney council to stop using glyphosate weedkiller on parks and gardens – to picnic where it's been sprayed, she said, 'is the shortest route to ingesting it bar drinking it straight from the bottle.'[23] When I ask what she's working on now she says, 'I'm trying to save the world, to stop us from making ourselves extinct.'

Career suicide

Wouldn't it be wonderful to win the bollworm war without toxic organochlorines? *Of course it would*, Monsanto agreed. But hang on, Monsanto makes those chemicals – won't that affect their profits? Aha! But what if they made and sold the cottonseeds? *Now there's an idea!* And what if they engineered the seeds to be resistant to a particular herbicide, one that they also made? That way farmers could liberally spray their fields with an organophosphate herbicide with no fear of damaging their crops. No more worms, no more weeds!

In 1997, Monsanto began open-field trials, in India, of their new Bt cottonseed. This seed is genetically modified to contain genes from a bacteria naturally found in soil that's toxic to the bollworm, as well as to be resistant to glyphosate – which most of us know as Roundup.

Ten years previously, the World Bank had put pressure on the Indian government to deregulate their domestic seed market, which was convenient when it came to selling the new Bt seeds to the second-largest cotton producer in the world. The situation was shaping up to be a win-win! A win for Monsanto, which could make more money, and for the farmers, who could rely on better yields. Or not. Depends who you listen to.

Anti-GM activist Vandana Shiva points out that farmers traditionally recycled their seeds or traded them between each other. The introduction of the new Bt seeds meant that 'seed which had been the farmers' common resource became the "intellectual property" of Monsanto'. So 'a renewable resource became a non-renewable, patented commodity'.

The new seeds were also more expensive, so, increasingly, farmers had to take on more debt to pay for them. On top of that, cotton crops, which had once been widely grown alongside food crops, 'now had to be grown as a monoculture, with higher vulnerability to pests, disease, drought and crop failure'.[24]

Those who oppose GM seeds in general fret about containment; they fear that the new Frankenplants will drift, spurring resistant 'super weeds', and stuffing up the entire ecosystem. But the big news story of 2008 was the Prince of Wales speaking by video to a conference in Dehli on the 'the truly appalling and tragic rate of small farmer suicides in India, stemming from the failure of many GM crop varieties'.

Was Bt cotton really causing farmers to take their own lives?

◉

It was Shiva who dubbed Maharashtra India's 'suicide belt', insisting that, 'Farmers are dying because Monsanto is making profits – by owning life that it never created but it pretends to create.' In 2014, she told the *New Yorker*'s Michael Specter that, '284,000 Indian farmers have killed themselves because they cannot afford to plant Bt cotton'.[25]

Talk of a 'seed dictatorship' is one thing – while it's emotive, the global agri-giants clearly do monopolise the Indian market – but Shiva also likens fertilisers to 'a weapon of mass destruction' and maintains that any messing with God's order of nature is unacceptable, despite global pressure to feed rising populations.

An independent report by the International Food Policy Research Institute (IFPRI) came out in 2008, citing significant average yield increases and a 40 per cent decrease in pesticide use as a result of Bt cotton crops. The report said it was 'simply wrong' to blame Bt cotton for farmer suicides: 'Despite the recent media hype ... there is no evidence in available data of a "resurgence" of farmer suicide in India in the last five years.'[26]

By 2014, when Specter interviews Shiva, seven million Indian farmers had planted Bt cotton, covering 90 per cent of the country's cotton fields. Things seem to be going pretty well, he decides. The suicide numbers only appear extreme because of the sheer numbers of people, and farmers, in India. In fact, the percentage of Indian farmers who kill themselves is no higher than it is for the French.

'At first, the new seeds were extremely expensive,' concedes Specter. 'Counterfeiters flooded the market with fakes and sold them, as well as fake glyphosate, at reduced prices. The crops failed, and many people suffered.' Dismissing Shiva's claim that since its commercial introduction in 2002, the price of Bt cottonseed had risen by '8,000 per cent' – a figure also quoted by Alexis Baden-Mayer, political director of the (US) Organic Consumers Association, in the documentary 100% Cotton: Made in India – Specter writes: 'In fact, the prices, which are regulated by the government, have fallen steadily. While they remain higher than those of conventional seeds, in most cases the modified seeds provide greater benefits.'

According to the IFPRI, while farmers spend more on the seed (about 15 per cent more) they spend much less on pesticides (about

50 per cent less). And they are still able to save and re-use their seed, argues Specter – it's just that most don't want to.

Specter visits Maharashtra, where farmers tell him they are healthier because they have to spray less. One says Bt cotton has turned his life around: 'Without it, we would have no crops. Nothing.'

But in *100% Cotton*, filmmakers Inge Altemeier and Reinhard Hornung visit farming families too, this time in Warangal, where they hear that expensive seeds unsuitable for low-water areas such as this lead to spiralling debt. One widow recounts how, 'People hear the banks are coming and they commit suicide out of fear'.

Monsanto acknowledges Indian farmers face 'hopelessness' but says it is 'lack of irrigation facilities, unavailability of timely credit and fluctuating cotton prices' that cause despair. Monsanto? They're the good guys – with Bt cotton resulting in better health, education, and nutrition among farming families.

Maybe farmers aren't killing themselves just because of Bt cotton, or any cotton, but they are killing themselves. There's evidence of official underreporting. In April 2015, the Maharashtra state government was in the news for admitting three famers suicided when bad weather ruined crops; the true figure, according to State Congress chief Ashok Chavan was 'about 1200' over just a few weeks. Revenue Minister Eknath Khadse countered that while a total of 601 farmers had officially committed suicide since the start of the year, only three deaths were due to damage caused by unseasonal rains. If only the weather was all they had to worry about.

In March 2015, the WHO released a report on the carcinogenicity of organophosphate pesticides previously thought to pose little or no risk to humans, linking glyphosate to non-Hodgkin lymphoma. Hamnett was right again.

Is there a better way?

Catarina Midby is talking me through the new H&M Conscious collection, holding up a pleated skirt made from vegetable tanned leather. 'The leather comes from a Swedish farm that raises cattle for organic meat,' she explains.[27] Next is a silky dress of blush Flamenco ruffles; Penelope Cruz wore a black version to the Vanity Fair Oscars party. 'This is recycled polyester,' she says.

Midby is an elegant blonde, who started out as a fashion journalist, and once worked at Swedish *Elle*. She says sustainability is 'one of H&M's most important values. We don't see it as separate to the rest of what we do.' Push her as to why, and she talks about the company values set by CEO Karl-Johan Persson, who in 2012 met with the prime minister of Bangladesh to lobby for an increased minimum wage. She says it's probably cultural, too. 'In Sweden we have this idea that nature belongs to everyone, which it literally does; I mean, you can camp anywhere. We are taught in school that it is our responsibility to take care of nature.'

The first Social Progress Index (2013), which judges countries by 'social and environmental measures that underlie wellbeing and opportunity' rather than GDP, ranked Sweden at number one. Although inequality is on the rise in Sweden, there is truth behind the cliché of a progressive nation where eco-aware fairness, social services and free camping are highly prized. They are big on recycling and renewable energy resources; only 1 per cent of solid waste goes into landfill in Sweden. And they are innovators – the Swedes invented Skype.

◉

There's some archival stuff in the H&M showroom, standout pieces from Conscious collections past. 'This was 2009, the first time we used hemp,' says Midby. 'And this one,' she holds up a multi-coloured dress, 'we had waste offcuts from our collaboration with Lanvin, so we made them into patchwork. In hindsight, it probably wasn't so great – too expensive, because it took a lot of work to sew, but the fabric was so nice, we had to try.'

I ask her how much difference this sort of thing can really make. Livia Firth, for example, maintains that fast fashion is simply incompatible with sustainability: 'It is admirable that H&M is doing so much work in sustainability, but all these brands – H&M, Zara, whatever – they are still producing in such volumes and at such ridiculous prices.'[28] And Shannon Whitehead, a consultant who works with sustainable fashion startups in the US, wrote on the *Huffington Post* of her personal experience asking for H&M Conscious in-store, and being met with 'a blank stare' from a sales assistant who clearly had no idea what she was on about.[29] That's happened to me too, although you can find shop assistants everywhere who don't know much about the product they sell. But what about the ratio between Conscious collection pieces and the rest? As Whitehead points out, H&M produces close to 600 million garments a year, just a small fraction of them from the eco line. Is it not just a marketing ploy?

'No,' says Midby emphatically. 'I really don't think so. Of course we can't make huge amounts of these collections; they are experimental for us. But using these fabrics is a way of starting the process. They trickle down into the main collections. In 2007 we did the first organic cotton pieces, back then that was very exclusive and surprising, but now we use organic cotton across the board.'

In 2014, H&M was the largest user of organic cotton in the world, and 21 per cent of their garments used either organic cotton, recycled or Better Cotton. They are aiming for 100 per cent by 2020.

Greenpeace publishes a Greenwashers list of fashion brands that talk the sustainability talk but have so far failed to deliver on promises to eliminate hazardous chemicals from their supply chains – Nike, for example, 'has made little progress,' they say, 'despite its fashion forward claims'.

Greenpeace also lists Detox Leaders. That's the list H&M is on. Says Greenpeace, 'H&M's action on toxic free fashion puts it firmly ahead of the pack.' This list also includes Inditex, Levi's, G-Star RAW, Burberry and Valentino.

There's a Detox Losers list too, which includes Hermès – a surprise to me. Greenpeace says Hermès, 'needs to come clean about its toxic supply chain and make a credible, individual Detox commitment,' after hormone-disrupting NPEs were found in Hermès baby booties.[30]

'It's hard to shift perceptions,' says Midby. 'Most people think lower price equals poorly made under bad working conditions. But over time things change. Of course our aim is to sell our collections. We would never say we don't want to be commercial because that would not be sustainable. We need to make a profit otherwise we wouldn't be where we are today.' H&M 'invests a lot in sustainability. We have been innovating in this space since the '90s.'

Along with IKEA, and Hamnett's bugbear Gap (on Greenpeace's Detox Losers list), H&M was one of the first brands to support the Better Cotton Initiative in 2005, in partnership with PAN UK, among others.

Says Midby, 'The idea was to try and do something about the [cotton] industry, because we know the use of chemicals is a problem, that it's not healthy to handle them, that it's expensive to buy them and that they contaminate local water systems.'

The Better Cotton Standard, run by a multi-stakeholder, not-for-profit association, requires growers to hit certain benchmarks. It trains farmers in things like drip feed and alternative furrow irrigation to reduce water use; the importance of protective clothing; and planting crops like corn and sunflowers that lure pests away. Midby says Better Cotton is grown with 'up to 70 per cent less chemicals, and up to 40 per cent less water. It's about using simple methods, so it could be that you plant crops that bloom earlier than the cotton flowers in between the rows of cotton plants so that the bugs favour these. Or you learn how to water from underneath.'

Until the end of 2015, Better Cotton did not allow for garment labelling, because the fibre is often mixed in with conventional cotton. That, they say, helps to keep costs low and maximise Better Cotton's introduction. Officially, they are 'neutral' on genetically modified Bt cotton and 'neither encourage farmers to grow it, nor seek to restrict their access to it'.

'Sustainability is complicated,' says Midby, 'and it can be difficult, but I firmly believe it will become normal. I tell my son that when I started working in magazines we had electric typewriters and he can't believe it. My grandchildren will smile at the idea of special collections for sustainability.'

CHAPTER 14

Dyeing Shame

Weekend rebels and the devil denim

There is surely no garment so iconic and yet so humdrum as the
denim jean. In 2007, British anthropologists Daniel Miller and Sophie
Woodward were investigating the culture of denim, inspired by the
idea that jeans have 'become the default choice' when we can't think
what to wear.

'We regard denim as an example of the "blindingly obvious"', said
the pair, 'something so taken for granted we fail to appreciate the fact
that one particular textile should come to dominate the world, when
there are so many other choices.'[1]

They travelled a lot while researching their book *Blue Jeans: The
Art of the Ordinary*, and got in the habit of totting up how many out
of the first 100 people they saw in any new city were wearing jeans.
The answer was usually at least half. They figure the average person
wears jeans for three-and-a-half days a week.

Historically, jeans were workwear, born either in the French city
of Nîmes, as hardy cotton drill pants popular with sailors, or in Italy,
as the working man's trouser choice. Did thrifty tailors order Genoa

cloth, which morphed into Genes, then jeans? Seventeenth-century paintings by an anonymous artist seem to prove the Italian theory, depicting peasants in blue trousers painted in indigo ink.

Whatever the truth, in 1873 it was Levi Strauss and Jacob Davis who began making men's workpants out of similar stuff in America. Like so many fashion revolutionaries who followed them, they were both Jewish immigrants from Europe: one a shopkeeper, one a tailor. They used natural indigo dye and reinforced their pockets with copper rivets to boost durability – cowboys loved their jeans, farmers and goldrushers too.

The HD Lee Mercantile Company was established in 1889. Henry Lee made overalls and jackets before jeans, but he was first to introduce the zip fly in the 1920s. Wrangler showed up in 1947. Levi's, Lee and Wrangler became the big three household names in American denim.

In the 1950s, rebellious teenagers adopted jeans as badges of outsider status, helped by Hollywood. John Wayne and Clint Eastwood wore denim; Elvis liked it; James Dean's was almost its own character in *Rebel Without a Cause*; Marlon Brando wore his with a leather jacket in *The Wild One*.

Over in Japan, kids saw these legends as personifying an idea of cool Americana style, and they wanted in. A few entrepreneurs imported American jeans, but others worked out they could use existing old Japanese textile looms, designed by the company that would become Toyota, to weave similar fabric – and make their own. This was the first Japanese selvedge denim.

Jeans soon became the youth culture uniform, and fashionistas clocked the significance. Diana Vreeland proclaimed blue jeans 'the most beautiful things since the gondola'; Yves Saint Laurent wished he'd invented them; Andy Warhol wanted to die in his.

Levi Strauss & Co. began advising customers to shrink their jeans to fit (by wearing them in a hot bath) in the '6os. And don't wash them at all until absolutely necessary, they said. Fast-forward to 2014 and Levi's CEO, Chip Bergh, a neat-looking baby boomer, admitted he hadn't washed his 501s in a year.

Genuine rebels wore their jeans until they developed a very personal patina of decay; you worked them hard, you wore them out. Californian surfers' jeans aged especially well thanks to sun and salt, while the '70s punks had it down – fight in them, pour bleach over them.

But come the '80s, with denim jeans *de rigueur* among all ages and sections of society, who had the time, or the inclination, to wear them in? If only you could buy your new denim pre-aged, like fine wine (or blue cheese). What? You can?

In the noughties, Jason Denham was the self-professed 'denim doctor' of Europe. 'I used to go into big companies and solve their denim problems,' he says.[2] He now helms his own brand, Denham the Jeanmaker, out of Amsterdam. I meet him one afternoon in one of his super-cool stores, and ask him for a lesson in the 'premium denim' pioneers. And how come a pair of artificially worn jeans can cost hundreds of dollars today? Exactly what do they do to them?

He shows me a book he put together to celebrate the fifth anniversary of his own line. 'I wrote letters to the people in the industry who have most inspired me,' he explains. 'I'm lucky I've got to know some of the greats'. Renzo Rosso, for example, who founded Diesel in Veneto in 1978 with a loan from his former boss Adriano Gold-schmied. Today Rosso's OTB Group controls high-end fashion houses Maison Margiela, Viktor & Rolf and Marni.

'Adriano Goldschmied – he's the guy behind Diesel and Replay,' says Denham. 'We have his company, The Genius Group, to thank

for the European denim revolution – before that, at the end of the
'70s, it was almost all American.'

The Italians built on Calvin Klein's idea of designer denim, and
bumped up prices while they were at it, developing new washes and
finishes. Thanks to them brands like Versace put denim on the runway. For US *Vogue*'s November 1988 cover, Anna Wintour's first as
editor, a model wore a $10,000 bejewelled couture jacket by Chris-
tian Lacroix with a pair of stonewashed Guess jeans. Denim wasn't
workwear anymore – it was serious fashion. 'The Italians started that
whole thing, but also in the '80s there was a surge from France, led
by François Girbaud,' says Denham.

He tells me about a conference in Europe where he and Gold-
schmied, Rosso and Girbaud spoke on a panel together. 'We were
talking about the future of the industry. Have you met Girbaud? He's
fucking mad, and he sat there, and he went, "It is all my fault! I killed
the fucking planet." He's the one who got the cement mixer at the end
of the '60s, threw in a pair of jeans and some pumice stones, and
that's why we've wasted so much water in the washing of jeans.'

Killer jeans

François Girbaud and his wife Marithé felt like rebels when they first
aged denim with rocks. 'We'd tried everything ... and found that
stones and water worked, what could be more natural?' he told the
website Denim Freaks.[3] 'Little did we know that we had innocently
started an inexorable process of destruction. We invented an industrialised stonewash, which no one else had ever done, but with it we
also created ... an industry that polluted every river on the planet.'

Multiple washing cycles removed solvents and chemicals from
the fabric's previous processing, and because almost no laundries had
wastewater pre-treatment systems before the 2010s, sent them down

the drain. The contaminated pumice sludge was left behind. This wasn't what the spirit of denim, or the Paris-based company Marithé + François Girbaud, was about.

The next trend was snow-wash, or acid-wash, which involves adding a bleaching agent such as potassium permanganate to the pumice stones. When the Berlin Wall fell, said Girbaud, and he saw 'hordes of communists [who] thought that jeans were *supposed* to have that shameful [snow-wash] colour ... It really shook us up.' He began to speak out, and soon there was a rift with his US licensing partners. In 1996, VF Corporation (owners of Lee and Wrangler) and Marithé + François Girbaud parted ways. 'I had offended the huge machine, I had overstepped the limits of the politically correct, but I refused to use the snow-wash like everyone else,' said Girbaud. 'I felt that we had contributed to a huge mistake and I didn't want to make jeans like that anymore.'

◉

Un-dyed denim is putty-coloured. They call it griege. Indigo or a synthetic equivalent will turn it blue. Washing it with lots of little volcanic rocks causes abrasion, which scuffs back the dyed surface of the fabric to fade it. Stonewashed denim is washed up to ten times; a water-intensive process for a product that is already far too thirsty. Until fairly recent recycling breakthroughs, denim laundries accessed their water by turning on the tap. In the 1980s and '90s, when the American industry was concentrated around El Paso in Texas, most garment-finishers used drinking-quality water from the city's municipal supply.

Girbaud is the only person I know of who's willing to shoulder blame for some of this, but the El Paso–based chemical engineer Claude Blankiet is also credited with inventing stonewash (these days he's a winemaker). Levi's reckon a guy called Donald Freeland was doing it in the '50s. Maybe, but there was barely any stonewash for sale in the US in 1981 when the four Marciano brothers ditched Marseille for LA, and began marketing it under their brand, Guess. By the end of the decade stonewash was the norm.

As both water and labour became more expensive in the 2000s, the big brands headed offshore. It is surely no coincidence that this was also when sandblasting took off, in places where occupational health and safety laws were laxer. I'm talking about firing abrasive sand at denim, to give it a worn look. There are mechanical booths for this, although the Clean Clothes Campaign (CCC) reckons these are often operated in unsealed areas.[4] The cheapest way to sandblast is to attach a hose to an air gun and pay some worker to fire it. It's cheaper again if you don't buy him protective gear.

In 2009, Turkey, then one of the biggest jeans exporters, banned manual sandblasting because of links to lung disease. Official figures showed forty-six Turkish denim workers had died of silicosis, and an estimated 5000 more were at risk. Alas the ban simply sent sandblasting elsewhere.

In Bangladesh, workers were found to be blasting away with just a cloth to cover their mouths. Some of them were shoeless. Bangladesh is now the second-biggest global denim producer; in first place, as usual, is China, but new territories are opening up all the time. Lesotho calls itself 'the jeans capital of Africa'. In Ethiopia the Indian-owned Kanoria Africa Textiles factory has the capacity to produce twelve million metres of denim annually out of Addis Ababa. And the industry is booming in Brazil.

In 2010, the CCC's 'Killer Jeans' campaign prompted sandblasting bans from some brands (Levi's, H&M, Versace, Gucci), the promise of action from others (Diesel, Inditex) and a big list of brands that declined to implement bans but claimed none of their suppliers did the bad thing (*it's not me, guv*). But subsequent reports showed reform was 'patchy', and that 'sandblasting units are still open in most factories', often at night to avoid the auditors. 'Almost half of the 200 million pairs of jeans exported from Bangladesh each year are sandblasted,' said the CCC in 2012.

Silicosis isn't the only health concern. As one Chinese factory supervisor quoted in the CCC report told investigators, 'Danger lurks in every stage of the denim treatment process.'

Your distressed jeans likely enjoyed a dousing with caustic chemicals and bleaches. Factories are often hot and poorly ventilated, and workers who remove their masks to beat the heat inhale microfibres and chemical dust.

In the good factories, workers spraying potassium permanganate wear vapour masks, rubber boots and aprons, and work in sealed areas. However, a third of workers interviewed by the CCC and labour groups for the 2013 report *Breathless for Blue Jeans: Health hazards in China's denim factories*, took their masks off whenever they got the chance – and 'many night shift workers take advantage of the more relaxed conditions to wear the more comfortable but less safe surgical masks'.[5] Many had 'no idea what kind of hazardous chemicals they were being exposed to', referring to them as 'magic water', 'white paste' and 'soft oil'.

One way to avoid all this is to return to the authentic 'distressing' that happens through real-life wear and tear. Ethical Swedish brand Nudie, a Fair Wear member committed to organic cotton, is pushing what they call Dry Denim – unwashed, fade it yourself. 'For some it's a hassle or the reason why their couch [turns] shades of blue,' they say. 'For others and ourselves it's the essence of denim and wearing jeans.'

The Spanish company Jeanologia distresses with lasers. They've worked with Levi's, H&M and Uniqlo and, in 2011, partnered with the Girbauds to create Wattwash, a 'clean' denim finishing process, using 70 per cent less water. Now consumers just need to catch up. In 2012, after forty years in business, Marithé + François Girbaud went bankrupt.

Cry me a river

'Most people have jeans in their closets, but they don't realise they're sending some river blue in China,' says Kelly Slater.[6] When we talk he is about to debut Outerknown, his Kering-backed 'coastal lifestyle label', designed by John Moore. It's no exaggeration to call Slater a hero – he is one of the greatest surfers the world has ever known. As of 2015, he's been crowned world champion a record eleven times, five of them in consecutive years. He is both the oldest and the youngest surfer to win a world title. He once dated model Gisele Bündchen, and his current partner, Kalani Miller, is a swimwear designer, but he concedes he has had to teach himself about the fashion system.

'Most of the money I've made has been from a clothing sponsor, and to be honest I didn't really know much about the whole process [of making clothes],' he tells me. Its impacts are out of sight, 'because production happens in China or Thailand or Taiwan, somewhere we aren't physically ... we're not privy to most of that information.'

For twenty-four years that clothing sponsor was Quiksilver. When they cut ties in 2014, Slater said there was 'nothing bad involved' in the decision, 'just certain circumstances happened that wouldn't allow for two things to be in the one area.'[7] He had his own fashion ambitions now, and he was excited that Outerknown was joining the Kering stable: 'They share my values,' he said.

John Moore, a former VP of mass-market streetwear brand Mossimo, is also ex-Quiksilver – he once designed their womenswear and Roxy Denim lines. But Outerknown, says Slater, is different. It's 'a brand that combines my love of clean living, responsibility and style', produced as ethically and sustainably as possible. They're working with Bluesign to avoid harmful chemicals in their supply chain, all their cotton is organic, and, for now at least, they have elected not to make blue jeans. 'I'm happy to not use denim at all until we can do it in a way that we feel is responsible,' says Slater.[8]

Is denim really turning rivers blue? I ask the expert Mark Angelo. 'Oh sure,' he says, 'that is absolutely true. A lot of the jeans producers in China, Bangladesh, India and Mexico release their dyes directly into the rivers. The wastewater doesn't go through any kind of treatment plant, so it's not just the colour that is coming out into the water, it's the bleaches and chlorines, and the heavy metals, things like mercury, cadmium, lead, copper.'[9]

Angelo has seen it first hand, and in some cases paddled through it in his canoe. No one knows rivers like Angelo, a conservationist guru and Canadian national treasure who has made it his life's work to explore and protect the world's rivers. He spent three years checking their health with cameras in tow for the 2016 documentary *River Blue*, which exposes some of the travesties wrought by fashion manufacturing on what Angelo calls 'the arteries of our planet, life-lines in the truest sense'.

Pollution stems not just from jeans and leather, he says, but textiles in general. 'In a number of places you can literally tell what trendy colours will be in fashion next season by the colour the streams are running.'

The Citarum River in Java is so filled with trash in places you can't see its colour at all. Local fishermen now catch garbage, which they sort and sell for recycling, and hundreds of textiles factories along the river's banks use it as a free dump. In 2014, one worker told a British journalist that his employers wait until nightfall to release poisoned wastewater into the river, which is the only source of water in his village. He wears gloves in the factory, he said, because the chemicals are dangerous, but then he goes home to bathe in that very same water. 'I am conflicted, but I need to eat so I have to work there.'[10]

Indonesia has tightened laws regulating industrial waste in recent years, but they are clearly not being properly enforced. It is up to the brands to do more. In 2013, Greenpeace exposed Gap as one of the companies then working with suppliers proven to pollute the Citarum.[11]

'The Citarum is disturbing,' says Angelo. 'Like the Buriganga in Bangladesh and the Pearl in China, it is in dire straits. But we should never give up on any river. When I first paddled the Thames [in southern England] forty-five years ago it was biologically dead. Now it has sprung back to life. If we make the right choices a river can heal.'

China's 'Jeans Town', Xintang, lies on the Dong River, one of the main tributaries of the Pearl. Official figures from 2008 show it produces around 260 million pairs of jeans a year, accounting for 60 per cent of China's total jeans production. It's safe to say the numbers have now increased. If there is denim in your wardrobe, there's a good chance it was made here.

The first laundries opened in the '80s, around the village of Dadun. By the late 2000s there were more than 3000 denim factories squashed into the small area. Pollution got so bad the government intervened, and much of the industry was relocated to the adjacent Xizhou village. What do you think happened then? Xizhou now faces the same problems as Dadun. The river runs blue. The dust in the streets is blue. When it rains, the puddles are blue too. The air stinks.

One local resident told Greenpeace that, 'every morning, at 4am when the waters recede, the odour is so nauseatingly foul that it nearly makes people vomit', while others reported fertility and respiratory problems, streaming eyes, itching skin.[12] Greenpeace investigators found high levels of lead and copper polluting the riverbed, with known carcinogen cadmium at levels 128 times the legal limit. No wonder the fish are dead.

'Over the past couple of decades I've seen many examples of this sort of thing, when travelling extensively in China, Mexico, India, Indonesia,' says Angelo. 'It always bothered me that the impacts related to textile production tended to fly under the radar. I've been involved in a lot of different river conservation battles related to things like dams, or pollution from sewage, mining or salination, or issues around the excessive extraction of water. Those issues have received a lot of notoriety, yet textile pollution is just as serious, and consumers hold the power to put it to a stop.'

We must hold brands to account, says Angelo. 'We need to think about the consequences of our actions. When we shop it's so important to think about how the products we choose impact on our global environment, which our children will inherit, and to think about public health in manufacturing countries. Everything is connected. As an example, toxins from Asian textile mills are now showing up in North American polar bears. Rivers flow into oceans. I feel so strongly that no one has the right to destroy a river. And when it comes to the fashion industry there is no excuse for it, we can do better.'

Does he still wear jeans? 'Of course.' He hopes to see wider use of cleaner technologies, and praises Jeanologia, Nudie, Tortoise and

Naked & Famous Denim. The last is a Canadian 'no wash' brand that uses only raw Japanese selvedge denim.

It's not just the Thames that can turn around. VF Corporation has lifted its environmental game – it uses Better Cotton, and, in partnership with universities, has developed the CHEM-IQ system to remove the most harmful chemicals from its supply chain.

Levi's is getting there, albeit in a zigzag fashion. I wish they'd try harder with organic cotton. They introduced organic jeans in 2006, indigo dyed and finished with starch, with buttons made from coconut shells and non-galvanised metal, but they are no longer available. Presumably we did not buy them in sufficient quantities.

After a Greenpeace *Toxic Threads* report exposed Levi's for continuing to pollute Mexico's rivers, despite earlier assurances of a clean-up, they heeded calls to detox in 2013 (they now star on Greenpeace's Detox Leaders list).[13] Their 'Water<Less' technology reduces water use in production through things like dry stonewashing, and combining multiple wet-washing processes into a single one. Around a quarter of Levi's denim is now Water<Less and they're aiming for 80 per cent by 2020.

'Tortoise is my favourite,' says Angelo. 'With something they call Wiser Wash, they use a very small amount of regenerated water, and all their wash agents are all natural and biodegradable. They use organic pigments, and no potassium permanganate, bleach or formaldehyde. This is the way of the future. Our film is not anti-jeans,' he says of *River Blue*. 'It's about changing the way they are made.'

CHAPTER 15

Slippery Customers

Go in peace

Lucy Tammam's shop is tucked away behind London's St Pancras Station, a lone fashion outpost among the office blocks and Edwardian apartment buildings. Tammam sells beautiful made-to-order wedding dresses. Her prices are similar to those of ready-to-wear garments sold by fellow Saint Martins alumni. Mary Katrantzou was in her year. Christopher Kane in the one above. So how come Tammam is holed up on a Bloomsbury backstreet, rather than glossy Mayfair, with Kane? How come her gear is not stocked in Liberty or Selfridges like Katrantzou's? 'I suppose what I do is quite niche,' she says.[1]

Tammam makes vegan wedding dresses. I know. When I first heard of them, from the animal rights campaigner Alicia Silverstone (she played Cher in *Clueless*), I thought the same. So what? So Tammam's gowns aren't trimmed in fur? Or cut from white leather or ivory wool crepe? You could say the same for London's more famous big day designers Jenny Packham or Alice Temperley. Or most of the gowns in the Victoria and Albert Museum's exhibition *Wedding Dresses, 1775–2014*, which I saw before I visited Tammam in autumn 2014.

Behind glass at the V&A were Gwen Stefani's pink-and-white dream dress by John Galliano, and Kate Moss's gown, also Galliano, inspired by *The Great Gatsby* and shimmering with 390,000 golden sequins. They, along with the 2,800 pearls on Moss's gown and lace 'Juliet cap' veil, took months to apply by hand; artisans spent 701 hours embroidering the dress, 253 more on the veil – but no puppies were harmed in the process. Short of finding genuine whalebones in Stefani's corsetry I couldn't think what about either of these outfits could possibly offend a vego.

'The silk,' says Tammam. 'Moths are boiled alive to make it.'

Silk is obtained from the cocoons of the domesticated silk moth, the *Bombyx mori*. Domesticated because it no longer exists in the wild. Silk farmers harvest the moth's eggs, and over a six-week period the larvae munch around 50,000 times their initial weight in mulberry leaves. Once properly fat, the worms spin cocoons to form a sort of sleeping bag, then begin the process of turning into moths.

In the wild they'd have broken free when they were ready, but the farmed moths must be prevented from damaging or soiling the cocoons, so the silkmakers kill the pupae with heat – they either boil or bake them. The undamaged cocoon can now be unraveled by machine to leave a continuous filament ready for spinning – and a dead worm. Mind you, those worms are rarely wasted. In China and Vietnam, they're roasted or fried to make a crispy treat. Koreans prefer their pupae boiled or steamed – the dish is called *Beondegi*, and it's a popular street food.

Silk producers separate off about 10 per cent of the moths to preserve for breeding, explains Tammam. 'These moths are allowed to emerge naturally, their empty cocoons can be processed and that's Ahimsa silk.' *Ahimsa*, she adds, means 'peace' in Hindi – Gandhi was a fan.

'But Ahimsa is still part of an industry which kills 90 per cent of the moths,' says Tammam, who was determined to find an entirely cruelty-free option. Enter Eri silk. 'The Eri moth naturally creates a cocoon that never completely closes,' she says. 'They emerge without breaking it – it's amazing.'

Most Eri silk in India is cultivated in the northeast, and some of the finest in Assam. The fibre, long appreciated by Buddhists and Jains for its non-violent origins, tends to be more 'cotton-like' or woolly than regular silk; some call it 'poor man's silk'.

'The cocoons are processed in a slightly different way,' says Tammam, 'treated more like a wool process. They kind of card it and brush it out, but they can spin it very finely to create beautiful fabric.'

How often, when Tammam explains all this, do people say, 'But it's just an insect?'

She sighs. Quite a lot then, eh? 'It's not just about the moth. It's about respect for the whole ecosystem. Anyway it depends on your point of view: to the moth, we're just humans.'

Sorry, but I don't believe they are thinking about us. 'Moths aren't thinking at all – at least not in the way that we understand the word,' I say.

'But how do we *know*?' says Tammam.

'Because moths don't use their brains the way we do.'

'We will never truly know without *being* a moth.'

I say I don't fancy being a moth, not least because they only live for two weeks, even if they don't end up as Beondegi.

Tammam says, 'If something came along and tried to kill all the humans to make clothes, we'd get pissed off, wouldn't we? It's not our place to say "You're just a moth," to rank life, to make that sort of distinction. We need to care about the entire ecosystem down to the smallest thing, including the moths and the less appealing creatures, the slugs and the snails. Everything exists for a reason.'

Tammam comes from rag-trade stock. Her grandfather was a tailor, her uncle owned a kidswear company. She was a vegetarian child. 'I did the Lisa Simpson thing: animals have personalities. I became a real eco-warrior as a teenager, I used to lobby outside McDonald's and hand out leaflets.' Indeed she looks quite the revolutionary today in all black: a beatnik vintage dress, tights and long rubber boots, a knit beret on the back of her head. Surely that's not wool? 'Synthetic,' she says. 'It's a bit pilled to be honest. I've had it for years.'

After college she started a sustainable fashion label called Tam & Rob, with her school friend Lucy Robinson. 'People are starting to use fashion as a platform to introduce political ideas to a wider audience now, but back then they weren't. Apart from People Tree, it felt like an empty space,' says Tammam.

It is impossible to write a book about ethical fashion without mentioning the UK-based ethical fashion brand People Tree. Founded by Safia Minney in the '90s, it's approach is similar to Maiyet's in that it designs 'up' from a base of artisan skill, although a People Tree organic cotton dress costs around £80, proving ethical can also be affordable. Minney's company keeps more than 7,000 people in work, and she has dragged collab culture into the eco-age, working with designers such as Orla Kiely and Zandra Rhodes.

Like Minney, Tammam worked with Fair Trade cooperatives in India – she spent a couple of years living in Bangalore. But it was a slog. After a few boutiques didn't pay their wholesale accounts, Tam & Rob folded. Tammam thinks it was ahead of its time. 'You have to be patient,' she says, 'hard for me because I'm a very impatient sort of a person. I was teased at uni for wanting to do this sustainable stuff. I remember saying, "It's really important we look at recyclable materials. We can do all this!" And the attitude was, "Yeah right, that's never going to catch on."

'I bumped into my course director Willie Walters a couple of years ago, and she said, "Lucy! I remember you. You were into sustainability – we're all about that now."' Today, Saint Martins offers entire courses on ethical fashion while the London College of Fashion's Centre for Sustainable Fashion has partnered with Kering. Students now have access to sustainable fashion awards, targeted curriculums, and, more importantly, jobs in the field when they graduate. Things have really changed on the education front.

Tammam shrugs; she likes to be an outlier. 'If everyone was doing it I would have found something else to be fussing about with. Obviously it would have been sustainable because that's intrinsic to me, but maybe it wouldn't have been fashion. I'd have found some other cause to fight.'

When friends asked Tammam to make them ethical wedding dresses she saw a business opportunity, although it's not easy money. 'People who are eco tend not to have huge budgets, they tend to be charity or NGO workers and want to spend 500 quid not six grand,' she says. And not everyone understands her passion for Eri silk.

'People will say, "No, no you don't want your silk from India! The best silk comes from China," but India is what I know.' Tammam visits often to work with the silk mills, embroiderers and beaders. 'I can check everything there. It's about more than just having a certificate; I have seen and trust the process. I can tell you the whole story. And it's fact, not fiction.'

Shanghai surprise

It's only recently that China has become a byword for cheap. In ancient times, it was a centre for near-unimaginable luxury. The

Chinese were the first to hit on the idea that the *Bombyx mori* existed to spin silk so that we might weave it into a cloth of the utmost opulence. Legend attributes this discovery to Xi Ling, the teenaged wife of the Yellow Emperor in the twenty-seventh century BC. Story goes that Xi Ling was in the palace gardens one day when a cocoon tumbled off a mulberry tree into her scalding hot tea. She poked it with her chopstick and it began to unravel, revealing itself to be damn good stuff for making posh frocks out of. By the first century BC the products of Chinese cocoon farming, known as sericulture, had reached the Mediterranean, and silk was traded as a luxury like gold.

The Romans thought silk grew on trees in the mysterious East – as Virgil remarked, 'What filmy fleeces from leaves the Serians cull?' – but prized it all the same for its grandeur. Not everyone was impressed with its clingy qualities. Seneca linked silk dresses with depravity, and whinged about contemporary fashionistas slutting about in their gossamer finery: 'Wretched flocks of maids labour so that the adulteress may be visible through her thin dress, so that her husband has no more acquaintance than any outsider or foreigner with his wife's body.'

Another tall tale has it that silk found its way into India after a Chinese princess smuggled cocoons into Central Asia inside her wig. For 3000 years sericulture's secrets were closely guarded; travellers were searched at boarder crossings and egg smugglers executed. The only way Westerners could get their paws on the slippery stuff was to pay top dollar to the traders who lugged it over the Silk Route, that ancient series of roads, tracks and river crossings which runs from Eastern China to the Med.

Silk production spread to Japan in the third century, and to the Byzantine Empire in the fifth. Europe had to wait until the Crusades to grow their own, when the Norman king Roger of Sicily invaded Thebes and shifted the local silk crops, and the workers, in a job lot to Palermo. So that's why the Italians are into their silk. The Popes, of course, were fans. Later, centres of weaving excellence were established in Lyons, so the French kings could dress the part too.

Wherever it wandered, silk was exclusive, pricey stuff. And when something's rare and expensive, there's always someone looking to get it – or something that might pass for it – on the cheap.

CHAPTER 16

Weird Science

They're coming to take you away, ha-haaa!

Fashion isn't the most obvious harbour for maths and science fans (although Hussein Chalayan once put animatronic dresses on his runway). Architecture, okay – Coco Chanel noted the parallels there when she said '[fashion] is a matter of proportions' – but physics, chemistry, biology … bacteria? Nah. Fashion people are famously right-brained: instinctive and visual, they deal in art, emotion and desire, inhabiting a parallel universe which the writer, former window-dresser and current impressive creative person at Barneys NY, Simon Doonan calls 'The Asylum'.[1] Fashion is not about laws and equations. It cannot be expressed in pie chart form.

You only have to look at its pet superlatives, it's all *sublime*, *divine*, *beyond*. It's about nonsense and poetry, air kissing and 'darhhhhling!' Confounding, inexplicable, profoundly unscientific, fashion is the place from which Doonan can say things like: 'Do not even think of leaving the house this season unless you are wearing a puce-coloured leotard and a scalloped zebra cape!' and get away with it, because he's parodying Diana Vreeland's 'Why Don't You?' columns from *Harper's Bazaar*, obvs.

Vreeland, the inimitable editor who went on to revolutionise the Costume Institute at the Met, was actually quite keen on science, at least the idea of it. In the 1960s, she commissioned a photoshoot of an eyelift operation for *Vogue*. It caused a lot of fuss, which she couldn't understand – she thought the 'pictures were *marvellous*' – anyway 'most of what looked like blood was Mercurochrome, because it's a special operation where the knife almost heals the blood flow'.[2] Then again, Vreeland's favourite phrase was 'I'm mad about ...'

Fashion's nebulous specialness, its sense of itself as a world apart – and yes, sometimes above – is one of the reasons it's so hard to start impactful conversations about sustainability and ethics inside it. While writing this book I've had many discussions about supply chains and the environment, some inspiring, some depressing, some, as you have seen, with international human-rights-lawyers-turned-luxury-sector-CEOs, but very few with creatives raised in fashion's inner circle.

As Stella McCartney puts it: 'It seems to me that fashion is the last industry on the planet to address ethics ... Sometimes you get the idea that all these designers are up on their high horses looking down on mere mortals, saying, "Fuck it, it's fur, it's beautiful darling!" Those people are out of touch.'[3]

There are exceptions – anyone sitting at the EFI table, as McCartney does for example, or Bruno Pieters or Livia Firth – but in general the sorts of people talking about these issues tend to be on the outside looking in, or on the outside looking somewhere else entirely, as many of the game-changers in the outdoorwear industry are.

Sustainability campaigners tend to think fashion is crazy town – I've heard many a well-meaning eco activist open a speech with the proviso: 'Of course *I'm* not into fashion but ...' Even Simone Cipriani says he is 'not a fashionable man'. The challenge is that fashion people aren't interested in listening to earnest lectures from those who don't know their peplums from their problems. You can attack the asylum from the outside, but it's much more effective to start your revolution from within.

Maybe the reason so few conversations about sustainability happen between fashion people is the same reason science doesn't tend to figure in their *tête-à-têtes*: the language barrier. 'How you say, *psyahnce*?' Translate 'sustainability' into fashion speak and you get 'I am not a plastic bag' embroidered on an Anya Hindmarch tote. Consider what happens when a bunch of fashion people plan a magazine cover inspired by technology: do they read *New Scientist* and add up the numbers? Nope. They grab the aluminium foil and scrunch it up behind a model, Cecil Beaton style; then they dress her in white go-go boots and a mirrored visor. It's the future, baby – without the maths.

And yet there's heaps of actual science behind the fashion scenes – even if the stars of the show don't know much about it. Take fabrics, for example. Ask your average designer where their cloth comes from and they might say 'the wholesaler' if it's made in China (or if they have no idea), or 'our Italian mills' if they buy it from somewhere more prestigious.

Push them to name a fabric that's kind to the environment, and they will likely plump for the 'natural' choice – which seems logical. But 'natural' is often misleading in this context: how natural is cotton that's been genetically modified or grown using synthetic pesticides? Or blended with spandex? Or backed with neoprene? How natural is wool or silk that's been dyed rainbow colours? Or waterproofed or made stain-resistant with PFCs (which are likely human carcinogens by the way). How natural is linen that's been shot through with metal lurex thread?

And anyway, how much do *you* know about how fabric is produced? I knew arse-all before I began this journey – and I used to make clothes for a living. ('Journey', by the way, is Anna Wintour's least favourite word.)

First the raw materials must be grown and harvested, or mined. The cotton must be picked (before which most of it is sprayed to absolute buggery with toxic pesticides, as we have seen); the wool must be sheared and the fleece scoured; the silk cocoons boiled and unravelled. The wood used in cellulose fabrics must be pulped, bleached and bathed in solvents; the crude oil that's the starting point for nylon and polyester must be refined.

And all this before any fibre is spun into yarn.

Unless it is yarn-dyed, woven fabric emerges from the looms in various shades of off-white known as greige ('Darling, you're looking a little greige today, you should get out more ...') and both natural and synthetic cloths are subject to finishing processes before dyeing: typically singeing, de-sizing, scouring, heat-setting, and bleaching, with multiple washes in between. Dyes are almost always synthetic, as are printing inks. An estimated 10,000 different substances can be used in the dyeing and printing of textiles, and at least 3,000 are in common use. Take a look at the care label in your shirt. What did you expect? No one lists them. Most designers wouldn't even know what they were.

The romanticised view of the artisan on his handloom or the block printer with his gentle vegetable dyes is a pretty one, but it has naff all to do with how most fabric gets made today. If it's a caricature you're looking for, try the bespectacled boffin in his lab.

Men in white coats and the quest for artificial silk
Before scientists managed to simulate silk in laboratories, merchants were on the hunt for ways to bump up the value of the real thing – and they too turned to chemistry. Textile dyers and finishers had been treating silk since forever. They used vinegar (or, sometimes,

stale wee) and tannins derived from various barks as a mordant to fix dyes. The tannins, as well as things like sugar and gum arabic, also added weight – because after washing, silk lost up to a quarter of its original volume as the naturally formed serecin gum was removed. Fraudsters sometimes tried to add still more weight with their waxes and sugars, but in general, early tannin processes tended only to bulk up the fibre to pre-serecin-removal levels.

The big trouble starts, as it usually does, after the industrial revolution. In the nineteenth century, manufacturers began to use metal salts for weighting. This lent silk that heavy, rustling quality familiar from *Downton Abbey* (Maggie Smith's stirring taffetas announce her presence before she speaks). Silk weighted in this way appeared luxurious and shoppers loved it, so the practice was widespread – even Queen Victoria was not exempt; one of her formerly black silk gowns, held by the Royal Trust Collection, is now brown and mottled, showing the tell-tale signs of having been finished with copper and iron salts.

An 1898 article in a New Zealand newspaper reported that, 'in much of the fabric sold today there is not more than 10 or 12 per cent of real silk, all the rest being extraneous matter applied to the fibre in the deceptive process of weighting' and noted that, 'skeins of German-dyed silk have been often found to be thus increased by 400 per cent of their original weight ... [which] swells up the tissue and pads the fabric like stuffing a cushion, giving it a *fictitious feel*'. ('Who d'you think you are in your fictitious silk, coming on all heavy 'n' stuff?') Here was a product 'of so combustible a nature that some have been known to take fire spontaneously' concluded the article.

Silk, always expensive and delicate to handle, was now dangerous too. And its supply was by no means assured.

In the 1850s, disease took hold in the silk-producing regions around Cévennes, southern France, and within a few years had spread to Italy and Spain. Silkworms discoloured, failed to spin cocoons, and died. French silk production collapsed, losing fourth-fifths of its output within three years. Something had to be done. In 1856, the government commissioned a report from a professor at the Sorbonne, who approached his former student for help. That student was Louis Pasteur.

Pasteur was the biologist whose investigations into the fermentation of beer and wine led to germ theory, vaccines and the milk pasteurisation process that bears his name. A workaholic – he had to be dragged from his lab on his wedding day – when Pasteur agreed to investigate the silkworm crisis, he didn't do so by halves. He moved his entire family to a remote village in the Cévennes for five years, and raised worms himself, eventually isolating the microbes that were causing their diseases. So in a sense Pasteur saved silk, but one of his assistants would do much to make it redundant.

Hilaire Bernigaud, comte de Chardonnet, studied under Pasteur, and learned a good deal about the behaviour of silkworms while he was at it. Chardonnet discovered his 'alternative silk' by chance when he knocked over a bottle of collodion (nitrocellulose dissolved in alcohol and ether) in a photography darkroom. He was a bit of a slouch in the cleaning department, and didn't get the rags out pronto, so the story goes. I like to think he ducked out for a cheese plate and a glass of burgundy, but whatever he did in the interim, when he returned the liquid had evaporated leaving a sticky residue formed of long, thin fibres.

The Swiss scientist Georges Audemars had already worked out that it was possible to produce filaments from a mixture of pulped mulberry bark and gummy rubber (he patented this in 1855), but while he got stuck trying to pull out his fibres with a needle, Chardonnet twigged that the answer lay in copying what silkworms do with their cocoons, and he pushed his fibres out through a hole. A dress made of 'Chardonnet silk' debuted at the Paris Exposition

Universelle of 1889, and two years later the comte opened the first commercial viscose factory in the French city of Besançon.

Now, all sorts of people had been messing about with nitrocellulose by this point. In the US, John Wesley Hyatt made billiard balls from a hardened form of it – they were cheaper than ivory, but liable to explode when hit. It was Hyatt who named this material celluloid, and he also used it to make false teeth (warning: be careful with those cigars). Fake tortoiseshell hair combs made from celluloid could catch fire when the wearer passed too close to a candle. Celluloid collars and cuffs, that convenient alternative to single-use starched cotton, regularly ignited when the wearer lit his pipe. Paris cabaret dancer Mademoiselle Zelle dressed her little dog in a celluloid collar, no doubt thinking he looked rather smart – until her 'cigarette touched the collar, and—pouf! It was all over.'[4]

Across the channel, Joseph Swan, a Geordie with a Father Christmas beard, worked out how to squirt a solution of nitrocellulose in acetic acid into a bath of alcohol to create a long thread. This was the first wet-spinning. Swan gave some of this magical yarn to his wife Hannah to crochet into doilies – an example of her handiwork was shown at the International Exhibition of Inventions of 1885.

The Brits finessed the manufacturing process – Chardonnet had failed to solve the flammability problem, and his factory closed after a couple of years – and in 1905 textile giant Courtaulds began producing viscose commercially for the apparel industry.

The way they did it then is pretty much the way it's done today – you take your wood (traditionally beech, but pine, spruce and eucalyptus are also used, and increasingly since the 1990s, bamboo), chip it, then boil it for several hours to form a sludge. Remove the big knots and major muck and that's pulp, which must be washed and bleached, pressed and dried to form cellulose sheets. These are steeped in caustic soda, then crumbed and bathed in solvent. Eventually you get a sort of gloop with the consistency of honey, and this is what you push through your holes – imagine a bank of shower heads; lots of little nozzles called spinnerets. The filaments that emerge on the other side are then plunged into an acid bath, where they solidify. Boom: fibre. Now you can spin it into yarn, and weave or knit it.

The Americans started calling their viscose 'rayon' from 1924, by which time it cost about half the price of silk, and fuelled the first wave of mass-manufactured fashion. It also, according to American OH&S pioneer Alice Hamilton's 1940 paper *Occupational Poisoning in the Viscose Rayon Industry,* could cause psychosis, dementia and motor paralysis in the factory workers who made it. The culprit was the solvent: carbon disulphide, a poison that acts on the central nervous system when inhaled, ingested or absorbed through the skin. It is still widely used by the modern textile industry.

Typically, 50 per cent of solvents used in the viscose process are now recycled – the rest must be disposed of. According to the WHO, 'the primary source of carbon dispulphide in the environment is emission from viscose plants, around which it is especially great' – carbon disulphide pollutes air, soil and waterways. Hopefully science, which got us into this mess, is the answer to getting us out.

Today, Europe's biggest cellulose yarn producer is the Austrian company Lenzing. With factories in Asia and Austria, they manufacture as sustainably as possible under the trademarks Lenzing Viscose, Lenzing Modal and Tencel (the name of their lyocell fabric, which is produced in a closed loop). Other companies make viscose and modal, without the same eco cred, so you need to check your labels. Also, Lenzing only manufactures yarn, not cloth, so it cannot control what happens to its product further down the chain.

Lenzing yarn production uses between ten and twenty times less water than cotton. They produce their own beechwood for pulp without using irrigation or fertilisers; half of this is grown in Austria, and most of the rest in Europe, and it's all certified by the Forest Stewardship Council. Tencel uses eucalyptus wood pulp, which Lenzing must buy on the open market from the Southern Hemisphere. They claim the plantations use only 'small amounts' of fertilisers, but not all this wood is FSC-certified.

Lenzing uses carbon disulphide in their viscose and modal processes – but they do so responsibly. About 70 per cent is recycled and reused, and the rest converted into sulphuric acid, which is also recycled. Tencel switches out the carbon disulphide entirely for a less toxic alternative, and 99 per cent of that is recycled. And Lenzing's Austrian Tencel plant runs on 100 per cent recovered energy from solid waste. Not perfect then, but pretty good.

Slime to the ridiculous

Name a raw material and chances are someone has tried to make clothes out of it. For his debut show in 1966, titled '12 Unwearable Dresses in Contemporary Materials', the Paris-based Spanish iconoclast Paco Rabanne strung aluminium plates, silver and plastic discs together to make Joan of Arc–style chainmail. You couldn't tumble-dry it.

Icelandic designer Sruli Recht pieces together sweaters from thin slivers of walnut wood. Karl Lagerfeld used wooden beads and paillettes in his Spring '16 Chanel couture collection. Vivienne Westwood added interest to early punk T-shirts by sewing chicken bones on them. Jean Paul Gaultier once exhibited a collection made out of bread. There's an iconic Alexander McQueen dress made from a carpet of real flowers, which tumbled as the model walked, but Dutch duo Viktor & Rolf went further, and used actual carpet to make their

Autumn '14 couture gowns. The thick bulky sort that belongs on floors. You couldn't sit down in it.

In 2012, a dramatic yellow cape conceived by artists Simon Peers and Nicholas Godley went on display at the V&A. It's woven from the silk of a million Madagascan golden orb-weaver spiders, 'borrowed' from the forest and 'milked'.

For 200-plus years women in the Philippines have been making cloth by hand from the leaves of pineapple plants. *Bashofu* is made from bananas, soy fabric from the discarded hulls of soybeans. Traditional Japanese *shifu* is made from twisted ribbons of *washi* paper (in 2013 Issey Miyake made menswear from it). The US brand Inego's linen-like cloth is derived from corn syrup. Taiwanese company Singtex markets a fibre made from coffee ground waste, which boasts 'natural odour control' properties.

Got an orchard? In 2014, Sicilian students Adriana Santonocito and Enrica Arena debuted Orange Fiber during Milan fashion week – the results of bashing up citrus fruit leftovers with a mortar and pestle at their kitchen table.

Meanwhile, British designer Suzanne Lee has been winning awards for BioCouture, which uses bacteria to 'grow' garments – one glitch: your coat may dissolve in the rain. At the University of Guelph in Canada, researchers are trying to work out how to replicate the fibrous slime of the bottom-dwelling hagfish on an industrial scale.

One of the weirdest fabric innovations happened in Holland as a result of snails invading artist Lieske Schreuder's garden. 'Walking outside, in the garden or in the streets, we are constantly walking on snail excrements,' she explains on her blog. 'But because these excrements are very small and look like normal dirt, we are not aware of this. This made me think of a situation where these excrements are in colour. This would be some sort of snail-excrements-carpet.'

Molluscs are cellulose-munchers, so Schreuder collected a bunch of her garden invaders, fed them coloured paper, then marvelled as they crapped red, yellow, blue, and 'grey excrements in case they eat recycled newspapers'. She built a machine to grind up their dried poo, and spin the resulting powder into a fibre, conveniently pre-dyed. She made tiles from it, or as she calls it, a 'semi-manufactured' alternative to lino.

Mad cow

'Yes, I have been eating it,' says Anke Domaske in her sing-song German lilt.

'A whole dress? Or just a tank top?'

Domaske seems to think I'm the crazy one.

'Just the fibre,' she says. 'Obviously. Out of the pan.'

It tastes like victory. Domaske has not been eating her Qmilk yarn because she's run out of pasta. 'Our idea was to create a fibre that is so natural you could eat it. We were told constantly, "This can never work".'[5]

Domaske runs her textiles company out of Hanover, where she moved from Leipzig after the Berlin Wall came down. As a kid she 'was really interested in bacteria. Somehow I found out about the work of Robert Koch. He is Germany's answer to Louis Pasteur,' she says. Koch, a fellow Hanoverian, won a Nobel Prize for his work on tuberculosis in 1905. 'He became my hero, I found this idea of a whole other world of bacteria totally fascinating.'

At sixteen Domaske went on a student exchange to a dairy farm in Idaho, and at college she studied microbiology. But the whole time she had a hobby, one that her science friends found unusual. 'My mother was a dress designer and as a teenager I would go with her to the fabric stores every weekend. In East Germany there was a sewing culture; everybody did it. I always loved fashion.' While still a student, Domaske started a clothing label. 'It was sustainable in that it was made in Germany with fabrics from Europe, but I wanted to know more about how fabric is produced.'

She was studying for a master's degree in textiles when her step-father was diagnosed with leukaemia and rushed into chemotherapy. 'It was dreadful. His immune system was so weakened he had to live in a sealed room. He seemed to be allergic to everything, and had constant skin rashes. He couldn't find any clothes to wear that didn't make them worse. It seemed ridiculous that he had this to contend with on top of being so sick.'

Domaske was researching non-irritant textiles when she read about an old process using milk. 'It was popular in the 1930s, because this was pre-nylon,' she explains. 'At one point, over 10,000 tonnes of milk wool were being produced in Europe each year. There were many brand names for it,' she says, reeling them off: Aralac, Lanital, Merivona. The raw material is casein, the main protein in cow's milk, which was used by the ancient Egyptians to make paint, and by the fashion industry in the first half of the twentieth century to make galalith for buttons – Coco Chanel turned it into costume jewellery.

Woo-hoo, thought Domaske, now convinced that the pesticides and chemicals used in conventional textile manufacturing were to blame for her stepfather's allergic reactions.

She thought of the Idaho dairy and of her beloved bacteria and the problem of the EU's notorious milk lakes – Germany alone dis-poses of 1.9 million tonnes of spoiled milk a year, she says – and she 'got goose bumps'.

Alas, like Chanel's galalith 'milk stone', 'milk wool' was processed with formaldehyde. The only modern milk fibre Domaske could find on the market was blended with acrylic. 'I was disappointed. They basically destroy something natural. It was far from environmentally friendly.' So she decided to make her own.

'We went to a grocery store and bought a mixer and a very big pan, the sort you use for marmalade, and spent the whole weekend trying to cook up success,' she says. 'That's how we got started. Literally created recipes in the kitchen. In the end it was simple, like creating noodles,' she insists, although she will not reveal the details of her award-winning sustainable process. 'Think of milk turning sour: at the bottom you have the whey, and at the top you have the white, you know, flakes, and this is the protein in the milk. Remove that, dry it and you have a protein powder. Now you add some other natural resources.'

'Like what?'

'I'm not telling you,' she says, like Colonel Sanders with his secret chicken spices.

'But can there really be no chemicals?'

'There can.'

Domaske claims Qmilk fibre is antibacterial, 'temperature regulating' and feels like silk. 'We produce in a closed loop, using very little water, just two litres for every kilogram of fabric. All our milk is waste; we don't use any milk that could be used for human consumption. Farmers had been either using it as animal feed or throwing it away.'

Domaske says her process allows for dyeing 'at the cookie dough stage', whatever that might be, and so far she's been using 'grocery dyes, vegetable or food colours, there are also natural colours like ashes for blacks'. She reckons you can wash Qmilk fabric, but I'd need to see it to fully believe it, given my own experiences with viscose (shrinks every time). I hope it works. If you tire of your dress made from Qmilk fibre, you can bury it in the garden. 'Totally compostable,' says Domaske.

Tights spot

It was possible to buy viscose stockings from around 1910. There's a pair in Sydney's Powerhouse Museum. Bagging ankles were one problem, but I'd have had something to say about their frumpy thickness too. Basically, they look like long white footballs socks. No wonder chicks rioted when nylons appeared.

Which brings us to one Dr Julian Hill – a man who liked birds, but the feathered lot, not the rioting ones. Hill was a twitcher on his days off; his days on were spent as research chemist at the DuPont Experimental Station in Wilmington, Delaware.

When Hill discovered nylon in 1930 ('by accident', as usual), he had no idea the trouble it would bring to his beloved birdlife, in the form of non-biodegradable trash bobbing about in the ocean.

A nylon fishing line can take up to 600 years to break down, giving it plenty of time to wrap around a pelican's beak or tangle in a seal's gut. Seabirds flying over the Eastern Pacific Garbage Patch, a vast area of marine debris roughly mid-way between California and Hawaii, feast on so many lonely lids, broken cartons and clothes pegs, and grocery bags, there's barely room left in their stomachs for real food or water. A survey funded by the US Environmental Protection Agency in the mid-'90s looked into the deaths of albatross chicks on Midway Atoll (about half way between North America and Japan) – less than 3 per cent had plastic-free digestive systems.[6]

We're all battling plastic rubbish in the twenty-first century, something Hill foresaw in 1988 when he said he feared 'the human race is going to perish by being smothered in plastic'.[7] But all this was to come. In 1930, Hill was just one member of the team, led by Wallace Carothers, investigating how molecules chain together to form polymers. Most of America's silk was then imported from Japan, and trade relations between the two nations had begun to sour. The bosses at DuPont were hoping to find a substitute.

It was slow work in the lab. Hill's early synthesised polyesters were unstable. Meanwhile, all eyes were on another member of the team, Arnold Collins, who developed the synthetic rubber we now call neoprene, imagining all sorts of serious uses for it (none of which were dresses by Dion Lee). So, for a while, rubber dominated the conversation, and Hill's synthetic silk was the wallflower at the party.

It was Carothers who made the breakthrough, in 1935, revisiting Hill's process to produce the first thin, strong, flexible polymer fibre that didn't melt in hot water. Two years later the first pair of 'nylon' stockings was made for DuPont by the Union Hosiery Company. 'Nylon' is a bastardisation of 'no-run'. The toe, heel and stocking tops were silk, and the back seam cotton. It's fair to say the ladies of Wilmington, first to try them out, went properly nuts for them. May 16th 1940 was proclaimed Nylon Day and four million pairs arrived in the nation's department stores. They promptly sold out.

The Second World War put the love affair on ice. Nylons were rationed, and women were back to browning their legs with tea or gravy powder and drawing on fake seams with kohl. Uncle Sam even asked women to give their old pairs back for use as gunpowder bags – department stores installed collection bins for recycling. However, once tried, nylons weren't easily forgotten; there was no wartime hardship like the lack of tights. When the market was freed, it was riot time again. The headlines were full of 'screaming mobs' rushing the counters. Outside one hosiery shop, reported the *Pittsburgh Press*, 'even at midnight, when the store closed, the line stretched for more than five blocks and included thousands'.

I think Carothers would have enjoyed all this, but sadly he missed it. He'd always been fragile, and was admitted to psychiatric hospitals at least twice in his life. In fact, he'd tried to turn down the DuPont gig citing 'neurotic spells', and one of the reasons he did eventually accept it was to get out of lecturing at Harvard.

In 1931, Carothers should have been excited about his team's breakthroughs, but instead he fretted over his colleagues going out and having fun 'while I, after my ancient custom, sit sullenly at home'. Although he no longer had to deal with those terrifiying rooms of blank-faced students, his position at the Experimental Station did entail public speaking — and he did dread it. He wrote to a friend that 'it was necessary to resort to considerable amounts of alcohol to quiet my nerves' when called upon to present. 'My nervousness, moroseness and vacillation get worse as time goes on. . . 1932 looks pretty black to me just now.'[8] He once showed Hill a cyanide pill he kept in his pocket.

In 1936, Wallace Carothers went missing while hiking in Austria. Weeks later he returned to his desk without explanation. In 1937, in a Philadelphia hotel room, he mixed his cyanide with lemon juice and drank it.

CHAPTER 17

You Should See Polythene Pam

Plastic soup

I'm alone. Somewhere between Australia and South America, on a beach on an island in the South Pacific, a stretch of shingly seafront formed from sun-bleached coral and volcanic rock. Unlike the rest of the swanky hotel complex it's part of, this particular bit of Bora Bora hasn't been tamed and it's glorious. I gulp the salty air and think how energising it is, how wild.

I do a bit of yoga-stretching, and am feeling mighty pleased with myself when I look down and realise that it's not only the sea-smashed bits of ex-reef that crunch underfoot but thousands of plastic fragments, some worn so small they resemble blue sand.

I start to sift, collecting the plastic so the birds and turtles don't bung up their poor stomachs with it. My hands soon fill, so I stuff the debris in my pockets until they too are laden. I try using a discarded bottle as a bin, shoving as much as I can through the neck but it's a losing battle, camel-through-the-eye-of-a-needle stuff, and the crosser I get, the more junk breaks free.

Nowhere is immune. In the Maldives, Thilafushi was once a

pristine lagoon. Now it is Rubbish Island – designated landfill to service the country's capital, and stretched way beyond capacity thanks
to millions of tourists. Migrant workers burn rubbish there in the
open air, while overflow has started to wash up in nearby resorts.

'Go to pretty much any beach or hike any trail and you will see
plastic trash,' Tim Coombs tells me.[1] He is a co-founder of the American company that makes Bionic Yarn, a blended polyester thread
that uses recycled ocean plastic as a raw material, and when we talk
I'm back from my holiday and he's back from his – in Costa Rica. 'It's
ridden with plastic,' he says of the Central American tourist mecca
famed for its biodiversity and jaw-dropping coastline. 'I've seen it in
Hawaii too, as bad if not worse.'

And I've seen it in Australia.

On New Year's Day I went for a swim with my husband on a Sydney beach. There were people everywhere: kids splashing, backpackers
sleeping, families picnicking, but the place was strewn with empty
bottles, fag ends and the coloured plastic shells of party poppers.

I totally flipped. 'WHAT IS WRONG WITH PEOPLE?' I shouted,
as I stomped past picking up what I could carry. 'HOW CAN YOU
JUST SIT THERE SURROUNDED BY GARBAGE LIKE IT'S A FUN
DAY OUT? HAPPY BLOODY NEW YEAR!'

Needless to say, swimming wasn't happening. My other half
clearly wanted the wheelie bin to swallow him whole, as the beach-
goers looked at me like I was the one with the problem. But the
problem belongs to us all, as well as to the seabirds and ocean creatures. How did we get here, to this place where we're so used to spoiling
nature that we don't even see it anymore?

The numbers are hard to fathom. There are over seven billion of
us on this planet – but five trillion bits of plastic in our oceans. A trillion is a thousand billion. It took less than the average human lifetime

to put them there. They travel through our stormwater drains and rivers, fall off boats, spill from factories and garbage heaps. Sometimes we toss them there on purpose. We add to this nightmare every second. By 2025 we'll be releasing eight million tonnes of plastic into the water EVERY YEAR, enough to cover 5 per cent of the earth's entire surface in clingwrap.

◉

Professional tidy-upperer Heidi Taylor is cross too. She and her teams remove about one tonne of debris per kilometre in remote Cape York at Queensland's northernmost tip whenever they run clean-ups there. It comes off boats or washes in from the Gulf of Carpentaria.

Taylor runs a charity called the Tangaroa Blue Foundation, which coordinates the Australian Marine Debris Initiative, dispatching teams of volunteers and rangers along Australia's coast to collect data and clean up. Their big-picture goal is to prevent rubbish from ending up in the ocean in the first place, but it's a Sisyphean task. The drink bottles make Taylor maddest.

'Plastic is an amazing material,' she says.[2] 'We need it for useful things like medical instruments and aeroplanes, but to use it to make some stupid pointless thing designed to be drunk out of once then tossed, but that will stick around in the environment forever, that doesn't make sense. I mean, what a dumb use of oil, which, we would do well to remember, is a finite resource. Sorry, did that sound cranky?'

'YES!' I say. 'I AM CROSS TOO. IT'S IMPOSSIBLE NOT TO BE.'

Taylor was working as a dive instructor in Western Australia in 2004 when she first started to worry about plastic debris. 'I spent a lot of time on the beach and kept coming across plastics washed up in the Leeuwin-Naturaliste National Park. I started hauling them back to my car,' she tells me. 'My friends couldn't believe how much

I found.' A hundred people showed when Taylor organised her first community clean-up. In 2007 she moved to Far North Queensland, and made the clean-ups a regular thing.

Coombs heard about Taylor through Parley for the Oceans, a hub that helps tell the story of our imperilled seas and works closely with the Sea Shepherd Conservation Society. In 2013, Tangaroa Blue started supplying them with plastic for recycling into Bionic Yarn.

Today it's PET bottles collected from beaches; tomorrow it could be polystyrene foam and plastic bags. There's no open ocean collection as yet, but they're working on it, says Coombs.

Bionic Yarn, which is backed by singer Pharrell Williams, takes that recycled raw material and turns it into thread. The basic technology is not new: the bottles are sorted, cleaned, chipped and melted, and then the regular polyester process works just fine, although Bionic blends theirs with other fibres. In its unblended form it uses no virgin raw material, and 30 to 50 per cent less energy than virgin polyester (although that's still more than cotton).

Patagonia has been using Repreve recycled polyester since 1993; that's made by the North Carolina–based firm Unifi, which also supplies Quiksilver, The North Face and Volcom. By 2016, Repreve had turned 630 million used PET bottles from rubbish into fibre. They also recycle polyester fabric waste. The big Korean polyester player Huvis makes a recycled yarn called Ecoever that is used by Nike. On a smaller scale, Thread is a social enterprise making recycled poly in Haiti.

Where Parley and Bionic Yarn are innovating is by using rubbish direct from beaches. So the very stuff Taylor's teams pick up off the sand ends up in your clothes. One of Bionic's most high-profile clients is the Dutch denim company G-Star. Add Pharrell to the mix, and you get a great swathe of people who wouldn't otherwise care suddenly ordering their denim with a side of happy oceans.

'I like the idea of turning this rubbish into something valuable, of course I do,' says Taylor. 'And if recycling can create jobs as well as diverting rubbish from landfill, that's good. But I'd prefer it if we didn't have a marine debris problem. Let me tell you a story: One Anzac Day, the Perth RSL decided they would release 1023 balloons into the sky to honour the Western Australian soldiers who died at Gallipoli. The balloons were a way to provide an emotional release. But they didn't consider what other things might occur as a result.'

Taylor went down there to tell them just what those outcomes might be: 'When the balloons reach a certain height, the air inside expands and they freeze and shatter. The remains look like jellyfish, which turtles eat. The ribbons, of course, are plastic so they don't biodegrade; they photo-degrade into smaller and smaller pieces. Except often before that happens, they tangle around birds' beaks and feet. So anyway the lady at the RSL tells me, "Don't worry, those were magic balloons; they disintegrate into nothing in the air."

I said, "You're kidding me, right?"

This lovely lady was convinced they would just disappear. People don't know, and they don't want to know.'

Don't mention the hat

To help spread the word about G-Star Raw for the Oceans (RFTO), Pharrell Williams has written a letter to humanity.

'Dear Human Beings,' he begins. 'We vacation by the oceans, we bathe in the oceans, we eat from the oceans but very few of us think of the oceans beyond what we want from it. The oceans need us now.'

The famous polymath – he of the multiple Grammys and CFDA fashion icon status, the Davos speeches, the production companies, clothing labels, and modelling for Chanel – reads the letter while a cartoon octopus called Otto, and a bunch of his ocean-dwelling buddies, nip about the deep blue sea collecting plastic bottles, and feeding them into something resembling the Beatles' Yellow Submarine, complete with gnashing teeth, which munch them magically into … jeans. It's a cute campaign with a serious message. As Pharrell points out, 'filling up [the ocean] with plastic is ruining the neighbourhood'.

'G-Star and Bionic Yarn want you to come together … and weather responsibility for the oceans,' says Pharrell. 'Happy life, happy human beings and happy oceans.'

❂

It's not easy to get Pharrell on the phone. And when you finally do, it's not easy to get him to talk. 'Not easy' is me being polite. Pharrell is a VIP – when he talks to someone, he wants it to be Oprah. But he is passionate about the G-Star project, so he is willing to submit to an interview for the magazine I'm working for. I am to be granted twenty minutes. There are, however, a few rules.

'No problem,' I tell the publicist. 'Although it is quite hard to get a cover story out of twenty minutes on the phone. Normally we'd need at least forty, preferably an hour, in person. I'd be happy to go to New York to see him.'

That's not going to happen.

'I'm really interested in G-Star,' I say. 'I don't think you'd find many journalists less interested in Pharrell's personal life and more interested in his denim.'

'Okay,' she says.

'So, what sort of rules?'

'He's happy to discuss anything about RFTO, why he's supporting it, working with Bionic Yarn, why he's leveraging his fame for a good cause,' she says. 'And he's happy to discuss how the relationship with Bionic Yarn and G-Star came about.'

'Anything else?'

She suggests I tread carefully with questions about his style.

'But it's a fashion story,' I say.

She thinks it would be a good idea if I avoid making puns about *Happy*.

'I thought he wanted us to make the oceans happy?'

She laughs, and politely reminds me of the importance of not mentioning the hat. What the publicist doesn't say, but what I can telepathically tell she is thinking is: Pharrell has had enough of the hat stuff, already. He's sick and tired of interviewers banging on about the bloody Vivienne Westwood Buffalo hat he wore to the Grammys, instead of asking him about the important stuff, like his music and his businesses, like how he lived in a neighbourhood called Atlantis as a kid and now he's trying to save the oceans, and why he thought that weird pink answer to Baileys was a good idea. Okay, maybe not that bit. Anyway, Pharrell isn't even wearing that hat anymore; he auctioned it off for charity.

'But it has its own Twitter account,' I say.

She suggests I ask how he likes Australia.

'I wasn't even thinking about the hat. Until you mentioned it.'

She is going to hang up.

'I can read your mind,' I say.

◉

'Regardless of what you believe, science tells us that we started out as primordial star slime,' says Pharrell down the line from LA. 'Things didn't have to work out for us, you know? I believe in a God, there are people who don't, but either way the earth is our home and that's something we can't dispute, and we need to take care of it.'[3]

Pharrell runs a community of companies called I Am Other, which includes his music and production interests and a bunch of creative ventures he's either backed as startups, or put his money and connections behind to take them to the next level. These include bicycle makers Brooklyn Machine Works, and Collaborative Fund, which provides seed capital for projects it deems likely to 'make this world a better place'.

Bionic Yarn is another. Its founders, high school friends Tim Coombs and Tyson Toussant, remember when Mayor Bloomberg slashed recycling services in New York City in 2002. 'It was amazing the amount of plastic being dumped in the streets and overflowing out of garbage cans,' says Coombs, who studied textiles at the FIT. Toussant was a biology major. They're both outdoorsy types.

'When it was being collected on schedule, we didn't notice it was an issue,' continues Coombs. 'Once it wasn't, we realised this was a disaster waiting to happen for the planet. It made us want to take matters into our own hands.'

At the time, they'd been focused on 'outdoor product design, tents, sleeping bags and such' and 'were aware of some textiles being made from plastic bottles, but they were low grade and more gim- micky,' says Coombs.

It took them six years to develop Bionic Yarn. Their first big cli- ent, in 2008, was Nike-owned shoe brand Cole Haan, which made a line of bags out of their yarn but didn't push its eco angle and barely mentioned Bionic. Never mind. Shortly afterwards, Coombs and Toussant met Pharrell. 'He saw the quality of the fabrics [and] showed them to some of his colleagues in the industry, who knew more about textiles than he did. They were super-impressed,' says Coombs. Pharrell's fashion connections stretch wide – from Adidas and Uniqlo to Louis Vuitton and Moncler.

'At the time I think he was starting to feel like something had to be something done for the environment,' says Coombs. According to *Forbes*, in 2009 Pharrell invested a high six-figure sum for 30 per cent equity in Bionic Yarn. With him on board as creative director, its next big client was footwear company Timberland, which Pharrell had been working with for a while through his Billionaire Boys Club clothing line. Moncler soon followed. The first G-Star RFTO collection dropped in 2014.

The following year, just as the White House stepped up its pledge to help America's beleaguered bee populations, Timberland produced a capsule collection of boots made with Bionic Canvas (a blend of recycled polyester and organic cotton) featuring honeycomb prints and bee graphics. It was Pharrell again, this time cross-pollinating his eco causes. He insists a man in his position must 'pay it forward'.

'It's about me personally saying thank you to the universe for giving me so much,' he says. 'What we have going on is a movement. I think it's really going to be effective.'

Bottle neck

'But what happens when you wash it?' says Mark Anthony Browne.[4] What he thinks happens, in the case of that eco darling, the recycled polyester fleece jacket, is that up to 1900 individual fibres detach themselves from the garment into the washing machine, and escape with the water down the drain. Literally come out in the wash. I say *thinks* because the companies that make the fleeces, and other garments out of synthetic textiles, haven't exactly been rushing to help him prove it.

Browne is a British scientist who spent his boyhood summers on the Cornish coast and wrote his first PhD on microplastics back in 2004. Browne and his team looked at 'shorelines from the poles to the equator, across the world', collected samples, and interrogated them with forensic techniques to identify the types of materials they contained. 'The big issue then was packaging,' explains Browne, 'and we expected to find loads of that broken down into irregular shaped fragments – and we did, but far more abundant were these polyester fibres, which were found in every single sample.'

Over several years he tested his hypothesis that these fibres might be coming from domestic washing machines. He roped in colleagues around the world. At one point he had fifteen people collecting his precious sand in foil takeaway tubs. What Browne concluded was that the same fibres were 250 per cent more concentrated near sewage dumps on the sea-floor, which suggested sewage as a possible pathway for these fibres into habitats. He found the same fibres in sewage effluent from treatment plants.

Next, his team tested the shedding rates of three common polyester textile items – a fleece jacket, a business shirt and a blanket – in the washing process. The fleece came off worst, but they still don't know exactly why or which other garments might pose the greatest problems. They need more resources to conduct wider testing.

New York–based sustainable fashion brand Eileen Fisher provided a grant. 'They are small but they are leaders,' says Browne, 'they are doing what they can and have been very receptive to receiving the information back so they can make better choices'.

The big guys have been less enthusiastic. 'Patagonia said they were really interested, but at the last minute said it was too expensive, so that was frustrating,' says Browne. Someone from Nike asked him, 'Do I think it's as bad as asbestos?' before declining to fund research due to other commitments. 'We've spoken to Polartec – no go. They seemed slightly annoyed that we'd done the research in the first place. I've lost count of all the approaches I've made over the last five years,' says Browne, 'probably ten a year, trying to find the correct person in these companies to make an inroad. It's pretty much always the same response.' No thank you, Dr Browne. Stop making a nuisance of yourself. He hasn't approached G-Star yet.

So why should consumers care? What happens when these fibres enter our water systems? 'Well, this is the question,' says Browne. 'They don't break down, at least not quickly, we know that. They are present in our seafood, there's been work done that quite clearly shows that. Humans take in these microfibres not just by inhaling them in house-hold dust but also through the food chain. That's where the concerns grow, because we've done work that shows that similar-sized particles can transfer into the tissues of organisms, and release toxic chemicals.'

Remember, ocean plastics look like dinner to a fish or a turtle or a bird. Eating them means eating the contaminants they contain, many of which bioaccumulate. 'I'll take the PCBs for entrée please. For dessert? I know I shouldn't but I'm thinking of the toxic flame retardants. Go on, *twist my arm*.' It's Rachel Carson's worst nightmare. Fancy fish and chips now?

As Browne points out, the fashion companies currently trying to clean up their eco act are focused on toxic chemicals in their supply chains, 'but ignoring the polymers themselves. With a fraction of what Nike is putting into its Bluesign project we could solve this issue quite easily,' he says. 'We have prototype washing machine filters; we just need to test them. We can collect samples from sewage works to see how different treatment would reduce emissions, and test emis-sions from various textile types to define which physical and chemical features cause the most problems,' he says.

'Why can't we have a productive, accountable textile industry that operates like the medical industry, whereby we have a policy in place that says you are not allowed to put a product to market until it has been adequately tested? That's what I mean by benign by design.' Why indeed?

CHAPTER 18

Waste Not, Want Not

Is recycling the answer?

'Most people don't understand how recycling works,' says Heidi Taylor. 'They think their responsibility ends with the bin at the end of their drive. If you recycle a plastic drink bottle that has a "1" on it, it can't be recycled into a new one. Did you know that?' Gah. No, I didn't.

The '1' in the little triangle is the resin identification code for PET, or polyethylene terephthalate, the most commonly recycled plastic. PET is semi-porous, so what they call 'post-consumer' PET – i.e. that bottle you sucked your juice out of – poses challenges for food safety. This means most of it is not recycled into a newer version of its old self. Who knew?

While we're on the subject, most recycling is manually sorted, at speed, so if a container isn't obviously made of one specific material, it will often be overlooked. Overlooked, means off to landfill. What about those plastic types with no viable market value to the recyclers? Landfill. Plastics that have been tied up in grocery bags before binning? Landfill. Bottle tops? Landfill. Polystyrene? Landfill.

'Recycling should be the last option,' says Taylor. 'We should be refusing, reducing, reusing.'

One example of reuse is vintage clothes – they find a new home but stick to their original intent. Re-purposing gives an item a new function. Upcyling gives it one better than its original, driving materials back up the supply chain.

That's what Ilaria Venturini Fendi does with her Carmina Campus accessories line. She no longer works in the family Fendi business. Instead she runs an organic farm just outside Rome, and designs handbags, made in Africa, from old truck tarpaulins and cast-off carpets, and once from car seat fabric left over from the Mini Cooper factory.

Petit h is the in-house atelier at Hermès which crafts one-of-a-kind bibelots from offcuts, discontinued colours and flawed skins, materials that other luxury houses routinely toss. It is here that Pascale Mussard, a descendant of the company's founder, makes very weird and very wonderful things, letting the materials guide her – a life-size tan leather bambi made from Birkin bag production scraps; little wooden boats with sails cut from imperfect silk scarves. Mussard's motto is 'we don't throw anything away.' Efficiency, creativity.

Recycling is something else entirely. It involves processing or breaking down a used item to extract the raw materials, which can then be made into something new: Bionic Yarn's polyester, for example, or Vivienne Westwood's EFI buttons made in Kibera by Steve Brass. Kit Willow's KITX label uses recycled metal buttons too – made in Cambodia, they were bullet casings in a former life.

Yvon Chouinard has been pushing the merits of this kind of thing for years. Time and again, when I interview people about sustainability, they mention Chouinard and his company Patagonia as leading the way.

Kelly Slater sought advice from Chouinard when he was setting up Outerknown. It's no coincidence that he hired Shelly Gottschamer, fresh from four years in sourcing at Patagonia, to be Outerknown's chief supply chain and sustainability officer. To launch his brand to the press, Slater posed on top of a pile of old fishing nets in a recycling facility in Slovenia. The nets, both rescued from the ocean floor and handed in by incentivised fishermen, are recycled into a nylon thread marketed as Econyl, which Outerknown is using to make boardshorts and windbreakers. Patagonia had already announced funding, though its $20 Million and Change Fund, for a Chilean startup that uses similar tech to turn old nets into skateboard decks.

Chouinard's company was raising awareness about ocean plastic back in 2006, as part of its Oceans as Wilderness campaign. They'd switched to organic cotton a decade before that. They've signed up for B Corporation status, and have worked with Bluesign since 2000. Patagonia was the first big clothing brand to push genuine supply chain transparency (you can see their Footprint Chronicles online). As Chouinard likes to say, the planet is his major shareholder. And the planet can't handle perpetual growth.

In 2011, to coincide with Cyber Monday, an online shopping drive by America's National Retail Federation, Patagonia booked a full-page ad in the *New York Times*, urging potential customers 'Don't Buy This Jacket'. The campaign detailed the 'astonishing' environmental cost 'of everything we make', and asked consumers to consider the pictured fleece jacket, 'one of our best sellers'. It took 135 litres of water to make it, 'enough to meet the daily needs (three glasses a day) of forty-five people. Its journey from its origin as 60 per cent recycled polyester to our Reno warehouse generated nearly twenty pounds of carbon dioxide, twenty-four times the weight of the finished product.'

Patagonia was asking readers to pledge for what they call the Common Threads Initiative, committing to 'reduce, repair, reuse, recycle, reimagine'. Over 60,000 signatories promised to 'use what I have, sell what I don't need, and buy used when I can' to 'keep my stuff out of landfills'. They're encouraged to trade their used Patagonia items on eBay under the Common Threads umbrella. Meanwhile Patagonia's Reno repair facility is the biggest in North America, and their 'Worn Wear' trucks drive around college campuses with sewing teams on board. They'll try to fix whatever clothing you bring – it doesn't have to bear a Patagonia label.

'That ad caused a stir,' says Chouinard. 'We got so much free press it was unbelievable, but that's not why we did it. It was honest.'[1]

In 2015, it wasn't the *Times* but the *Wall Street Journal* running a story titled 'Why Fashion Insiders are Buzzing about Patagonia'. The article describes hipster execs teaming their old Patagonia fleeces with box-fresh ACNE and Opening Ceremony, and quotes designer Patrik Ervell on the venerable Californian outdoorwear brand: Patagonia 'has a kind of romance to it'. Over at Louis Vuitton, for Autumn '15, menswear designer Kim Jones seemed to be inspired by Patagonia – and its 'styles, which are only occasionally updated for fit' – perhaps in a nod to the normcore trend: 'To dress normcore is to appropriate relatively mundane items most popular in the 1990s as fashion pieces.'[2]

I ask Chouinard himself – a man who believes in function over form, in tools not toys – how he feels about the fashion world embracing activewear with no intention of breaking a sweat, and he laughs. 'Like urbanwear?' he says. 'And lumbersexuals! Or is it lumberjack-sexuals? That's a trend, I hear. We don't pay much attention to that, we just do our own thing.' I don't mention normcore.

When we speak, Chouinard says he is preparing another shit-stirring ad campaign. He plans to run it in *Vogue* of all places. 'I'm starting to realise that we have a lot more power and influence in this company than we're using, so we're going to start using it,' he says. 'Fashion is a very powerful force.'

His idea takes aim at distressed denim. 'To put brand new jeans in these machines with pumice and rocks? That is so stupid and bad for the environment,' he says. 'We're going to do an ad that shows a model with a pair of those jeans on, and it's going to say "BOUGHT", then another model with patches sewn all over her jeans, and that picture is going to say "EARNED". We're going to ridicule people who think it's cool to buy this crap.'

Chouinard says he is not trying to get *Vogue* readers to buy Patagonia's jeans (at the time of writing their website displays just two women's denim styles, both out of stock). 'The purpose is not to market Patagonia,' he says, but to help shift thinking away from irresponsible consumption. Chouinard is often described as anti-fashion, even allergic to it – they whisper that, behind closed doors, Patagonians refer to fashion as 'the F word'. It is his beloved 'athletes', especially climbers, walkers and surfers, that Chouinard wants to sell to – the people he went into business for back in the '60s. People like him.

In his 2005 autobiography *Let My People Go Surfing* (so named after a company culture that says, when the surf's up, we surf), he wrote: 'All our customers are not equal in our eyes. There are indeed some we favour more than others. These are our core customers, those for whom we actually design our clothes.'

Chouinard says he never wanted to run a company. Another line from his book: 'No young kid growing up ever dreams of someday becoming a businessman. He wants to be a fireman, a sponsored athlete or a forest ranger.' As a boy Chouinard thought being a fur trapper might be neat. 'After that I had no idea what I wanted to do. I still don't,' he tells me.

His family moved from Maine to California when he was about eight. As a teenager he read about falconry in an old *National Geographic*. 'I thought they were the coolest looking birds.' He joined a falconry club, with some other boys and 'two or three' adults. 'They were the father figures we all needed.' They taught the boys to rappel, moving down rock-faces with the help of a double rope, in order to reach the birds' nests. It was the journey that got them hooked. (A Chouinardism for you: 'More important than getting to the summit is how you do it.') The boys taught themselves to climb up, and were soon tackling tough ascents in Yosemite.

Chouinard's own father was a handyman. 'What I learned from my father was how to work with my hands, to really enjoy that,' he tells me. 'I don't think he ever went to a movie in his life, I don't know if he ever went to a restaurant. He worked really hard and came home and drank and went to sleep. My mother was the adventurous one, but she never had the opportunity.'

In the '50s, climbers used soft iron pitons, which they hammered into the rock, and left behind. Chouinard thought he'd try making his own, harder and reusable. He taught himself to be a blacksmith, and by the early '60s was selling his pitons from the back of his car. In 1965, he went into business with a climbing buddy Tom Frost. They made the gear they needed to help them be better climbers. Within five years they were the biggest producers of climbing hardware in the US. Chouinard says it was never about profits, although they rolled in.

When they realised pitons were damaging mountains, they introduced aluminium chocks that didn't require hammering. They started talking about 'clean climbing' and the need to protect the rock so that future climbers would have a more 'natural' experience.

'We met resistance because here are these climbers pounding in these big steel pitons with a hammer. All of a sudden we're saying,

"Hey, we have these chocks you stick in with your fingers and then you take 'em out with your fingers, and they're just the same, but faster and cheaper and they don't hurt the rock." Well, it was a stretch. We had to lead by example. I went with a friend and we climbed this big rock El Capitan without a hammer. I think people thought, "Jeez, if those guys came back to tell the tale I guess I could do my sixty metre climb [that way].'"

On a trip to Scotland, Chouinard bought a traditional rugby shirt because it seemed like a better prospect than the thrift store business shirts he usually climbed in. He imported a few and they sold out, so he had some made. Next came durable corduroy pants and canvas shorts – again, classic British gentlemen's outfits ideal for climbing but not widely used by American sportsmen. 'This is back when the outdoor industry only [sold] forest green, rusty red and blue [clothing]. We came out with all these wild purples, lime greens, fuchsia. [Think about] climbers sitting on a storm for a week at a time, it gets pretty dreary, you want a bit of colour to help your mentality.' By this time Frost had moved on, and Chouinard was in the apparel game – not fashion, *never* fashion – by accident. 'How many blacksmiths make clothes?' he laughs. 'But it turned out alright.'

His wife Malinda came up with the prototype polar fleece, looking for a quick-dry fabric for some sample jackets. At a store downtown, she found a roll of fake fur of the sort mums use for fancy-dress costumes for their kids. Those first jackets were ugly but cosy, and unlike wool jackets they didn't hold water or easily freeze. So what if they made you look like a yeti?

Chouinard's team started working with fabric suppliers to develop synthetics for underwear and insulating layers, as well as jackets. Initially they were focused on performance; they made clothes to please the hiker, the fisherman, the camper, the mountaineer, but then something happened that showed greater factors than mere pleasure were at play here.

In 1988, at the new Patagonia store in Boston, staff complained of headaches. An engineer came to check the air-conditioning system, and concluded that it was carrying chemical fumes up from the basement stockroom. That room was filled with new Patagonia clothing. It was probably the formaldehyde, said the engineer.

Best known as a preservative used in mortuaries (the pathologist on call when Einstein died popped the great man's brain in a jar of it), the lesser-known uses of this supremely nasty chemical include keeping fabrics wrinkle-free, stain-resistant and colourfast, and preventing mildew during shipping. In the short term, exposure can make you feel sick and headachy, cause rashes and red eyes – in the long term it's a known human carcinogen.

Now it was about making a product that didn't screw up the environment and make people sick. So Chouinard commissioned a study into the various fibres Patagonia used. Formaldehyde was only part of the story. Like Katharine Hamnett, when Chouinard found out exactly how conventional cotton is farmed he spat the dummy.

He acknowledges you can't mass manufacture without creating harm, so he talks in terms of 'no unnecessary harm' and 'natural growth'. While he dismisses the capitalist system as 'a Ponzi scheme', he stays in business, he says, because 'this is my resource to do good. It sounds kind of corny, but, well, this is about the fate of the planet. I have a simple life, I drive an old beat-up car, and I don't need more money.'

A 2015 story in the *New Yorker* questioned how Patagonia could convincingly urge people to buy less, while trying to sell them products. It pointed out that the company's profits continue to grow, while plenty of customers buy in to the brand's image without setting foot in the great outdoors: 'Visit the company's stores in locations like the

Upper West Side, Hong Kong, and Chamonix, and you will also see the affluent recreational shoppers who helped to inspire the nickname Patagucci.'[3] How, then, to reconcile all this with Chouinard's vision for buying less, buying with purpose, and responsible growth?

For starters, Patagonia donates 1 per cent of sales to grassroots environmental groups – so more sales mean more donations. Inside the company, Chouinard's 'do good' ethos covers the obvious things like decent pay, onsite childcare, flexible working hours and that famous go-surfing-when-you-feel-like-it policy, but looking outward it's also about product innovation and market education. Patagonia makes the learnings from things like its Traceable Down Standard and the plant-derived Yulex rubber they're using as an alternative to neoprene wetsuiting, available to other companies to try to spark broader change.

Chouinard had a phase of talking to fellow CEOs 'about greening their companies' (in a 2007 speech at Google's Mountain View HQ, he mentioned Rupert Murdoch and Steve Jobs) but tells me that he's 'kind of given up' on that. 'What's happening right now with these public companies is that they are making attempts to look green but they're not really serious, so it's a waste of our time trying to deal with them. I mean, we spent a lot of our time trying to influence Walmart, but it's only the small private companies that are really trying to do the right thing.'

I ask if he thinks Kering's new focus on sustainability is meaningful, and he says, 'It's very hard [for an existing public company] to change its business culture. It takes a huge educational campaign. But it's good business to change because customers want it.' Then he tells me about the burgeoning market for vintage Patagonia, and how there are stores in Japan that sell only that. 'The prices are going through the roof. There are jackets going for $5,000.'

I say it's cool that so much value is being attributed to something that not so long ago would have been chucked in the bin, and he says, 'Yeah! That stuff never ends up in the dump anymore that's for sure. It's only in the last 150 years we've had the resources to fuel this consume–discard society. Well, guess what? That party's over.'

A hole in one

I wondered, at the beginning of this book, who darns? And I expected the answer to be no one, obviously. But repair culture is gaining traction, whether as a genuine attempt to conserve natural resources, a backlash against the crap value of disposable goods, or a reaction to economic insecurity. Green shoots can be found in the premium denim industry.

Nudie has standalone repair shops. They post out sewing kits for DIY, accept used Nudies for resale, and have worked with students to upcycle samples. Dutch brand (and B Corporation) MUD Jeans allows customers in Europe to lease their jeans. And if you do decide to buy, they offer free repairs. When customers return past-it jeans they no longer love, MUD sends them back to their Italian factory to be shredded and re-spun. There are repair services at Denham stores and at some Levi's flagships, while Levi's also directs customers to sewing tutorials online.

'Mending used to be normal,' says Orsola de Castro. 'Somehow we lost the skill and the will.'[4] De Castro is the Italian-born Londoner behind upcycled brand From Somewhere, which she stepped away from in 2015 after eighteen years. 'I have closed the door but not locked it. I feel somehow that I am saving it for posterity,' she tells me. For now she's focused on Fashion Revolution, which she co-founded, and on mentoring students at Saint Martins. Like Chouinard, she is convinced the next generation will be the one to solve fashion's sustainability crisis. 'But I think now is the worst possible moment because the consumer is terrified that this bonanza of cheap is going to end,' she says.

From Somewhere began in the mid-'90s with holes in a jumper. De Castro was crestfallen at the prospect of bidding goodbye to her favourite pullover. 'It was me being stubborn and not wanting to let it go' that led her to crochet around every hole, making a feature of them. Sam Robinson at The Cross boutique in Holland Park encouraged de Castro to make more of her peculiar sweaters for the store. De Castro put a call out for people with crochet skills, and began sourcing used knits from 'huge second-hand warehouses' and 'adding value through design'. This wasn't vintage dealing – 'it was upcycling, although we didn't use that name then.'

◉

The concept of old clothes as a fashion statement was born in 1960s London, when the rocker boys and model girls paraded down the King's Road in Art Deco outfits and antique military jackets bought from Portobello markets or boutiques like Granny Takes a Trip. The dealers bought from old ladies' attics, from estate and jumble sales.

Red or Dead's Wayne Hemingway was one of the first to see the possibilities in the old shoddy and mungo yards up north. 'They were the prototype recycling yards, in these big old industrial buildings, with these old ladies who'd sit on a conveyor belt. They'd put blue cotton down one side, red wool down another, sort it all out, and it would get compressed into bales.'[5] Cotton items were removed for rags or, traditionally, paper production, while the wool was shredded and re-spun.

'We used to leave them examples of 1950s clothing, tip them to save it, then we'd pay for it by weight,' says Hemingway. He and his wife Gerardine ran a stall on Camden market in the early '80s before designing their own collections. 'There was no one else doing it. We'd fill two enormous vans a week. I was a jumble sale fan as a teenager,' says Hemingway. 'I made all my old punk clothes from jumble, adding bondage straps and stuff. I learned how to take a sow's ear and turn it into a silk purse – that's what me nan used to say.'

Club kids, students, struggling families and starving artists bought second-hand clothes because they were cheap, plentiful and offered endless styling possibilities. In the 1990s, grunge fans bought their Courtney nighties and Kurt sweaters from charity shops, and Kate Moss combed flea markets for bits of old tat with fashion potential. But in the 2000s, as new clothing production increased, second-hand lost some of its appeal. When you can buy a new blouse in Zara for $10, why buy a used one in Oxfam for the same money? So much unwanted fashion piled up outside charity shops that third parties started selling it to pre-Zara economies.

In his book *Clothing Poverty*, Dr Andrew Brooks describes how less than 30 per cent of clothes donated to charities in the UK, US and Canada gets sold in local charity stores now – the rest heads to Eastern Europe and Africa by the bale, to be sold for a profit. In 2013 the second-most-popular destination for Britain's piles of donated old clothes was Ghana.

Meanwhile, the quality of those donations was in free fall. Much of it's such rubbish, charity stores must fork out to send it to landfill. They rarely see the top stuff anymore. Grandma's designer handbags, the Art Deco tea dresses, wartime coats, '50s suits and '60s minis command silly money, and get whisked off to destination stores in the fashion capitals. The famous New York vintage store What Goes Around Comes Around has opened an outpost in Kuwait that sells second-hand Chanel bags for $5,000. Decades in LA outfits

Hollywood startlets in pre-loved red carpet gowns that cost as much as new ones. Even high street gear from twenty years ago costs a pretty penny from boutique resellers. De Castro would've had a hard time finding a jumper worth upcyling from her local vintage warehouse when Brooks was writing his book.

Luckily, she and her business partner Filippo Ricci had moved on by then – to 'pre-consumer waste' in the form of factory surplus. First, it was garments: the high street chain Jigsaw provided her with reject knits, which she upcycled for sale through their stores. Next came waste fabric, rolls and rolls of it – considered rubbish, though it had never been used.

'We were the one upcycled fashion brand absolutely capable of producing collections,' says de Castro. 'We built unique relationships with suppliers. We had an Italian agent and before the GFC we sold very successfully. We were never a big brand, but we were big enough.'

In 2006, the British Fashion Council approached them to help promote sustainable design at London fashion week, and the Esthethica hub was the result. De Castro and Ricci set up a sub-label called Reclaim to Wear, which partnered with mainstream brands to make collections from remnants, offcuts and factory surplus fabric. There were capsule collections for Topshop and Speedo, and in 2009 de Castro talked Tesco into selling a recycled fashion line. Yes, well, we remember what happened with Katharine Hamnett bedded down with the supermarket giant, don't we?

De Castro says the general focus on post-consumer waste means the pre-consumer picture remains shadowy. Official figures are scant. 'We do know that anything between 5 and 15 per cent is offcut waste in any garment production. Then there's waste at the mill, in the form of defective rolls – fabric can be the wrong shape or colour, or it doesn't pass some kind of a washing test. That gets warehoused and potentially it's sold, but who knows in what quantities? There is no story. In humid countries, use your imagination as to what happens to fabric in those damp warehouses. Often they incinerate it.'

Surplus garments suffer a similar fate. 'When Tesco orders 50,000 T-shirts, which is their minimum, the factory will produce 70,000 in case there's a re-order. That's standard,' she says. 'But if Tesco only sells 30,000 of those shirts, then not only the leftovers [on the shop floor] but also the extras will be waste.' Pretty much no one recycles them, she says. The technology for recycling blended fabrics is in its infancy, 'and even 100 per cent cotton shirts are sewn with polyester thread. Is a worker going remove the threads and labels from 40,000 T-shirts? It's not economically viable.'

Some factories have their own lines, she adds, so when they are left with surplus garments, they can try to on-sell them. 'But the big brands have very strict controls. They insist factories destroy every single defective branded item, and this applies to fabric too. I have seen it, and I know people who work in factories who see it every day.'

De Castro tells me about visiting a Sri Lankan mill in search of surplus fabrics to buy. 'I found myself in a warehouse, I won't say it's as big as a football field, but it's totally damn gigantic, there were hundreds of thousands of metres of surplus fabrics there. I said, "What happens to this?" They said, sometimes they sell it by the container. When it's been stored for more than a year, that's trickier. And every day, more arrives. They have to make space.'

De Castro was livid; why wasn't this story being told? 'So I went back to Sri Lanka with a journalist,' she says. The fabric was gone, like it had never been there, like she had dreamed it or was a crazy hallucinating person. 'They told me, "Sorry, we don't produce any waste. We do not have a warehouse."'

Circle of life

In 2014, H&M collected 7,600 tonnes of unwanted old clothes for recycling through its store-drop-off program, and made their first garments from 100 per cent recycled cotton from the results. The challenge is to work out how to do this again and again, because with each new life cycle the fibres get shorter and weaker, which is why they are generally blended with virgin material during recycling.

The following year H&M joined forces with Kering to work with British startup Worn Again, which is streamlining a process for separating blended fibres, and extracting the cotton and poly from old clothes for re-spinning. Their long-term aim is to 'eradicate textile waste' completely.

Until that happens there's always crochet.

'Crochet is inherently sustainable,' says Katie Jones, a Saint Martin's graduate knit-whiz who had a helping hand from de Castro when she started out. 'It's a zero waste craft because you create the piece as you go, you don't cut anything out or throw any of it away. It just is.'

Jones has no labour supply chain issues because every piece is made by her and her mum. It takes ages to make a Katie Jones flouncy cream poncho with a black-and-purple frilled hem and a high, Elizabethan-style collar, edged with a Pepto-Bismol pink ruff. Ages more to make the matching knickerbockers.

'It's my job,' says Jones, 'it's full time, so it's fine.'

She could spend eight hours of her day networking or compiling spreadsheets or liaising with factory managers offshore, or she could spend them with a crochet needle in her East London studio. It's a matter of choice, albeit one that rules out the potential big bucks that come with economies of scale, or even the modest bucks that come with regular wholesale orders.

At the time of writing, Jones has a stockist in Toyko and one in Shenzhen, plus she makes-to-order for private clients. 'It gives me freedom,' she says. 'I can do everything bespoke.' No excess stock for Jones, no rushing new styles out to be on trend. She laughs when I say 'trend': 'I don't think "hand knit" and "fast fashion" are words you often hear in the same conversation.'

Anyway, you can't unravel a pile of faulty Sonia Rykiel knits *fast*. 'I sometimes buy factory rejects, knits that have been nearly made but were stopped when a fault was spotted, or unfinished garments with dropped stitches. I unravel the yarn and reuse it.' De Castro helped Jones source factory surplus yarns and unwanted end rolls. One time, Jones made a whole collection out of the wool from unravelled Arran sweaters, because she kept finding them in charity shops.

Jones's pieces are expensive and hard to acquire, so hopefully treasured. But if they're not, maybe they too will be unravelled, and reworked into something new. Maybe something even more eccentric.

◎

Back home in Sydney, I nip out to buy a Kit Kat and on my way meet a flame-haired lady in a wheelchair who calls herself Queen Babs.

'You're the guerrilla knitter!' I say, having often seen her rainbow-hued handiwork hugging lampposts and railings near my house. She hands me a woolly love-heart from the bag in her lap.

'Crochet actually,' she corrects, with a big wobbly laugh. 'I'm the Redfern yarnbomber.' She suffers from fibromyalgia, which leaves her largely house-bound. Babs taught herself to crochet after seeing the work of other yarnbombers around the city. 'I do it because it makes me happy, and it makes other people happy – people I don't know and never see.' Volunteers help install her work; there are six of them today.

I ask Babs where she gets her wool, and she says from donations, through social media and word of mouth, mostly from people who've bought it to knit with, then never bothered. It's not only fashion people who hoard. 'Oh they have the best intentions,' laughs Babs, 'but the yarn ends up in a bag behind the couch. We give it a new life.'

I wonder what happens to the sweaters she's dressing the tree trunks in today, you know, later on. Will a Katie Jones–type come and unravel them?

'What, when the trees get bored of them? Ho ho! No, love, I know what you mean. Do we come and take it all away? We don't get chance. Most of it gets stolen.' Not recycling perhaps, but passing on, reusing then, with a criminal edge. Whatever it takes – waste not, want not.

A local pops by to thank Babs for beautifying the neighbourhood. 'Ooh you should have seen them kids the other day, trying to steal your crocheted bees!' she says.

'Nevermind,' says Queen Babs. 'What goes around comes around. I'm going to make a ladybug next.'

CHAPTER 19

Raising the Baa

Needs must

Those 'shoddy yards' Wayne Hemingway frequented weren't chic places, and the cloth that resulted from their pickings was poor, but they owed their existence to wool's high value. Yorkshire weaver Benjamin Law developed the shoddy cloth process during the Napoleonic wars, when local mills ran short on virgin wool. Ragmen collected old used textiles door to door, and sold them to the shoddy yards, where armies of young women sorted them by quality and colour to be shredded and re-spun. Mungo was the name for the better quality cloth made from unused tailors' offcuts.

In Prato, Italy, the Calamai mills, which now supply Yvon Chouinard's Patagonia with reclaimed wool, were doing a similar thing during WWI. By the 1930s wool was engaged in a war of its own, under siege from synthetics. To fight back, the International Wool Secretariat (IWS) was formed, and growers, initially from Australia, New Zealand and South Africa, paid a levy towards marketing their product as naturally beautiful, versatile, and *très très chic*. After all, wool was the favoured daywear cloth of Paris couturiers.

The IWS launched what's known today as the Woolmark Prize in 1953 (the Woolmark logo didn't appear for another decade or so). Almost no one remembers who won the first year because the next one was the biggie. When Pierre Balmain and Hubert de Givenchy and the rest of the competition judges delivered their verdict for 1954, the course of fashion's future shifted. Winner of the dress design category was a shy, lanky French-Algerian genius. He drew gorgeous pictures and seemed afraid of his shadow. He was the eighteen-year-old Yves Saint Laurent.

Who do you think won the next most important prize that year? Don't say runner-up. Someone not keen on that sort of language, thank you very much. Okay, so who won the coat design category? He who once said: 'I'm not a second option person.' It was Karl Lagerfeld.

Today's reconfigured prize includes regional heats and a menswear category, and is run by the IWS's modern incarnation Australian Wool Innovation (which owns Woolmark). In 2014, the overall winner was Rahul Mishra, a physics major from a village near Kanpur, who fell into fashion by way of Gandhi.

'I always wanted to be an artist,' says Mishra, 'physics was my father's choice.'[1] Mishra got the science out of the way then won a postgrad place at the National Institute of Design in Ahmedabad. 'That's where I came across the ideology of Gandhi, and homespun.'

Homespun, or *khadi*, is cotton, and from the 1920s Gandhi made it into a symbol of independence when he encouraged Indian nationalists to spin and weave their own in order to boycott imported – and heavily taxed – British cloth. That such cloth was woven in the mills of northern England using cotton grown in, and bought cheaply from, India added insult to injury, said Gandhi.

What Mishra took from the great man's teachings and applied to his fashion practice was not the politics, but 'the beauty, value and tradition of craft'. For basic cotton, Mishra substituted Indian hand-loomed silk, and also a fine blend of wool with silk. He added intricate embroidery in unusual weights and configurations, worked in knob-bly wool to push traditional techniques into new territory.

Mishra was inspired by group of Keralan weavers he'd worked with at design school. They were in crisis, he explains. 'So much over-stock, nothing is selling; saris aren't selling.'

Surely the sari is India's blue jeans?

'Not at all; blue jeans are India's blue jeans,' he smiles. 'Fashion is all about newness – nobody wants to carry the baggage of tradition. So fashion is one of the biggest challenges to craft, but also one of its only solutions.'

Mishra launched his label in Mumbai with the idea of 'evolving craft' to make an elevated product that's luxurious, light and modern. Even in the hallowed world of Paris couture, he says, 'most of the fabrics are machine-made now, so handwork is vanishing'.

In Mishra's processes 'many people work together on an embroi-dery, they sit together, perhaps four people around one frame, and they work with great skill. That's what I want to promote: the unique possibilities of that.'

He made his Paris fashion week debut for Spring '15, and as part of his Woolmark prize won contracts to supply some of the world's leading department stores. He flew to Australia to see David Jones, and took in a tour of a Merino station in the New South Wales South-ern Tablelands.

'I started weaving with wool because I love the idea behind it, and there is no killing involved as, for example, there is with non-Ahimsa silk,' he says. 'Growing a fleece takes almost a year; a slow fibre for my slow fashion.'

There are prizes for wool growers too, and they centre on Australia, which produces around 90 per cent of the world's fine apparel wool (although it consumes less than 1 per cent of the finished product). The best stuff comes from the Merino breed, and the best of that from the Superfine Merino.

In 2015, there were around 75 million sheep in Australia. 'That's down from a 1970 high of 180 million, thanks to competitive fibre use,' says Stuart McCullough, CEO of AWI. He's talking about all that polyester and conventionally grown cotton. 'It's a pretty simple equation: if consumers choose other fibres then the price of wool won't flow back to growers' pockets, and they will say, "Bugger this, let's use our land for something more profitable."'[2]

The price of fine wool has bucked up since McCullough came on board in 2010. AWI, which is not-for-profit, now spends 60 per cent of grower levies on marketing (pre-2007, it all went on research and development) – the Woolmark Prize is a big part of that, as is the Campaign for Wool, which aims to bridge the gap between fashion and farm.

Personally, I'm a fan. Wool is a natural fibre and unlike, say, conventionally grown cotton, it needs only water and grass to grow. It is renewable – sheep grow new fleeces every year. Wool breathes, it biodegrades, it's gorgeous. Like any other fibre it runs into potential problems during processing – the scouring and dyeing processes in particular tend to use harsh chemicals – but the European mills are ahead of the game when it comes to waste and water management.

'We've got to make the consumer aware where the fibre comes from, and the farmer aware where it sells to,' says McCullough. And so Woolmark brings sheep into unlikely locations for the cameras – on the roof of the Musée d'Art Moderne with the Eiffel Tower in the background, for example, or posing with Alexander Wang in a graffiti-ridden alley near his New York office.

The Prince of Wales is patron of the Campaign for Wool – and he is keen to reboot the British wool industry. Although farmers continue to struggle, there is money to be made.

I was among the thousand guests at the Sydney party for the fiftieth anniversary of the Ermenegildo Zegna Wool Trophy in 2013. Lavish doesn't do it justice; there were rivers of champagne, and chefs cooking paella in giant pans as if expecting *Thor* himself to turn up for supper. Actually, he did – Chris Hemsworth walked the runway, in three-piece houndstooth. He was flanked by 60 male models, more than half of them flown in especially from Europe.

Zegna is the biggest menswear brand in the world, and the Ermenegildo Zegna Group turns over €1.2 billion a year. Based in Italy, it's a vertical operation, so it owns the mills that weave the cloth for its suits, and as of 2014 it owns the farms that grow the wool too – at least, 60 per cent of one of the farms: Achill station in New South Wales. They plan to invest in more properties down the track. A Zegna suit costs several thousand dollars, and although more wool cloth is now woven in China than Italy, the Italians still supply the biggest luxury players, particularly in menswear, and operate the poshest mills. Zegna's produce fabric for high-end tailors, as well as the likes of Gucci and Tom Ford. Their rival, the ultra-luxe Loro Piana mill (cashmere expert, now 80 per cent owned by LVMH), sells to Brioni and Brooks Brothers. The Italians compete for the lowest micron (diameter) Superfine, use high-tech and often eco-aware processes, and push the idea that 'provenance is the new luxury'.

The Zegna trophy is prestigious, but more lucrative for winning growers is the fledgling gong awarded by another Italian mill, one that's been around for more than 350 years, Vitale Barberis Canonico. Their Wool Excellence Award recognises 'wool produced under natural pastoral and grazing conditions with the highest regard for the environment and the animal'. To launch it in 2014, they held an elaborate dinner in the private dining room at Sydney's Quay restaurant, an establishment that serves things topped with foam and seaweed and calls its cream 'cultured'. I sat across from Tasmanian growers Simon and Ann Louise Cameron, and their farm manager Lyndel Poole, who were in the running with the clip (wool shorn in one season) from Kingston in Tasmania. They came third, but if they were disappointed they didn't show it as they cheered for the victors.

First prize was a trip to Italy, and 'a monetary reward equivalent to the full delivered value of the wool purchased from the winning clip by Vitale Barberis Canonico' that season. Double your money. Third place won a plaque.

What the butt?

Storm has a great bum. There are three of us squinting at it, as we lean, elbow-to-elbow, on a gate. In fact, Storm, a Superfine Merino ram, is a bit of a looker all round. It was love at first sight when Lyndel Poole first spotted him at the Bendigo Sheep and Wool Show.

For months Poole had been looking for the ideal ram to take back to Kingston, an historic 8,000-acre property near Campbell Town, Tasmania. Ideal meant big and healthy with a tidy backside – what's known as plain-bodied. Wrinkly folds in the skin can collect moisture and dirt, and attract the blowflies. 'Cutting them off [mulesing] is not a nice process,' says Poole.[3]

The female blowfly likes to lay eggs in wet wool, around those folds under the tail and along the sheep's back. The eggs hatch into maggots, which feed on skin and flesh. Left untreated, most affected sheep will slowly die. Mulesing is generally performed on lambs between two and twelve weeks old.

'When I first came to Kingston, the mulesing contractors wanted to work at their own pace, which in our case meant doing the job in one day,' says Poole. 'We had to spend more money to make sure those sheep healed, they took a lot of looking after. Some died, they'd been treated so badly. The next time we tried a different contractor, and they were good, but I still felt that I didn't want to do it. And this is in the broader context of pressure on the industry from the animal rights people.'

What attracted Poole to Storm was the likelihood of wrinkle-free offspring.

'We don't push the land. We select the genetics that are suited to it,' says Simon Cameron. He owns the place; Poole runs it. 'So Lyndel is breeding the best sheep for the property.'

Kingston is lucky as far as elevation goes; it tends towards cooler and drier, but flies do breed in the grass here when it's wet. 'We have to monitor the sheep and keep them clean around the crutch,' says Poole. If necessary, they apply a topical fly dressing as prevention and treatment. 'Because of our target market, mulesing is not a choice for us now.'

In fact, while only wool from non-mulesed sheep is accepted for competition by Zegna, Barberis is less strict – a clip from a mulesed flock is eligible, as long as growers have used a registered pain relief product for at least three years. The RSPCA claims the pain involved 'is similar to that of castration, but it lasts longer (up to forty-eight hours)' and causes the animal suffering and distress. They say it should be a farmer's 'last option'.

PETA wants it banned altogether. At the height of their anti-mulesing campaign, when they pushed for a boycott on Aussie wool and AWI tried to sue them, a bunch of brands including H&M and Hugo Boss announced they'd stop using wool from mulesed flocks. AWI introduced labelling in 2007, but it's voluntary. 'If you don't declare you're non-mulesed, it's obvious you're not,' says Poole.

But, she adds, it's not always an easy call for growers. Flystrike is horrible 'and all farmers care about the animals. Sheep grown under some conditions – and I have to be a bit careful here because I haven't experienced them – but where pastures are watered, for instance, big irrigators; or where the climate is humid, the flies love all that so it would be much harder to have the right husbandry for non-mulesed sheep.'

◎

When Poole arrived at Kingston eight years ago, 'plenty thought I'd last about eight minutes. People don't think a woman can run a farm.' She knew better. Her grandmother ran her own farm on Tasmania's east coast. 'She drove a bullock team, she was a formidable woman.' Takes one to know one.

Cameron inherited Kingston in 2004, but it didn't make financial sense to leave his Sydney IT business to run the place full time. 'I wish it did,' he says. 'I'd like more flexibility to put more cerebral horsepower into what we do.' He needed a farm manager, someone who shared his big ideas. He needed Poole.

Cameron's great-grandfather had bought Kingston as a 'bolt-on property' for grazing in 1905. It's tough land – hilly, rugged – so no one bothered to plough it up, but it was ideal for Merinos with wattle to chomp on and plenty of kangaroo grass, *Themeda triandra*.

Poole lives in the old cottage, which dates from John Batman's grazier days. Batman lived here in the 1820s with his convict wife Eliza, before founding the settlement that would become Melbourne; 'founding' makes it sounds nice but it wasn't. Batman was a brutal bastard who did unspeakable things to indigenous people. (He is no relation to the Camerons.) Now we are sitting in the pretty back parlour. There's a spider the size of a cat on the ceiling.

Cameron chooses a cake from a plate piled high, takes a sip of his tea and says, 'That wonderful Dorothea Mackellar poem about Australia – the sunburnt country, the wide brown lands – she wasn't talking about the dustbowl, she was talking about the Themeda. A lot of it has been lost because it's not a highly productive grass. In Tasmania as a whole, there's about 3 per cent left of what was here when the whites came.'

'Simon, I just want to pull you in about Themeda being unproductive,' says Poole. 'Actually it's the best summer grass we've got. When those exotic species they spend so much money planting are dying, Themeda is flourishing. All it needs is a light shower.'

Much of the land around Kingston has been artificially transformed into verdant crop fields – washed through with irrigation water that grows saltier by the year, and treated with superphosphate fertilisers. Cameron's inheritance is some of the only pristine grassland left in the region.

He reaches for a map, smooths it out across the table between us. 'Each one of those coloured dots is a threatened or endangered species,' he says, explaining that in 2005 some senior government botanists conducted a natural values survey here. He has a copy of the report to show me, and he reads a bit out: '"Kingston is one of the few remaining arable valley flats in Tasmania to retain native vegetation at a landscape scale. Kingston retains roughly 8 per cent of all kangaroo grass in Tasmania and roughly 1 per cent of the tussock grass. It is highly likely that the natural values retained on Kingston make this property of national significance." It's pretty hard to plough it up when somebody has put that in a document! I have had proposals to chop into it.'

A three-dollar mining company wanted to put down exploratory drill holes across the conservation area that comprises 30 per cent of Kingston, and Cameron fought them tooth and nail and won – for now at least. The day-to-day battles are less dramatic, but nothing is easy. 'There's a lot of farming people who would say, "Let's just make this place as productive as we can for now," but I've got a longer term view,' says Cameron. 'I have a responsibility. Once this goes, that's a large chunk of biodiversity shot to pieces. If we didn't graze it, or manage it somehow, the land would become overgrown with one thing,' he says. 'We've got big job to manage out imported invasive species like willows, hawthorns, briars and gorse.'

They must cull the roos that overgraze the Themeda, and they worry about a parcel of land on their border that was planted with pine by collapsed timber giant Gunns. And yet the pros outweigh the cons. There are wedge-tailed eagles and peregrines on Kingston, and Tassie bettongs. 'They're like a very tiny roo,' says Poole. 'Some people want to call them a potoroo, but they're not; these guys look like they're wearing mascara.' And there are wonderful wildflowers. Cameron's eyes sparkle as he describes them.

'Now, look at these fantastic things here,' he says, showing me a blown-up photograph of a tiny lily. 'They're about the size of your fingernail. See the raindrop on that one, gives you an idea. You don't set out to find them.'

'You come across them,' says Poole.

'This blue flower – do we know what this is?' says Cameron.

'*Dianella tasmanica*,' says Poole. 'And that's *Pterostylis commutata*.'

'Otherwise known as a Midland Greenhood,' says Cameron. 'Again, it's tiny. You don't find them until you're on your hands and knees. Sorry but you're a bit late for them, come back in spring. Now this one, it's a sundew, carnivorous.'

'They live off flies,' says Poole.

'And look at all this Wahlenbergia,' says Cameron, 'like bluebells. In lots of places you find them in ones and twos – in Kingston you get great lumps of stuff. This, now, this is my favourite, it epitomises the farmer: it's a really optimistic plant, what's it called? Ar … starts with an A—'

'*Arthropodium minus*,' says Poole. 'The purple flowers are the most resilient.'

'Why it's so optimistic,' says Cameron, 'is, this is where they grow – a rock with a bit of dirt. Soon as it dries out they're gone. Why would something so beautiful turn up in such an inhospitable place? Farmers are like that. Perennial optimists. I think there's a parallel there.'

◉

The Camerons and Lyndel Poole are those rare folk who are interesting and interested, and they want to know all about what I do and what makes the fashion industry tick, so I tell them about Stella McCartney, because I think she would appreciate their approach to growing wool.

They've never heard of Stella, so I tell them she's Paul and Linda's daughter, and they know about Linda's vegetarian sausages, because everyone of a certain age does. I explain about Stella's vegan ethics and her industry clout. And the fact that she has a carefully considered sustainability policy, and is probably the leading ethically minded fashion designer in the luxury bracket. That basically Stella rules.

The sun is low now and through the window the valley dips, and the gums frame the scene. As Ann Louise pours me a glass of wine, we look up Stella's website, scrolling through pictures of beautiful coats that cost more than the Camerons get at auction for a whole bale of their wool. You could make about 100 coats from one bale, Cameron says. We read about how Stella McCartney has partnered with the Nature Conservancy to use wool from a flock of sustainably grazed, non-mulesed sheep in Argentina. The program, which operates with a local B Corp partner called Ovis 21, aims to restore depleted grasslands in the Patagonia region, which sounds kind of like Kingston's approach albeit on a much bigger scale.

'But why Argentina?' says Poole.

I tell her I have no idea, beyond the fact that this faraway grass evidently needs some love. I tell her that Stella McCartney is a British label, headquartered in London, although it is owned by Kering, which is based in Paris. Surely McCartney could find a happy flock on home turf which would help the Campaign for Wool *and* make Prince Charles happy, and maybe give his great sheep hope, the Bowmont, a lovely luxury market for their coats. Maybe she'll do that next time. Or maybe she'll read this and Google 'SustainaWOOL' to find accredited Aussie suppliers like Kingston. Or call up Simon Cameron direct (Stella, please call up Simon Cameron direct! I will give you his number.)

There's a photo online of a mob of the Patagonian sheep, their little white faces jostling for position. Poole tuts.

'What?'

'Look at that!' she says. They've been branded with blue paint, which can damage the fleece. 'Tell Stella Mcwhatsit that you won't find me doing that to our girls.'

Eight months after my visit to Kingston, PETA released video footage allegedly showing farms that are part of the Ovis 21 network mistreating sheep. McCartney immediately cut ties with them, and announced she was looking into vegan 'wool' now.

Tour de Sheep

It was a covert op. Crews arrived at 10.30 p.m. to clear London's Sav-ile Row of parked cars. 'Some of them had to be towed,' explained Mark Gregory, an affable grey-haired gent in a high-vis vest. They put down 1,000 metres of turf and set up pens in the road outside Gieves & Hawkes and Hardy Amies, preparing for the 7 a.m. arrival of the stars of the show: a flock of Exmoor Horn and Bowmont sheep.

The Savile Row ring-ins weren't the first sheep to hit the capital that October for the 2010 launch of the Campaign for Wool. The day before, fifteen of their mates, dyed Selfridges yellow, paid a call on that department store in a stunt that would have made Harry Self-ridge proud. Vogue threw a Wool Week party at the restaurant in Selfridges' shoe department (lamb canapés were on the menu). 'All we are saying,' quipped Condé Nast's Nicholas Coleridge, 'is give fleece a chance.'

Wool Week in the UK now attracts all sorts of fun. One Sunday morning during the 2014 event, modern Miss Marples in checked capes, hipsters in Fair Isle vests and more fellows in tweeds than I'd thought were left in the world cycled down the Strand. It was the inaugural Wool Ride. The Tour-de-Sheep. Of course it was. And at the end of the thirteen-mile route that passed Big Ben and Bucking-ham Palace, there was a prize for best outfit.

This was also the week that the jumpers Prince Charles had bur-ied in his garden were dug up – one pure wool, one grotty synthetic, dispatched to their earthly graves four months previously so see how they fared breaking down. The wool number was on its way to mulch; the synthetic one, perky as the day it was born.

CHAPTER 20

Can We Really Change Our Ways?

Selling ideas vs. selling out

Dame Vivienne Westwood is giving an interview on camera.[1] She's on the lawn at Clarence House, London, where the Prince of Wales is about to host yet another eco-aware event. Not the Campaign for Wool this time, but his Garden Party to Make a Difference, in support of sustainable living. Westwood's carrot-coloured hair is swept up becomingly. Her dangly earrings swing. She is clearly in a good mood, smiling and flirtatious.

Her dress is made from the wool cloth known as Prince of Wales check (after Edward VII before he was crowned). It is, remarks Westwood, 'a very traditional English thing', although it's actually Scottish: tradtional Glen plaid from Inverness-shire, where the Countess of Seafield, a Kiwi by birth, dressed her gamekeepers in it.

Less traditional is the cut of Westwood's frock. You can see the men's boxers she's wearing underneath it. If she were younger, she explains, she wouldn't bother with underwear. Then she reconsiders, and says: 'I think it's really cool wearing these boxer shorts ... Borrow your husband's!'

Westwood is keen on the sustainable possibilities of wearing clothes already in existence. 'Buy less, choose well,' she urges, in the soft Derbyshire accent she has never quite lost. 'And also, do it yourself. So for example, I went down a discotheque with a towel [on] instead of a coat. My friend said to me, "Oh don't go out with that towel. I can lend you a cashmere shawl." I said, "No, no this is much more chic." As it happens somebody spilt wine on me, which was quite good.' Whether it was good because the wine stained the towel and not the cashmere, or because it lent her look a daredevil edge, we can only guess.

Vivienne Westwood was always an unconventional fashion designer. She began her working life as a school teacher, and sees her collections as agents for social change, not trends. As far back as 1976, she was claiming that her aim wasn't to sell, 'but to convert, educate, liberate'.

It was around 2006 when Westwood started to tell people to buy less for the sake of the environment. She publically dismissed 'the drug of consumerism' and launched her Get A Life manifesto calling for people to spend more time in art galleries to 'become more cultivated and therefore more human'.

Her Spring '07 collection, titled 'I am Expensiv' [sic], explored the idea that if fashion could talk it might say 'I'm a spoilt little girl, I come in a package all wrapped up like Barbie and I am supported and subsidised by all the poor people in the world.'

Now she was reading the work of geophysicist James Lovelock, who had developed his Gaia theory – essentially that the Earth is alive and therefore subject to disease as well as good health – back in the '70s.

By the 2000s, Lovelock was a leading bell ringer for climate change. In an article for the *Independent,* the self-styled 'planetary physician' announced that his patient suffered from an imminent 'morbid fever', predicting 'before this century is over, billions of us will die and the few breeding pairs of people that survive will be in the Arctic'[2] (an idea that in 2012 he recanted, saying that while climate change remains a problem, he'd been alarmist about the timing).

Westwood's response was to step up the campaigning. In 2011, she pledged £1 million to the charity Cool Earth. Her runway shows encourage her audiences to support the Green Party and help save the rainforests. She once took a shower on camera for PETA to push the idea that meat production uses too much water. In 2015, she drove a tank to UK Prime Minister David Cameron's country house to 'declare war on fracking'. Westwood has advice for all sorts: from the Duchess of Cambridge (who should wear things 'over and again because that's very good for the environment') to those who can't afford organic food ('eat less'). But no matter how loud this chatter gets, her 'buy less' message rings above it all. She has promised to inscribe those two little words above her Rue Saint Honoré shop when it opens in Paris in 2016.

Guests at the Autumn '13 show for her second line, Vivienne West-wood Red Label, received a copy of Westwood's own Climate Revolution Charter, including a checklist on *How to Join the Revolution*. Point number one: 'Money is a means, not an end in itself'. Two was 'Quality v. Quantity'. Point number three read 'Buy less, choose well, make it last (we don't want the "latest thing" just for the sake of it).'

But while writing such a slogan above the door of your flash new Paris shop is a bold move, it doesn't change the fact that *it's still a flash new Paris shop*. Last time I looked, shops were in the business of selling. It's that thorny issue raised by the *New Yorker* with reference to Patagonia: how can a clothing brand convincingly deliver the anti-consumerist message? Is it not absurd for them to even try?

When Greenpeace quoted Westwood's catchphrase on its Face-book page in November 2014, there was a torrent of vitriol, most about the fact that Westwood is 'rich' and successful. She was called 'snotty, elitist and right wing', and 'a purveyor of scandalously over-priced shite'. Accused of 'lecturing people from millionaires' row [while] selling her clothes for big bucks', and being a 'total hypocrite'; 'the woman who made flipping great wodges of cash out of commercialising punk? Ha!'

Yvon Chouinard has more chance of making the 'buy less' message stick because his anti-fashion claims stack up (tools not toys). It is even harder to take an eco stand as a runway darling. The fashion fans aren't listening, while the Greenpeace fans think you're a depraved capitalist pig for daring to make frivolous clothes in the first place. Viv saying poor people should eat less didn't help. The only way to avoid charges of hypocrisy is to stop selling fashion altogether.

Wayne Hemingway closed Red or Dead because he hated the game. Jean Paul Gaultier retired from ready-to-wear (in 2014) to escape its frenzied limitations: 'I love fashion but not the route it is taking,' he told *WWD*. 'Commercial constraints as well as the frenetic pace of collections don't leave any freedom, nor the necessary time to find fresh ideas.' Viktor and Rolf cited similar reasons for bowing out of ready-to-wear shortly after.

Orsola de Castro shuttered From Somewhere because she 'wanted to not compromise ... I'm forever trying to make my clothes cheaper to compete with things that I shouldn't be trying to compete with.' When I asked if she thought the fashion system was broken she said, 'It's a thriving machine geared to make us consume, so we cannot say it's broken, but it has become disassociated from its vital organs: it is no longer feeling, it no longer has a heart. Above all, it no longer has any shred of common sense.'

And yet those who work within it, and indeed anyone who has ever been smitten by the power of glamour and clothes, find it hard to go cold turkey.

Katharine Hamnett says, 'Fashion as a concept will always interest me. Apart from keeping us warm and protected, it's status; it's about finding a mate, it's about dressing up as someone you'd like to be, it's fascinating. Fashion will always exist, and I am glad about that. But the fashion *industry* needs to be reformed.'

Hamnett believes consumers have the power here. 'So, how about "buy right"?' she says. 'Buy thoughtfully. Buy consciously. First of all look at vintage, that's the easiest, because then you can cheat. If you buy a vintage dress you're let off the hook in some ways, because you're not buying something that has damaged the planet just for you.

'Then ask questions, ask for organic, don't buy things like PVC. Be informed. And don't look frumpy,' is Hamnett's parting shot, 'because it will make you miserable.'

What has been green cannot be ungreen

'Oh. My. God,' I say.

'Hello to you too,' says Sarah Wilson, who has just walked into the café I'm brunching in.

'B-b-but ...'

'But what?'

'THE SHORTS!' I feel a need to grab the shorts, to touch them, to prove to myself – and perhaps to Wilson – that they are in fact what they seem – i.e. not the old ones – and so I lurch up from my chair, knocking it flying. At the next table, a child begins to sob.

It's a scorcher of a Sydney day and Wilson is wearing a brand new pair of shorts. They are not green, but black.

'Ah,' she says, glancing down and recoiling slightly. I swear she'd forgotten they were there. 'They did come from a shop, but I had a voucher. I held out as long as possible.'

Wilson has ethical objections to clothes shopping. She believes that the acquisition of fashion and other consumer goods is wasteful and that 'giving a shit about consumption and the planet broadly isn't about de-cluttering; it's about not buying stuff in the first place'. Having to make a trip to The Shops, she says, 'insults' her, and robs her of time she could spend doing something she enjoys, like hiking or riding her bike, or promoting her *I Quit Sugar* empire.

A few weeks before our encounter, she wrote on her blog about her old green shorts, which she'd bought eight years ago, on sale, at American Apparel. She wore them for four years 'every day, until the holes became obscene'[3] then recycled them into a grease rag for her bike. Out of necessity, she replaced the original green shorts with a second pair; out of choice she went for the exact same style: 'Same size, same colour, no need to try them on' and had worn them 'virtually every day since – hiking, at yoga, at the gym, to the pool'.

The blog post was inspired by the fact that this second pair was now nearing the end of its productive life, and then some. Strangers had begun to comment on their decrepitude. Because Wilson was rarely seen in anything else, someone started the hashtag #greenshorts on social media.

At Wilson's fortieth birthday dinner, her family pulled out the shorts and made her wear them on her head for a photo (along with her childhood eye-patch – thanks mum and dad). Even in the eye patch, Wilson looked gorgeous. She was in a fancy strapless bronze bustier dress with a complicated draped skirt that could've been by Westwood; but no – Wilson bought it when she was 18 from a reclaim outlet at a Canberra rubbish dump. It cost $4. Twenty-two years later it was still going strong.

The dress fit the theme of the birthday party, which was sustainability. Wilson didn't want to throw a wasteful bash that would give her an ethical hangover, so she had her tables decorated with twigs, branches and flowers collected 'from the side of the road'[4] and designed a menu of foraged, local or organic booze and food (including 'Tuna Trash Tartare' – the chef 'took a tuna carcass from Cleanfish Australia, that would otherwise be turfed and, using a spoon, scraped off all the flesh from around the bones to create [it]'). Guests were asked to bring containers to take leftovers home. Napkins were washable linen. Needless to say, the cake was sugar-free.

Anyway, twelve months after this soiree, Wilson's colleagues were threatening to frame the decaying second-coming-of-the-shorts and hang them in the office as an artwork. She knew their days were numbered, but she wasn't happy about it.

'I like to fend,' she wrote. 'I like to work from leftovers, scraps, rejects. I like to avoid shopping, partly because it takes up valuable time. And Things make me unhappy. It's the bother of having to store them and account for them and think about them. It all interrupts the flow of a morning. And of a life well-lived.'

I first met Wilson ages ago when she was editor of the Aussie edition of *Cosmopolitan*, and my first impression was one of shimmering glamour – and great legs. In my memory she is forever striding through parties on her model-worthy pins, tanned from Bondi summers and clad in smart little shorts of various kinds. Was it possible there were some made from leather? And sequins? 'It's possible,' she concedes.[5] I seem to recall a lot of wedge heels; this she denies – 'I've always been a flat sandals person.' Okay, but Wilson does have quite a fashion-y past. After her magazine life, she co-presented *Master-Chef Australia*, necessitating a wide and varied TV-appropriate wardrobe. 'None if which I bought,' she says. 'I insisted it was all borrowed. My life in minimalism came after that, but I personally never bought into the consumerist ideal.'

She grew up on a farm, where growing food and making stuff was the norm. 'I worked in magazines to tell stories,' she says. As an editor, she was offered the usual freebies from fashion brands. 'I was offered gifted handbags and I turned them down. I just wasn't into it. In fact I don't think I've ever bought a handbag. I was once given one by the *Cosmo* team in the US, which I used. At the moment I have a bag I had made from excess material from my couch. For three years the only one I had was canvas from Byron Bay markets. People have enormous complicated backpacks but I've hiked with just that cloth bag.' Not that she wants you to chuck yours out if you have one.

'This idea that minimising is about, "Oh I've got too many things! I should get rid of them!" That is the most ridiculous thing I ever heard. People get rid off all this stuff, then they find they have "gaps in their wardrobe"; they don't have the long-sleeved top they need to wear under their whatever, so off they go and buy more. I would say people need, what? Ten per cent of the clothing they buy? Fending is one of the greatest things you can do. And you know what? We enjoy it,' she tells me. It makes us more creative, and that makes us feel proud of ourselves. 'You know how food tastes great when you go camping, and you've only got a little stove and a few veggies and some cabanossi but you make something everyone loves. It's the same when you don't have a lot of clothes.'

Dismiss fashion's prescription and you have to dig deeper to define your own style. You could indeed be camping on your weekend, or picnicking, or dancing or exercising or reading. Why would anyone *choose* to fall victim to the gruen transfer instead, asks Wilson. It's a fair point.

'I am oblivious to all that until I go to a mall,' she says. 'Then, like everyone else I feel it, I get sucked in, I see all these people with [carrier] bags and see things hanging seductively in the windows and I start to want them, and to question myself: I'm feeling a bit out of touch now. Should I be updating my look? That is deeply annoying. And it's also nonsense, so I avoid it. If you don't go to the shops, it doesn't happen.'

Just say no

In 2009, Brooklyn-based creative director Sheena Matheiken launched the Uniform Project, which entailed her wearing the same little black dress, in creative ways, for 365 consecutive days.

She did this to promote the idea of sustainable fashion, and also to raise money for a not-for-profit organisation called the Akanksha Foundation, providing education to underprivileged children living in Indian slums. Matheiken's quest was reported from CNN and the BBC to *Teen Vogue* and *Elle*, and people donated not just money (over $100,000 for Akanksha) but alo second-hand garments and accessories for Matheiken to dress her dress up with. At the end of the year these were auctioned off.

But people, being people, weren't content just to watch and learn – they wanted the dress for themselves. They just couldn't help wanting to shop, even as that funny little cap-sleeved A-line dress, designed to be worn either forwards or backwards, or even undone as a jacket, 'grew beyond simply being a dress, becoming more of a symbol of social change for the community of supporters around the world'.[6] Matheiken found herself in the curious position of considering manufacturing and selling the very thing she had cast as her 'statement against overconsumption'.

She decided to harness the consumer desire she had unwittingly created and milk it for the sake of Akanksha, and had a limited edition of 365 dresses made up to sell to fans, diverting the profits to the fund. Those who missed out could download the pattern for free from the Uniform Project website, and make their own.

The same year Matheiken was pushing her LBD to the limits, 20 or so people joined an online group committing to the Great American Apparel Diet – a year-long 'fast' from buying new clothes. Within a few months their numbers swelled to 300.

Six Items or Less also explored the 'shopping diet' idea. Around 100 people initially took up the challenge, and the *New York Times* commented: 'Though their numbers may be small, and their diets extreme, these self-deniers of fashion are representative ... of a broader reckoning of consumers' spending habits. As the economy begins to improve, shoppers of every income appear to be wrestling with the same questions: Is it safe to go back to our old, pre-recession ways? Or should we? The authors of these diets – including some fashion marketing and advertising executives, interestingly enough – seem to think not.'[7]

In Melbourne, former consumer PR Tamara DiMattina had just completed a nine-month fellowship at the Centre for Sustainability Leadership, and was buzzed about conscientious consumption. If she could encourage people to stop shopping for new stuff for a month, she decided, that might get them thinking longer term about how and why they bought things, and about more sustainable alternatives.

Her national campaign, Buy Nothing New Month (BNNM), was in its third year when it came onto my radar – and I took it personally. At that time, 2012, I was running my fashion business, and had a shop on Sydney's Oxford Street. Financially I was struggling, and I wasn't the only one. There seemed to be another 'For Lease' sign every time I looked.

One morning I picked up a newspaper to find a dirty great photograph of our embattled block inside. Once 'Sydney's premier shopping destination for fashion lovers', it was now branded 'a ghost town'. I don't mind telling you that I put my head in my hands and cried. It was a shit climate to run a small business in, and the effing last thing I needed was some anti-capitalist Melburnian hippie rallying people to stop shopping. Not, from where I was standing, that they needed much encouragement.

The press smelled a story when the City of Sydney allowed BNNM to install an exhibition at the Custom's House, Circular Quay. The installation was designed to show visitors sustainable home ideas and promote second-hand goods, but NSW Premier Barry O'Farrell pronounced the whole thing 'nuts', and said that 'shop less, live more' could soon become 'shop less, live poor' for the third of the city's workers who are employed by the retail sector.

Daily Telegraph columnist Miranda Devine suggested we boycott the boycott and start a counter campaign called 'Don't pay rates for a year'. DiMattina, who had until now tried to stay in the background, found herself on the news trying to explain that her idea was not anti-retail. 'I'm actively promoting the second-hand retail sector,' she says.[8] 'Think of the millions of dollars spent promoting fashion brands; this is one girl with a laptop. If people are threatened by me with no money and no office, saying, "Hey, let's think a bit more about our stuff," seriously, *that's nuts*. And also bad luck – if what you are doing is not sustainable, I want you to change that.'

Eighteen months later, having returned to my first career as a journalist, I wrote a magazine feature called 'Closed For Business?' It told of an unprecedented number of independent Australian brands (including Collette Dinnigan, Lisa Ho, Kirrily Johnson, Ksubi, Alannah Hill, Bettina Liano) either closing or going into receivership over a five-year period. Competition from online and fast fashion, plus high rents and rampant sale culture were making it increasingly hard to stay in the black. No wonder retailers got their backs up about BNNM.

Second-hand but not second rate

Tamara DiMattina answers the door to her Melbourne townhouse wearing a crisp cotton sundress and jewelled Mary Janes. A bulldog at her feet beats the floor with his tail, and gives me a gappy grin.

'This is Leopold,' says DiMattina. 'Don't mind him, he's just had his teeth out.'

The dog notes the slightest inclination of my head, and bounds toward me.

'Leopold was second-hand,' she says. 'Best pre-loved treasure I ever got.'

This is not what I expected. I don't want to like DiMattina, business ruiner, anti-shopping nutter. But I do. I totally love her. And Leopold. They're legends.

We settle down in her kitchen (lots of wood and glass, doesn't look vintage) and I explain all this. 'I'm used to the haters,' she says. 'But you have to ask yourself, why do you have all this baggage?'

I tell her that BNNM felt like an affront to me, and she says, essentially, good; because the whole idea was to ignite reactions. 'That's why it's called Buy Nothing New Month. If it was called Second-hand September or Op Shop October, who would listen? The idea is that it's pointy, we want to jolt people.'

But second-hand isn't the only sustainable shopping choice. What about the ethical fashion retailers and the eco-vendors who sell new product?

'I like them,' she says.

'But you are saying don't shop there for a month, either. What if the store is tiny, and can't support four weeks of crap sales?'

'It's not like everyone's going to listen to me.'

'But you want them to.'

'Of course.'

'But if no one shopped for new stuff, then no one would make it, so no one would pass it on, and there wouldn't be any second-hand stuff. And then the economy would melt down and there would be riots and war, probs. And we'd have to live in caves making fire with sticks.'

'That's so dumb,' she laughs, pouring me some coffee from a second-hand pot. 'I don't think that's a likely outcome.'

'It's complicated,' I say. 'Is this coffee new?'

'It's actually very simple. I am not saying don't spend. I am saying spend more consciously; try buying experiences and services over stuff you don't need, see how you go. You might like it.'

◎

DiMattina can't pinpoint the exact moment the idea for BNNM hit, but in hindsight it seems like her whole life was gearing up for it. 'As a kid, when we'd drive around at night I remember looking at all the lights left on in the shops and getting stressed out; I'd go on about how wasteful it was. And I'd see all the sale signs, 50 per cent off, and think, where does all that stuff go?'

Her grandmother was a designer. DitMattina likes fashion; she even considered studying it, but did an arts degree instead. As a student in Melbourne she 'shopped at Witchery, without thinking much about it', but when she moved to London in her early twenties, money for clothes was tight. 'I shared a bedroom in Kensington with a girl-friend. It was around 1998, I was working at Sotheby's on Bond Street. It was all very lovely but I couldn't afford to dress as smartly as I needed to. A lot of trust fund people work there, ha ha! That wasn't me. Sometimes I couldn't pay my rent.'

She bought a sewing machine on eBay and became a thrift-store shopper. 'It was more "make-do" than joyful. I felt like I wasn't good enough because I wasn't earning enough.' DiMattina brought her op-shopping habit back to Melbourne. 'But I didn't want to be that person who had to buy stuff in a charity store – I would look around and make sure no one saw me go in. That's basically the opposite of what I feel now. Actually I'd probably feel ashamed to walk into a high street store now.'

Guilt and shame. Powerful incentives, both. DiMattina was also feeling increasingly guilty about her job in consumer PR. 'I got paid to encourage people to sbuy things they don't need. It made me feel sick, knowing how much rubbish we were creating. In those days, I'd sometimes mentioned to my boss little things we could do to be more environmentally aware, like switching the brand of paper we used in the printer, and I'd get called the herbal hippie.'

She left the agency and started taking on her own clients with an ethical agenda: a women's centre, a mental health association. Enter the environmental scientist boyfriend who encouraged her to take a trip to Antarctica. She went for two weeks, and came back set on using her marketing skills to reduce our impact on the environment. 'I think a lot of people have an emotional shift there, when they see how beautiful and pristine the natural world can be.'

The idea behind BNNM is to encourage us to think about how and why we consume. Let's start with her.

'There is, um, quite a lot of stuff in this apartment,' I say.

'Oh I know, I do love stuff. I have absolutely far too much of it. Ironically I'm a hoarder. I am a creative person. What can I say? Minimalism doesn't serve my soul.'

'So you buy all this second-hand stuff because it defines you creatively?'

'I'm a hunter-gatherer. I like the joy of the hunt. I just don't want that to screw up the environment any more than it has to,' she says, before describing a trip she made with her father to Mumbai's Dharavi slum, a place where even rubbish has value.

'Have you ever been to a tip?' she says. 'Go check one out and you will see truck after truck ploughing our stuff into the ground. You buy cheap clothes in your lunchbreak then your wardrobe overflows so you dump them outside a charity store, but they're worthless – they can't sell them. The Salvos tip fees for Melbourne alone are $3 million a year. The UK is going to run out of landfill space by 2018. What's it all for?'

For the first BNNM campaign, in October 2010, DiMattina partnered with Salvos stores nationally to promote shopping second-hand, and she dressed breakfast telly stars in vintage outfits. 'I wanted to show that second-hand is not automatically second rate.'

By 2012, she'd talked the Grand Hyatt into helping her furnish a 'second-hand' show home with beds and linen. 'When you book into a luxury hotel, you're not given brand new sheets, are you? You are using a towel that's been used by someone else, then laundered – and you do that happily, right? It's all about how we sell the message. No one goes to a restaurant and thinks, eiww, that cutlery has been used before, and yet people think it's gross to buy it second-hand. What's with that?'

'I am no expert in sustainability,' says DiMattina. 'I'm just one person who thinks that through some very simple changes we can do better by ourselves and the planet.'

Couldn't have put it better myself.

Acknowledgments

I am lucky indeed to work with the exceptional Jeanne Ryckmans, Sophy Williams, Samantha Forge and the team at Nero – thank you for believing in this project. Without you, it simply would not be. And thanks, of course, to my fantastic family, friends and colleagues for your invaluable support. Sarah Wilson, what can I say? I am thrilled you wrote my foreword.

This book is about the people. So many were generous in sharing their time and knowledge. Hurray for Lucy Siegle, who on a busy trip to Sydney made time to meet a total stranger (me) for coffee. Thank you to Simone Cipriani and Chloé Mukai from the Ethical Fashion Initiative for all your help. And to Melinda Tually – a brilliant mentor.

I am grateful to all who submitted to my interview questions, or shared experience, contacts and leads, and in particular: Bethlehem Tilahun Alemu, Mark Angelo, Mark Anthony Browne, Joan Burstein, Sally Campbell, Orsola de Castro, Yvon Chouinard, Tim Coombs, Rosario Dawson, Jason Denham, Tamara DiMattina, Anke Domaske, Pamela Easton, Abrima Erwiah, Ben Esakoff, Betty Halbreich,

Katharine Hamnett, Wayne Hemingway, Barbara Hulanicki, Stella Jean, Katie Jones, Melody MacMillan, Stuart McCullough, Catarina Midby, Rahul Mishra, Kate Muir, Lydia Pearson, Roopa Pemmaraju, Gosia Piatek, Marisa Regozo, Liane Rossler, Annelinde Rossman, Jackie Ruddock, Guillaume de Seynes, Kelly Slater, Riz Smith, Carry Somers, Doug Stephens, Lucy Tammam, Heidi Taylor, Karen Walker, Kit Willow, Valentina Zarew, and Paul van Zyl.

Special thanks to Pierre Gryzbowski, who travelled to NYC from Washington especially to take me shopping; and to Simon and Ann Louise Cameron and Lyndel Poole, who invited me to beautiful Kingston in Tasmania to see what it's really like out there on the land.

Further Reading

Websites

bcorporation.net

bluesign.com

cleanclothes.org

ethicalfashioninitiative.org

fashionrevolution.org

greenpeace.org

parley.tv

patagonia.com/us/footprint

stellamccartney.com

thenewjoneses.com

Books

Bringing Home the Birkin, by Michael Tonello (Harper, 2008)

Cheap: The High Cost of Discount Culture, by Ellen Ruppel Shell (Penguin, 2010)

Chic Savages, by John Fairchild (Simon & Schuster, 1989)

Coco Chanel: The Legend and the Life, by Justine Picardie (It Books, 2010)

Committed: A Rabble-Rouser's Memoir, by Dan Mathews (Simon & Schuster, 2007)

David Jones: 175 Years, by Helen O'Neill (NewSouth, 2013)

Deluxe: How Luxury Lost its Luster, by Dana Thomas (Penguin, 2007)

Dior by Dior, by Christian Dior (Penguin, 1957)

Overdressed: The Shockingly High Cost of Cheap Fashion, by Elizabeth L. Cline, (Portfilio, 2013)

Shopping, Seduction and Mr Selfridge, by Lindy Woodhead (Profile Books, 2007)

Silent Spring, by Rachel Carson (1962, Houghton Mifflin)

The Asylum, by Simon Doonan (Blue Rider Press, 2013)

The Opulent Era: Fashions of Worth, Doucet and Pingat, by Elizabeth Ann Coleman (Thames & Hudson, 1989)

To Die For: Is Fashion Wearing Out The World?, by Lucy Siegle (Fourth Estate, 2011)

Vivienne Westwood: An Unfashionable Life, by Jane Mulvagh (HarperCollins, 1998)

Notes

Introduction

1 Lucy Siegle, To *Die For: Is Fashion Wearing Out The World* (Fourth Estate, 2011), p3

2 Ellen Ruppel Shell, *Cheap: The High Cost of Discount Culture* (Penguin, 2010), p202

Chapter 1: Behind the Seams

1 Nicholas Coleridge, *The Fashion Conspiracy* (William Heinemann, 1988), p131

2 Joan Burstein, interview with author, January 2015

3 Charles Manning, 'I DIYed clothes for John Galliano', cosmopolitan.com, 15 April 2014

Chapter 2: The Couture Effect

1 Claude Baillén, *Chanel Solitaire* (Collins, 1973), p57

2 Justine Picardie, *Coco Chanel: The Legend and the Life* (HarperCollins, 2010), p21

3 Ernestine Carter, *The Magic Names of Fashion* (Weidenfeld & Nicolson, 1980), p58

4 Beryl Jents, *Little Ol' Beryl from Bondi* (Macmillan Australia, 1983), p39

5 Jonathan Walford, *Forties Fashion: From Siren Suits to the New Look* (Thames & Hudson, 2008), p145

6 Christian Dior, *Dior by Dior* (Penguin, 1957), pp21–26

7 Jents, *Little Ol' Beryl*, ibid.

Chapter 3: More Please, Sir

1 Ben Summerskill, 'Shopping Can Make You Depressed', *The Guardian* (UK), 6 May 2001

2 Livia Firth, 'More Fashion Mileage Per Piece', *Business of Fashion*, 8 May 2014

3 Rebecca Lowthorpe, 'Is this the most provocative man in fashion?', *Elle* (UK), September 2014

4 Karl Lagerfeld, 'Paris Fashion Week: Is Karl Lagerfeld off his trolley? Audience strips shelves after show', video interview, *The Independent*, 30 September 2013

5 Suzy Menkes, interview with Imran Amed, *Business of Fashion*, 10 June 2014

6 Evan Osnos, 'Your cheap sweater's real cost', *Chicago Tribune*, 16 December 2006

7 Olivia Lidbury, 'George at Asda recreates the Chanel supermarket', *The Telegraph* (UK), 5 March 2014

8 'British brands linked to Bangladesh factory that burnt down', ITV.com, 10 October 2013

Chapter 4: Status Anxiety

1 Isabel Wilkinson, 'Paris when it glitters', *New York Magazine*, 28 July 2014

2 Annette Tapert and Diana Edkins, *The Power of Style* (Crown, 1994), pp15–28

3 Georgina Goodman, 'Pietro Yatorny', *Love Shoes and Other Stories*, 30 August 2013

4 Paulina Szmydke, 'Mouna Ayoub's moving sale', *WWD*, 19 March 2014

5 Thomas Adamson, 'Meet Mouna Ayoub: the billionaire haute couture collector', *The Telegraph* (UK), 20 February 2014

Chapter 5: Because You're Worth It

1 Sarah Jessica Parker, 'Sentimental, lady, modern – and surprisingly timeless', *The Financial Times*, 11 May 2012

2 Guillaume de Seynes, interview with author, October 2014

3 Kamel Hamadou, interview with author, October 2014

4 Michael Tonello, *Bringing Home the Birkin: My Life in Hot Pursuit of the World's Most Coveted Handbag* (Harper, 2009), p42

5 Lauren Sherman, 'Fashion Inflation: Why Are Prices Rising So Fast?', *Business of Fashion*, 2 August 2013

6 Dana Thomas, *Deluxe: How Luxury Lost its Lustre* (Penguin, 2007), pp8–9

7 Karen Walker, interview with author, October 2014

Chapter 6: What's in a Name?

1 'Lagerfeld's High Street Split', vogue.co.uk, 18 November 2004

2 arcadia.co.uk/fashionfootprint

3 'Fashion's Dirty Secret', *Dispatches*, Channel 4 (UK), directed by James Jones, first broadcast 12 November 2010

4 Jane Gibson, 'Stella event's a real rip off', *The Sydney Morning Herald*, 12 March 2007

5 Daisy Buchanan, 'Peter Pilotto for Target is good in theory, but there's a snag', *The Guardian* (UK), 8 February 2014

6 Karen Walker, interview with author, October 2014

7 Claude Baillén, *Chanel Solitaire*, p85

8   Richard Morais, *Pierre Cardin: The Man Who Became A Label* (Bantam Press, 1991), p90

9   Ibid., p128

10 Betty Goodwin, 'Yves Saint Laurent Lights a Spark of Controversy', *The Los Angeles Times*, 25 January 1985

11 Veronica Horwell, 'Yves Saint Laurent: Obituary', *The Guardian* (UK), 2 June 2008

12 Cathy Horyn, 'Yves of Destruction', *The New York Times Magazine*, 24 December 2000

13 Diane Von Furstenberg, *The Woman I Wanted To Be* (Simon & Schuster, 2014), p164

14 Ibid., p166

15 Ibid., p171

16 Ibid., p176

17 'I've got you labelled', *The Economist*, 31 March 2011

Chapter 7: Revolution Baby

1   Kyle Stock, 'How Wall Street puffed up sales of $800 down parkas', *Bloomberg*, 10 December 2014

2   Betty Kobayashi Issenman, 'The Art and Technique of Inuit Clothing' (Musée McCord, 2007)

3   Melody MacMillan, interview with author, April 2014

Chapter 8: The Dog Fur Private Eye

1   wearefur.com/our-trade/about-the-fur-trade

2   'Fur fashion is here to stay', wearefur.com, 15 May 2014

3   Eric Wilson, 'Fashion Feels Fur's Warm Embrace', *The New York Times*, 10 March 2010

4   Carole Cadwalladr, 'Peta's Ingrid Newkirk: making the fury fly', *The Guardian* (UK), 31 March 2013

5   peta.org/features/ingrid-newkirks-unique-will

6   Alix Sharkey, 'Peta: the fur will fly', *The Telegraph* (UK), 6 July 2008

7   Suzanna Andrews, 'There's Something about Gisele', *Vanity Fair*, October 2004

8   Clare Press, 'Kandy Girl', Sunday Style, 14 September 2014

9   Miles Socha, 'Fendi Fetes Karl Lagerfeld Charm', *WWD*, 9 July 2014

10 Pierre Grzybowski, interview with author, May 2015

11 Karl Lagerfeld, as quoted in fendi.com/ii/the-magic-of-fendi/fur-atelier/Karl-Lagerfeld-e-Fendi-Fur, video interview

12 Imran Amed, 'CEO Talk: Pietro Beccari, Chief Executive Office, Fendi', *Business of Fashion*, 13 May 2014

13 Ingrid Newkirk, 'Why We Euthanize', peta.org, 21 March 2013

14 'Animal Rights Uncompromised: "Pets"', PETA, available at peta.org/about-peta/why-peta/pets/

15 Cadwalladr, 'Peta's Ingrid Newkirk', *The Guardian*

16 Catarina Midby, interview with author, 2014

17 Meaghan Agnew, 'One Woman Is Revolutionizing the Fur Industry By Using Road Kill', *Modern Farmer*, 2 December 2014

Chapter 9: Counter Culture: How Retail Evolved

1 Betty Halbreich, interview with author, November 2013

2 Jane Austen, *Emma* (Oxford University Press, 1999), p215

3 Lindy Woodhead, *Shopping, Seduction and Mr Selfridge* (Profile Books, 2007), p17

4 Ibid., pp19–20

5 Ibid.

6 Bonnie English, *A Cultural History of Fashion in the 20th and 21st Centuries: From Catwalk to Sidewalk*, (Bloomsbury, 2013), p14

7 Woodhead, *Shopping, Seduction and Mr Selfridge*, p3

8 Crystal Gaylean, 'Levittown: The Imperfect Rise of the American Suburbs', *U.S. History Scene*, 13 August 2012

9 Ruppel Shell, *Cheap*, p93

10 Ibid., p38

11 Ibid., p94

12 Barbara Hulanicki, interview with author, August 2014

13 Martin Pel & Barbara Hulanicki, *The Biba Years: 1963–1975* (V&A Publishing, 2014), p33

14 Ibid., p35

15 Ibid., p127

16 Zandra Rhodes, interview with author, September 2014

17 Pel & Hulanicki, *The Biba Years*, p31

18 James Brady, *Superchic* (Little, Brown, 1974), p153

19 Ibid.

20 Janet Mulvagh, *Vivienne Westwood: An Unfashionable Life*, (HarperCollins, 2003) p88

21 Lee Siegel, 'The Department Store's Magic, Dispelled by Online Shopping', *The New York Times*, 23 November 2012

22 Lisa Wang, 'Reinventing the Department Store', *Business of Fashion*, 8 October 2014

23 Doug Stephens, interview with author, March 2015

24 Ruppel Shell, *Cheap*, pp112–113

25 Robert Lewis, as quoted in 'A Dying Breed, The American Shopping Mall', *CBS News*, 23 March 2014

26 Janice Bree Burns, 'How Melbourne's Megan Quinn and Net-A-Porter Pioneered Online Shopping', *The Sydney Morning Herald*, 5 July 2012

27 Rebecca Burn-Callander, 'Net-A-Porter merges with Italy's Yoox', *The Telegraph* (UK), 31 March 2015

28 Brooke Moore, 'Eyes on the future', *Los Angeles Times*, 13 April 2008

29 Megan Quinn quotes from Saxton Corporate Luncheon speech, Melbourne, September 2012

30 Eva Wiseman, 'One Click Wonder: the rise of Net-A-Porter', *The Guardian*, 11 July 2010

31 Brooke Moore, 'Eyes on the future', *Los Angeles Times*, 13 April 2008

32 Dana Thomas, interview with author, February 2014

33 Suzy Menkes, 'Condé Nast Invests in eCommerce', *The New York Times*, 3 March 2013

Chapter 10: Seventh Heaven?

1 Malcolm Gladwell, *Outliers: The Story of Success* (Allen Lane, 2008), p144

2 Ibid., p149

3 Oprah Winfrey, 'Oprah talks to Ralph Lauren', *O Magazine*, October 2002

4 Michael Gross, 'The Latest Calvin: From Bronx to Eternity', *New York Magazine*, 9 August 1988

5 Rosemary Feitelberg, 'The House That Calvin Built', *WWD*, 19 October 2011

6 Anne-Marie Schiro, 'Mildred Custin, 91, Made Bonwit's Fashion Force', *The New York Times*, 1 April 1997

7 Ingrid Sischy, 'Calvin to the Core', *Vanity Fair*, April 2008

8 Kate Betts, 'Donna's Day', *The Daily Beast*, 9 October 2010

9 John McDonnell as quoted in Nicole Crowder, 'When the American designer rose to prominence in fashion', *The Washington Post*, 19 February 2015

10 Jean Appleton, 'Needles Threads and New York History', *The New York Times*, 1 August 2012

11 Joshua Levine, 'A Homegrown Fashion Mogul', *WSJ Magazine*, 5 April 2012

12 Ralph Blumenthal, 'When the Mob Delivered the Goods', *The New York Times*, 26 July 1992

13 Ibid.

14 Charles Kingsley, 'Cheap Clothes and Nasty', *The Christian Socialist: A Journal of Association*, 1850

15 Woodhead, *Shopping, Seduction and Mr Selfridge*, p100

16 Robert J. S. Ross, 'The World', PRI, radio interview, 23 March 2011

17 'When Will the Apparel Quota System Finally Go Out of Style?', Knowledge@Wharton, University of Pennsylvania, 29 June 2005

Chapter 11: Grand Social

1 Rosario Dawson, interview with author, September 2014

2 Abrima Erwiah, interview with author, September 2014

3 John Colapinto, 'Just Have Less', *The New Yorker*, 3 January 2011

4 Horacio Silva, 'Inside Bottega Veneta's New Atelier', *Departures*, August 2014

5 Eve Ensler, 'Rape in the Congo', *Glamour*, August 2007

6 Simone Cipriani, interview with author, January 2014

7 'Boomtown slum', *The Economist*, 22 December 2012

8 Jacob Balzani Lööv, 'I work for Vivienne Westwood', jacobbalzaniloov.com, 25 July 2013

9 Simone Cipriani, interview with author, January 2014

10 'Stella McCartney in Conversation with Imran Amed', *Business of Fashion*, 25 March 2015

11 Bethlehem Alemu, interview with author, May 2015

Chapter 12: The Ethical Runway

1 Paul van Zyl, interview with author, March 2014

2 Suzy Menkes, 'Maiyet Embraces the Human Touch', *The New York Times*, 14 November 2012

3 Suleman Anaya, 'The Luxurious Goodness of Maiyet', *Business of Fashion*, 9 April 2013

4 Maya Singer, 'Spring 2015 Ready-to-Wear: Maiyet', Style.com, 27 September 2014

5 Suzy Menkes, 'Suzy Menkes at Paris Fashion Week: Day Four, Maiyet: Fashion's Bravehearts', vogue.co.uk, 6 March 2015

6 Nicole Phelps, 'Fall 2015 Ready-to-Wear: Maiyet', Style.com, 6 March 2015

7 Vanessa Friedman, 'Maiyet Names New Creative Director; Get Ready for Change', *The New York Times*, 20 April 2015

8 Ibid.

9 Maya Singer, 'Resort 2016: Maiyet', 8 June 2015

10 Rachel Dodes, 'Out of Africa, Into Asia', *The Wall Street Journal*, 10 September 2010

11 Amy Verner, 'Ali Hewson and Danielle Sherman Open Up About Edun's Future', Style.com, 24 July 2014

12 Ellie Pithers, 'Ali Hewson: "It's not a business unless people want to buy it and wear it and live in it"', *The Telegraph* (UK), 16 September 2016

13 Emily Cronin, 'Meet the masterminds Behind Maiyet', *The Telegraph* (UK), 29 June 2013

14 Orsola de Castro, 'Q&A', *1 Granary*, Central Saint Martins student magazine, 2 February 2015

15 Eviana Hartman, 'Duro Olowu, Inspired by the World,' *T Magazine*, 5 June 2015

16 Marion Hume, 'Threads of Change,' *Time*, 1 April 2009

17 Kit Willow, interview with author, April 2015

18 Carry Somers, interview with author, September 2014

19 Pamela Easton & Lydia Pearson, interview with author, October 2014

20 Roopa Pemmaraju, interview with author, March 2014

21 Orsola de Castro, 'Q&A', *1 Granary*, Central Saint Martins student magazine, 2 February 2015

22 Wayne Hemingway, interview with author, June 2015

Chapter 13: Silent Spring/Summer

1 Katharine Hamnett, interview with author, May 2014

2 Ellie Pithers, 'Lessons from the stylish: Katharine Hamnett, 66, fashion designer', *The Telegraph* (UK), 17 May 2014

3 Katharine Hamnett, interview with author, May 2014

4 Barney Hoskyns, 'ZZT: Every record company panicked after Two Tribes', *The Guardian* (UK), 1 January 2013

5 Bernadine Morris, 'British fashion rises and shines', *The New York Times*, 20 March 1984

6 Ibid.

7 Ella Bonner, '25 Years On, What is the Iron Lady's Legacy to Britain and the World?', *The Sunday Telegraph* (UK), 1 May 2004

8 Hermione Eyre, 'Katharine the Great', *The Independent*, 12 October 2008

9 'Katharine Hamnett interviews Vivienne Westwood', katharinehamnett.com, 31 March 2014

10 Nicholas Coleridge, 'Fashion For Aid', *The Spectator*, 16 November 1985

11 Katharine Hamnett, interview with the author, May 2014

12 Rachel Carson, *Silent Spring* (Penguin, 1962), p21

13 Ibid., pp46–47

14 Ibid., p132

15 Ibid., p133

16 Ibid., p121

17 Laura Orlando, 'Industry Attacks on Dissent: From Rachel Carson to Oprah', *Dollars & Sense*, 2002

18 Mark Hamilton Lytle, *The Gentle Subversive: Rachel Carson, "Silent Spring", and the Rise of the Environmental Movement*, (Oxford University Press, 2007)

19 Sean Hamill, 'Was Rachel Carson Right?', *Pittsburgh Quarterly*, Summer 2012

20 Katharine Hamnett, interview with author, May 2014

21 Lynn Barber, 'She used to get mad ... now she's getting even', *The Observer*, 15 April 2007

22 Richard Fletcher, 'Hamnett pulls out of Tesco range', *The Telegraph* (UK), 28 September 2007

23 Josh Loeb, 'Katharine Hamnett CBE slams council use of weedkiller on London Fields wildflower meadow', *Hackney Citizen*, 13 May 2014

24 Vandana Shiva, 'The Seeds of Suicide: How Monsanto Destroys Farming', *Global Research*, Centre for Research on Globalization, 13 March 2014

25 Michael Specter, 'Seeds of Doubt', *The New Yorker*, 25 August 2014

26 James Randerson, 'Indian farmer suicides not GM related, says study', *The Guardian*, 6 November 2008

27 Catarina Midby, interview with author, March 2014

28 Yermi Brenner, 'Greenwashing: Consumers confronted by dubiously "conscious" fashion', *Aljazeera America*, 19 May 2014

29 Shannon Whitehead, 'H&M's "Conscious" Collection? Don't Buy Into the Hype,' *Huffington Post*, 24 May 2015

30 'A Little Story About a Fashionable Lie', Greenpeace International, greenpeace.org, 17 February 2014

Chapter 14: Dyeing Shame

1 Daniel Miller & Sophie Woodward, Global Denim Project, University College London, 2007 and 'A Manifesto for a Study of Denim' *Social Anthropology* 2007 15: 335–351

2 Jason Denham, interview with author, October 2014

3 Axel Butchison & Victor LeGreige, 'Francois Girbaud', DenimFreaks.com

4 'Deadly Denim: Sandblasting in the Bangladesh Garment Industry,' Clean Clothes Campaign, March 2012

5 'Breathless for Blue Jeans: Health Hazards in China's Denim Factories,' IHLO, Campaign for Clean Clothes, War on Want, June 2013, p18

6 Kelly Slater, interview with author, April 2014

7 Kelly Slater, Facebook statement, 1 April 2014

8 Kelly Slater, interview with author, April 2014

9 Mark Angelo, interview with author, June 2015

10 Seyi Rhodes, in 'The World's Dirtiest River', *Unreported World*, Channel 4 (UK), first broadcast 11 April 2014

11 Greenpeace International, 'Polluting Paradise: A story of big brands and water pollution in Indonesia', *Toxic Threads*, greenpeace.org, April 2013

12 Greenpeace International, 'Chapter 1: A Description of Xintang and Gurao', *Intimate Pollution*, 2010

13 Greenpeace International, 'Under Wraps: Exposing the Textile Industry's Role in Polluting Mexico's Rivers,' *Toxic Threads*, greenpeace.org, December 2012

Chapter 15: Slippery Customers

1 Lucy Tammam, interview with author, September 2014

Chapter 16: Weird Science

1 Simon Doonan, *The Asylum: A collage of couture reminiscences ... and hysteria* (Blue Rider Press, 2013)

2 Diana Vreeland, *Allure* (Chronicle Books, 2010), p136

3 Stella McCartney, 'Q&A with Stella', stellamccartney.com, accessed January 2016

4 Jane E. Boyd, 'Dangerous Materials?', Chemical Heritage Foundation, chemheritage.org, 13 February 2013

5 Anke Domaske, interview with author, December 2014

6 Heidi J. Auman et al., 'Plastic ingestion by Laysan albatross chicks on Sand Island, Midway Atoll, in 1994 and 1995', Albatross Biology and Conservation, (Surrey Beatty and Sons, 1997)

7 David Stout, 'Julian W. Hill, Nylon's Discoverer, Dies at 91', *The New York Times*, 1 February 1996

8 Matthew E. Hermes, *Enough For One Lifetime: Wallace Carothers, Inventor of Nylon* (American Chemical Society and Chemical Heritage Foundation, 1996), pp140–144

Chapter 17: You Should See Polythene Pam

1 Tim Coombs, interview with author, January 2015
2 Heidi Taylor, interview with author, May 2015
3 Pharrell Williams, interview with author, November 2014
4 Mark Anthony Browne, interview with author, June 2015

Chapter 18: Waste Not, Want Not

1 Yvon Chouinard, interview with author, June 2015
2 Lauren Sherman, 'Why Fashion Insiders are Buzzing about Patagonia', *The Wall Street Journal*, 9 January 2015
3 J. B. MacKinnon, 'Patagonia's Anti-Growth Strategy', *The New Yorker*, 21 May 2015
4 Orsola de Castro, interview with author, April 2015
5 Wayne Hemingway, interview with author, May 2015

Chapter 19: Raising the Baa

1 Rahul Mishra, interview with author, October 2014
2 Stuart McCullough, interview with author, August 2014
3 Lyndel Poole & Simon Cameron, interview with author, January 2015

Chapter 20: Can We Really Change Our Ways?

1 'Vivienne Westwood Talks Eco Friendly Fashion', video interview, The Fashion 411, accessed 15 February 2016, https://www.youtube.com/watch?v=HQaPlyLNNXg
2 James Lovelock, 'The Earth is about to catch a morbid fever that may last as long as 100,000 years', *The Independent*, 16 January 2006
3 Sarah Wilson, 'Why I Wore the Same Pair of Green Shorts for 8 Years', sarahwilson.com, 17 December 2014
4 Sarah Wilson, 'How to Host a Sustainable Dinner Party', sarahwilson.com, 31 January 2015
5 Sarah Wilson, interview with author, March 2015
6 Sheena Matheiken, 'The Little Black Dress', theuniformproject.com/about-2/, accessed 1 February 2016
7 Eric Wilson, 'Shoppers on a "Diet" to Tame the Urge to Buy', *The New York Times*, 21 July 2010
8 Tamara DiMattina, interview with author, January 2015